Advanced Topics in Java

Core Concepts in Data Structures

Noel Kalicharan

Apress®

Advanced Topics in Java: Core Concepts in Data Structures

ISBN-13 (pbk): 978-1-4302-6619-8

ISBN-13 (electronic): 978-1-4302-6620-4

President and Publisher: Paul Manning
Lead Editor: Steve Anglin
Development Editor: James Markham
Technical Reviewers: Jim Graham, Massimo Nardone, and Manuel Jordan
Editorial Board: Steve Anglin, Mark Beckner, Ewan Buckingham, Gary Cornell, Louise Corrigan, Jim DeWolf, Jonathan Gennick, Jonathan Hassell, Robert Hutchinson, Michelle Lowman, James Markham, Matthew Moodie, Jeff Olson, Jeffrey Pepper, Douglas Pundick, Ben Renow-Clarke, Dominic Shakeshaft, Gwenan Spearing, Matt Wade, Steve Weiss
Coordinating Editor: Kevin Shea
Copy Editor: Kim Wimpsett
Compositor: SPi Global
Indexer: SPi Global
Artist: SPi Global
Cover Designer: Anna Ishchenko

Distributed to the book trade worldwide by Springer Science+Business Media New York, 233 Spring Street, 6th Floor, New York, NY 10013. Phone 1-800-SPRINGER, fax (201) 348-4505, e-mail orders-ny@springer-sbm.com, or visit www.springeronline.com. Apress Media, LLC is a California LLC and the sole member (owner) is Springer Science + Business Media Finance Inc (SSBM Finance Inc). SSBM Finance Inc is a Delaware corporation.

For information on translations, please e-mail rights@apress.com, or visit www.apress.com.

Apress and friends of ED books may be purchased in bulk for academic, corporate, or promotional use. eBook versions and licenses are also available for most titles. For more information, reference our Special Bulk Sales–eBook Licensing web page at www.apress.com/bulk-sales.

Any source code or other supplementary material referenced by the author in this text is available to readers at www.apress.com/. For detailed information about how to locate your book's source code, go to www.apress.com/source-code/.

To my children

Who have been a perennial source of joy, laughter, and friendship

The reliable, diligent, disciplined Anushka Nikita

and

The enigmatic, free-spirited, will-o'-the-wisp Saskia Anyara

Contents at a Glance

Contents

About the Author

Dr. Noel Kalicharan is a senior lecturer in computer science at the University of the West Indies (UWI) in St. Augustine, Trinidad. For more than 36 years, he has taught programming courses to people at all levels, from children to senior citizens. He has been teaching algorithms and programming, among other things, at UWI since 1976.

In 1988, he developed and hosted a 26-program television series entitled *Computers: Bit by Bit*. This series taught computer literacy and programming to the general public. He is always looking for innovative ways to teach logical thinking skills that go hand in hand with programming skills. His efforts resulted in two games—BrainStorm! and Not Just Luck—which won him the Prime Minister's Award for Invention and Innovation in 2000 and 2002, respectively.

He has written 17 computing books and is a computer science author for Cambridge University Press, which published his international successes, *Introduction to Computer Studies* and *C by Example*. The C book has received glowing reviews from readers from diverse countries such as Australia, Brazil, Canada, France, India, and Scotland. Many rate it as having "the best treatment of pointers," one of the more difficult programming topics to master. *Advanced Topic in Java* is written in a more leisurely style.

In 2010, Kalicharan was designated as a Trinidad & Tobago Icon in Computer Science by the National Institute for Higher Education, Research, Science, and Technology (NIHERST). In 2011, he was bestowed with a National Award, the Public Service Medal of Merit (Gold), for his contribution to education. In 2012, he was given a life-time award for Excellence in Education by the Ministry of Education of Trinidad & Tobago.

In 2012, he created a system called DigitalMath (`www.digitalmath.tt`). DigitalMath is an ingenious way to do arithmetic with your hands. With it, you can do addition, subtraction, multiplication, and division quickly, accurately, and with confidence, using just your fingers.

Born in Lengua Village in Princes Town, Trinidad, he received his primary education at the Lengua Presbyterian School and his secondary education at Naparima College. He is a graduate of the University of the West Indies in Jamaica, the University of British Columbia in Canada, and the University of the West Indies in Trinidad

About the Technical Reviewers

Jim Graham received a bachelor of science in electronics with a specialty in telecommunications from Texas A&M and graduated with his class (class of '88) in 1989. He was published in the International Communications Association's 1988 issue of ICA Communique ("Fast Packet Switching: An Overview of Theory and Performance"). His work experience includes working as an associate network engineer in the Network Design Group at Amoco Corporation in Chicago, IL; a senior network engineer at Tybrin Corporation in Fort Walton Beach, FL; and as an intelligence systems analyst at both 16th Special Operations Wing Intelligence and HQ US Air Force Special Operations Command Intelligence at Hurlburt Field, FL. He received a formal letter of commendation from the 16th Special Operations Wing Intelligence on December 18, 2001.

Manuel Jordan Elera is an autodidactic developer and researcher who enjoys learning new technologies for his own experiments and creating new integrations. Manuel won the 2010 Springy Award – Community Champion and Spring Champion 2013. In his little free time, he reads the Bible and composes music on his guitar. Manuel is a senior member in the Spring Community Forums known as dr_pompeii. Read and contact him through his blog at http://manueljordan.wordpress.com/ and follow him on his Twitter account, @dr_pompeii.

Massimo Nardone holds a master's of science degree in computing science from the University of Salerno, Italy. He worked as a PCI QSA and senior lead IT security/cloud architect for many years, and currently he leads the security consulting team in Hewlett Packard in Finland. With more than 19 years of work experience in SCADA, cloud computing, IT infrastructure, mobile, security, and WWW technology areas for both national and international projects, Massimo has worked as a project manager, software engineer, research engineer, chief security architect, and software specialist. He worked as a visiting lecturer and supervisor for exercises at the Networking Laboratory of the Helsinki University of Technology (Helsinki University of Technology TKK became part of Aalto University) for the course Security of Communication Protocols. He holds four international patents (PKI, SIP, SAML, and Proxy areas.

Preface

This book assumes you have a working knowledge of basic programming concepts such as variables, constants, assignment, selection (if...else), and looping (while, for). It also assumes you are comfortable with writing functions and working with arrays. If you are not, it is recommended that you study *Java Programming: A Beginner's Course* (www.amazon.com/Java-Programming-Beginners-Noel-Kalicharan/dp/1438265182/) or any other introductory Java programming book before tackling the material in this book.

The emphasis is not on teaching advanced concepts of the Java language, per se, but rather on using Java to teach advanced programming concepts that any aspiring programmer should know. The major topics covered include elementary sorting methods (selection, insertion), searching (sequential, binary), merging, pointers (called *references* in Java), linked lists, stacks, queues, recursion, random numbers, files (text, binary, random access, indexed), binary trees, advanced sorting methods (heapsort, quicksort, mergesort, Shell sort), and hashing (a very fast way to search).

Chapter 1 revises some basic concepts you should know. It deals with sorting a list using selection and insertion sort, searching a list using sequential and binary search, and merging two ordered lists.

Java is considered an object-oriented programming language. At the core of its being is the notion of classes and objects. Chapter 2 gives a detailed introduction to these concepts.

Chapter 3 deals with linked lists—an important data structure in its own right but also the foundation for more advanced structures such as trees and graphs. We will explain how to create a linked list, how to add to and delete from a linked list, how to build a sorted linked list, and how to merge two sorted linked lists.

Chapter 4 is devoted specifically to stacks and queues, perhaps the most useful kinds of linear lists. They have important applications in computer science. We will show you how to implement stacks and queues using arrays and linked lists and how to evaluate an arithmetic expression by converting it to postfix form.

Chapter 5 introduces a powerful programming methodology—recursion. There is no doubt that recursion takes a bit of getting used to. But, once mastered, you would be able to solve a whole new world of problems that would be difficult to solve using traditional nonrecursive techniques. Among other interesting problems, we will show you how to solve the Towers of Hanoi problem and how to escape from a maze.

We all like to play games. But what lurks inside these game-playing programs? Random numbers. Chapter 6 shows you how to use random numbers to play some simple games and simulate real-life situations. We will explain how to write an arithmetic drill program, how to play the perfect game of Nim, and how to simulate a queue at a supermarket checkout counter or bank, among others. We will also discuss a novel use of random numbers—estimating numerical values like π (pi).

Almost anything we need to store on a computer must be stored in a file. We use text files for storing the kinds of documents we create with a text editor or word processor. We use binary files for storing photographic image files, sound files, video files, and files of records. Chapter 7 shows how to create and manipulate text and binary files. And it also explains how to work with two of the most useful kinds of files—random access and indexed.

Chapter 8 provides an introduction to that most versatile data structure—the binary tree. A binary tree combines the advantages of an array and a linked list without the disadvantages. For example, a binary search tree allows us to search in "binary search time" (as with a sorted array) and insert/delete with the facility of linked lists.

The sorting methods (selection, insertion) discussed in Chapter 1 are simplistic in that they get the job done but will be slow if given a large number of items (one million, say) to sort. For example, they will take about six days (!) to sort a million items on a computer that can process one million comparisons per second. Chapter 9 discusses some faster sorting methods—heapsort, quicksort, and Shell sort. Heapsort and quicksort will sort the million items on the same computer in less than a minute while Shell sort will take slightly more than one minute.

Chapter 10 is devoted to hashing, one of the fastest ways to search. It covers hashing fundamentals and discusses several ways to resolve collisions, which is the key to the performance of any hashing algorithm.

Our goal is to provide a good grasp of advanced programming techniques as well as a basic understanding of important data structures (linked lists, stacks, queues, binary trees) and how they can be implemented in Java. We hope that this will whet your appetite for deeper study of this exciting, essential area of computer science.

Many of the exercises require you to write a program. Not providing answers for these was deliberate. My experience is that, in our fast-food culture, students do not spend the necessary time to figure out the solutions when answers are available. In any case, the idea of the programming exercises is for *you* to write the programs.

Programming is an iterative process. When you compile and run your solutions, you will know whether they are correct. If they are not, you must try to figure out why the program does not work, make improvements, and try again. The only way to learn programming well is to write programs to solve new problems. Providing answers will short-circuit this process without any benefits.

The programs in *Advanced Topics in Java* will compile with any version of the Java Development Kit (JDK) from 5.0 and newer. The programs are self-contained. They do not require, for instance, someone to provide a class to do basic input/output. They will run "right out of the box."

The code for the examples shown in this book is available on the Apress web site, `www.apress.com`. A link can be found on the book's information page on the Source Code/Downloads tab. This tab is located in the Related Titles section of the page.

Thank you for taking the time to read and study this book. We trust that you will enjoy your experience here and will get to the point where you can continue your programming journey in a painless, pleasant, enjoyable, and rewarding way.

—Noel Kalicharan

CHAPTER 1

■ ■ ■

Sorting, Searching, and Merging

In this chapter, we will explain the following:

- How to sort a list of items using selection sort

- How to sort a list of items using insertion sort

- How to add a new item to a sorted list so that the list remains sorted

- How to sort an array of strings

- How to sort related (parallel) arrays

- How to search a sorted list using binary search

- How to search an array of strings

- How to write a program to do a frequency count of words in a passage

- How to merge two sorted lists to create one sorted list

1.1 Sorting an Array: Selection Sort

Sorting is the process by which a set of values are arranged in ascending or descending order. There are many reasons to sort. Sometimes we sort in order to produce more readable output (for example, to produce an alphabetical listing). A teacher may need to sort her students in order by name or by average score. If we have a large set of values and we want to identify duplicates, we can do so by sorting; the repeated values will come together in the sorted list.

Another advantage of sorting is that some operations can be performed faster and more efficiently with sorted data. For example, if data is sorted, it is possible to search it using binary search—this is much faster than using a sequential search. Also, merging two separate lists of items can be done much faster than if the lists were unsorted.

There are many ways to sort. In this chapter, we will discuss two of the "simple" methods: selection and insertion sort. In Chapter 9, we will look at more sophisticated ways to sort. We start with selection sort.

Consider the following list of numbers stored in a Java array, num:

num

57	48	79	65	15	33	52
0	1	2	3	4	5	6

Sorting num in ascending order using selection sort proceeds as follows:

1ˢᵗ pass

- Find the smallest number in the entire list, from positions 0 to 6; the smallest is 15, found in position 4.

- Interchange the numbers in positions 0 and 4. This gives us the following:

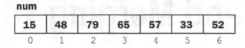

2ⁿᵈ pass

- Find the smallest number in positions 1 to 6; the smallest is 33, found in position 5.

- Interchange the numbers in positions 1 and 5. This gives us the following:

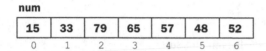

3ʳᵈ pass

- Find the smallest number in positions 2 to 6; the smallest is 48, found in position 5.

- Interchange the numbers in positions 2 and 5. This gives us the following:

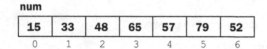

4ᵗʰ pass

- Find the smallest number in positions 3 to 6; the smallest is 52, found in position 6.

- Interchange the numbers in positions 3 and 6. This gives us the following:

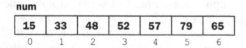

5ᵗʰ pass

- Find the smallest number in positions 4 to 6; the smallest is 57, found in position 4.

- Interchange the numbers in positions 4 and 4. This gives us the following:

num

15	33	48	52	57	79	65
0	1	2	3	4	5	6

6th pass

- Find the smallest number in positions 5 to 6; the smallest is 65, found in position 6.

- Interchange the numbers in positions 5 and 6. This gives us the following:

num

15	33	48	52	57	65	79
0	1	2	3	4	5	6

The array is now completely sorted. Note that once the 6th largest (65) has been placed in its final position (5), the largest (79) would automatically be in the last position (6).

In this example, we made six passes. We will count these passes by letting the variable h go from 0 to 5. On each pass, we find the smallest number from positions h to 6. If the smallest number is in position s, we interchange the numbers in positions h and s.

In general, for an array of size n, we make n-1 passes. In our example, we sorted 7 numbers in 6 passes. The following is a pseudocode outline of the algorithm for sorting num[0..n-1]:

```
for h = 0 to n - 2
    s = position of smallest number from num[h] to num[n-1]
    swap num[h] and num[s]
endfor
```

We can implement this algorithm as follows, using the generic parameter list:

```
public static void selectionSort(int[] list, int lo, int hi) {
//sort list[lo] to list[hi] in ascending order
    for (int h = lo; h < hi; h++) {
        int s = getSmallest(list, h, hi);
        swap(list, h, s);
    }
}
```

The two statements in the for loop could be replaced by the following:

```
swap(list, h, getSmallest(list, h, hi));
```

We can write getSmallest and swap as follows:

```
public static int getSmallest(int list[], int lo, int hi) {
//return location of smallest from list[lo..hi]
    int small = lo;
    for (int h = lo + 1; h <= hi; h++)
        if (list[h] < list[small]) small = h;
    return small;
}

public static void swap(int list[], int i, int j) {
//swap elements list[i] and list[j]
    int hold = list[i];
    list[i] = list[j];
    list[j] = hold;
}
```

3

To test whether selectionSort works properly, we write Program P1.1. Only main is shown. To complete the program, just add selectionSort, getSmallest, and swap.

Program P1.1

```java
import java.util.*;
public class SelectSortTest {
    final static int MaxNumbers = 10;
    public static void main(String[] args) {
        Scanner in = new Scanner(System.in);
        int[] num = new int[MaxNumbers];
        System.out.printf("Type up to %d numbers followed by 0\n", MaxNumbers);
        int n = 0;
        int v = in.nextInt();
        while (v != 0 && n < MaxNumbers) {
            num[n++] = v;
            v = in.nextInt();
        }
        if (v != 0) {
            System.out.printf("\nMore than %d numbers entered\n", MaxNumbers);
            System.out.printf("First %d used\n", MaxNumbers);
        }
        if (n == 0) {
            System.out.printf("\nNo numbers supplied\n");
            System.exit(1);
        }
        //n numbers are stored from num[0] to num[n-1]
        selectionSort(num, 0, n-1);
        System.out.printf("\nThe sorted numbers are\n");
        for (v = 0; v < n; v++) System.out.printf("%d ", num[v]);
        System.out.printf("\n");
    } //end main

    // selectionSort, getSmallest and swap go here

} //end class SelectSortTest
```

The program requests up to 10 numbers (as defined by MaxNumbers), stores them in the array num, calls selectionSort, and then prints the sorted list.

The following is a sample run of the program:

```
Type up to 10 numbers followed by 0
57 48 79 65 15 33 52 0

The sorted numbers are
15 33 48 52 57 65 79
```

Note that if the user enters more than ten numbers, the program will recognize this and sort only the first ten.

1.1.1 Analysis of Selection Sort

To find the smallest of k items, we make k-1 comparisons. On the first pass, we make n-1 comparisons to find the smallest of n items. On the second pass, we make n-2 comparisons to find the smallest of n-1 items. And so on, until the last pass where we make one comparison to find the smaller of two items. In general, on the jth pass, we make n-j comparisons to find the smallest of n-j+1 items. Hence, we have this:

total number of comparisons $= 1 + 2 + ...+ n\text{-}1 = \frac{1}{2}\, n(n\text{-}1) \approx \frac{1}{2}\, n^2$

We say selection sort is of order $O(n^2)$ ("big O n squared"). The constant ½ is not important in "big O" notation since, as n gets very big, the constant becomes insignificant.

On each pass, we swap two items using three assignments. Since we make n-1 passes, we make $3(n\text{-}1)$ assignments in all. Using "big O" notation, we say that the number of assignments is $O(n)$. The constants 3 and 1 are not important as n gets large.

Does selection sort perform any better if there is order in the data? No. One way to find out is to give it a sorted list and see what it does. If you work through the algorithm, you will see that the method is oblivious to order in the data. It will make the same number of comparisons every time, regardless of the data.

As we will see, some sorting methods (mergesort and quicksort; see Chapters 5 and 9) require extra array storage to implement them. Note that selection sort is performed "in place" in the given array and does not require additional storage.

As an exercise, modify the programming code so that it counts the number of comparisons and assignments made in sorting a list using selection sort.

1.2 Sorting an Array: Insertion Sort

Consider the same array as before:

num

57	48	79	65	15	33	52
0	1	2	3	4	5	6

Now, think of the numbers as cards on a table that are picked up one at a time in the order they appear in the array. Thus, we first pick up 57, then 48, then 79, and so on, until we pick up 52. However, as we pick up each new number, we add it to our hand in such a way that the numbers in our hand are all sorted.

When we pick up 57, we have just one number in our hand. We consider one number to be sorted.
When we pick up 48, we add it in front of 57 so our hand contains the following:

48 57

When we pick up 79, we place it after 57 so our hand contains this:

48 57 79

When we pick up 65, we place it after 57 so our hand contains this:

48 57 65 79

At this stage, four numbers have been picked up, and our hand contains them in sorted order.
When we pick up 15, we place it before 48 so our hand contains this:

15 48 57 65 79

When we pick up 33, we place it after 15 so our hand contains this:

15 33 48 57 65 79

Finally, when we pick up 52, we place it after 48 so our hand contains this:

15 33 48 52 57 65 79

The numbers have been sorted in ascending order.

The method described illustrates the idea behind *insertion sort*. The numbers in the array will be processed one at a time, from left to right. This is equivalent to picking up the numbers from the table one at a time. Since the first number, by itself, is sorted, we will process the numbers in the array starting from the second.

When we come to process num[h], we can assume that num[0] to num[h-1] are sorted. We insert num[h] among num[0] to num[h-1] so that num[0] to num[h] are sorted. We then go on to process num[h+1]. When we do so, our assumption that num[0] to num[h] are sorted will be true.

Sorting num in ascending order using insertion sort proceeds as follows:

1st pass

- Process num[1], that is, 48. This involves placing 48 so that the first two numbers are sorted; num[0] and num[1] now contain the following:

The rest of the array remains unchanged.

2nd pass

- Process num[2], that is, 79. This involves placing 79 so that the first three numbers are sorted; num[0] to num[2] now contain the following:

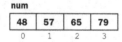

The rest of the array remains unchanged.

3rd pass

- Process num[3], that is, 65. This involves placing 65 so that the first four numbers are sorted; num[0] to num[3] now contain the following:

num

48	57	65	79
0	1	2	3

The rest of the array remains unchanged.

4th pass

- Process num[4], that is, 15. This involves placing 15 so that the first five numbers are sorted. To simplify the explanation, think of 15 as being taken out and stored in a simple variable (key, say) leaving a "hole" in num[4]. We can picture this as follows:

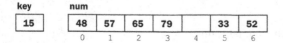

The insertion of 15 in its correct position proceeds as follows:

- Compare 15 with 79; it is smaller, so move 79 to location 4, leaving location 3 free.
  This gives the following:

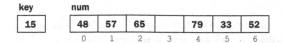

- Compare 15 with 65; it is smaller, so move 65 to location 3, leaving location 2 free.
  This gives the following:

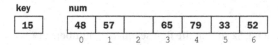

- Compare 15 with 57; it is smaller, so move 57 to location 2, leaving location 1 free.
  This gives the following:

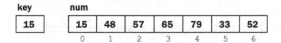

- Compare 15 with 48; it is smaller, so move 48 to location 1, leaving location 0 free.
  This gives the following:

key		num						
15			48	57	65	79	33	52
		0	1	2	3	4	5	6

- There are no more numbers to compare with 15, so it is inserted in location 0,
  giving the following:

key		num						
15		15	48	57	65	79	33	52
		0	1	2	3	4	5	6

- We can express the logic of placing 15 (key) by comparing it with the numbers to its left, starting with the nearest one. As long as key is less than num[k], for some k, we move num[k] to position num[k + 1] and move on to consider num[k-1], providing it exists. It won't exist when k is actually 0. In this case, the process stops, and key is inserted in position 0.

5th pass

- Process num[5], that is, 33. This involves placing 33 so that the first six numbers are sorted. This is done as follows:

  - Store 33 in key, leaving location 5 free.

  - Compare 33 with 79; it is smaller, so move 79 to location 5, leaving location 4 free.

  - Compare 33 with 65; it is smaller, so move 65 to location 4, leaving location 3 free.

  - Compare 33 with 57; it is smaller, so move 57 to location 3, leaving location 2 free.

  - Compare 33 with 48; it is smaller, so move 48 to location 2, leaving location 1 free.

- Compare 33 with 15; it is bigger, so insert 33 in location 1. This gives the following:

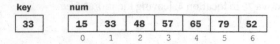

- We can express the logic of placing 33 by comparing it with the numbers to its left, starting with the nearest one. As long as key is less than num[k], for some k, we move num[k] to position num[k + 1] and move on to consider num[k-1], providing it exists. If key is greater than or equal to num[k] for some k, then key is inserted in position k+1. Here, 33 is greater than num[0] and so is inserted into num[1].

6th pass

- Process num[6], that is, 52. This involves placing 52 so that the first seven (all) numbers are sorted. This is done as follows:

  - Store 52 in key, leaving location 6 free.

  - Compare 52 with 79; it is smaller, so move 79 to location 6, leaving location 5 free.

  - Compare 52 with 65; it is smaller, so move 65 to location 5, leaving location 4 free.

  - Compare 52 with 57; it is smaller, so move 57 to location 4, leaving location 3 free.

  - Compare 52 with 48; it is bigger; so insert 52 in location 3. This gives the following:

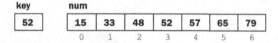

The array is now completely sorted.
The following is an outline of how to sort the first n elements of an array, num, using insertion sort:

```
for h = 1 to n - 1 do
    insert num[h] among num[0] to num[h-1] so that num[0] to num[h] are sorted
endfor
```

Using this outline, we write the function insertionSort using the parameter list.

```
public static void insertionSort(int list[], int n) {
//sort list[0] to list[n-1] in ascending order
    for (int h = 1; h < n; h++) {
        int key = list[h];
        int k = h - 1; //start comparing with previous item
        while (k >= 0 && key < list[k]) {
            list[k + 1] = list[k];
            --k;
        }
        list[k + 1] = key;
    } //end for
} //end insertionSort
```

The while statement is at the heart of the sort. It states that as long as we are within the array (k >= 0) and the current number (key) is less than the one in the array (key < list[k]), we move list[k] to the right (list[k+1] = list[k]) and move on to the next number on the left (--k).

We exit the while loop if k is equal to -1 or if key is greater than or equal to list[k], for some k. In either case, key is inserted into list[k+1].

If k is -1, it means that the current number is smaller than all the previous numbers in the list and must be inserted in list[0]. But list[k + 1] *is* list[0] when k is -1, so key is inserted correctly in this case.

The function sorts in ascending order. To sort in descending order, all we have to do is change < to > in the while condition, like this:

```
while (k >= 0 && key > list[k])
```

Now, a key moves to the left if it is *bigger*.

We write Program P1.2 to test whether insertionSort works correctly. Only main is shown. Adding the function insertionSort completes the program.

Program P1.2

```
import java.util.*;
public class InsertSortTest {
    final static int MaxNumbers = 10;
    public static void main(String[] args) {
        Scanner in = new Scanner(System.in);
        int[] num = new int[MaxNumbers];
        System.out.printf("Type up to %d numbers followed by 0\n", MaxNumbers);
        int n = 0;
        int v = in.nextInt();
        while (v != 0 && n < MaxNumbers) {
            num[n++] = v;
            v = in.nextInt();
        }
        if (v != 0) {
            System.out.printf("\nMore than %d numbers entered\n", MaxNumbers);
            System.out.printf("First %d used\n", MaxNumbers);
        }
        if (n == 0) {
            System.out.printf("\nNo numbers supplied\n");
            System.exit(1);
        }
        //n numbers are stored from num[0] to num[n-1]
        insertionSort(num, n);
        System.out.printf("\nThe sorted numbers are\n");
        for (v = 0; v < n; v++) System.out.printf("%d ", num[v]);
        System.out.printf("\n");
    } //end main

    public static void insertionSort(int list[], int n) {
    //sort list[0] to list[n-1] in ascending order
        for (int h = 1; h < n; h++) {
            int key = list[h];
            int k = h - 1; //start comparing with previous item
            while (k >= 0 && key < list[k]) {
                list[k + 1] = list[k];
                --k;
            }
```

```
            list[k + 1] = key;
        } //end for
    } //end insertionSort

} //end class InsertSortTest
```

The program requests up to ten numbers (as defined by MaxNumbers), stores them in the array num, calls insertionSort, and then prints the sorted list.

The following is a sample run of the program:

```
Type up to 10 numbers followed by 0
57 48 79 65 15 33 52 0
The sorted numbers are
15 33 48 52 57 65 79
```

Note that if the user enters more than ten numbers, the program will recognize this and sort only the first ten.

We could easily generalize insertionSort to sort a *portion* of a list. To illustrate, we rewrite insertionSort (calling it insertionSort1) to sort list[lo] to list[hi] where lo and hi are passed as arguments to the function.

Since element lo is the first one, we start processing elements from lo+1 until element hi. This is reflected in the for statement. Also now, the lowest subscript is lo, rather than 0. This is reflected in the while condition k >= lo. Everything else remains the same as before.

```
public static void insertionSort1(int list[], int lo, int hi) {
//sort list[lo] to list[hi] in ascending order
    for (int h = lo + 1; h <= hi; h++) {
        int key = list[h];
        int k = h - 1; //start comparing with previous item
        while (k >= lo && key < list[k]) {
            list[k + 1] = list[k];
            --k;
        }
        list[k + 1] = key;
    } //end for
} //end insertionSort1
```

We can test insertionSort1 with Program P1.2a.

Program P1.2a

```
import java.util.*;
public class InsertSort1Test {
    final static int MaxNumbers = 10;
    public static void main(String[] args) {
        Scanner in = new Scanner(System.in);
        int[] num = new int[MaxNumbers];
        System.out.printf("Type up to %d numbers followed by 0\n", MaxNumbers);
        int n = 0;
        int v = in.nextInt();
        while (v != 0 && n < MaxNumbers) {
            num[n++] = v;
            v = in.nextInt();
        }
```

```
    if (v != 0) {
        System.out.printf("\nMore than %d numbers entered\n", MaxNumbers);
        System.out.printf("First %d used\n", MaxNumbers);
    }
    if (n == 0) {
        System.out.printf("\nNo numbers supplied\n");
        System.exit(1);
    }
    //n numbers are stored from num[0] to num[n-1]
    insertionSort1(num, 0, n-1);
    System.out.printf("\nThe sorted numbers are\n");
    for (v = 0; v < n; v++) System.out.printf("%d ", num[v]);
    System.out.printf("\n");
} //end main

// insertionSort1 goes here

} //end class InsertSort1Test
```

1.2.1 Analysis of Insertion Sort

In processing item j, we can make as few as 1 comparison (if num[j] is bigger than num[j-1]) or as many as j-1 comparisons (if num[j] is smaller than all the previous items). For random data, we would expect to make ½(j-1) comparisons, on average. Hence, the average total number of comparisons to sort n items is:

$$\sum_{j=2}^{n} \frac{1}{2}(j-1) = \text{½} \left\{1 + 2 + \ldots + n-1\right\} = \text{¼} \, n(n-1) \approx \text{¼} \, n^2$$

We say insertion sort is of order $O(n^2)$ ("big O n squared"). The constant ¼ is not important as n gets large.

Each time we make a comparison, we also make an assignment. Hence, the total number of assignments is also ¼ n(n-1) ≈ ¼ n².

We emphasize that this is an average for random data. Unlike selection sort, the actual performance of insertion sort depends on the data supplied. If the given array is already sorted, insertion sort will quickly determine this by making n-1 comparisons. In this case, it runs in $O(n)$ time. One would expect that insertion sort will perform better the more order there is in the data.

If the given data is in descending order, insertion sort performs at its worst since each new number has to travel all the way to the beginning of the list. In this case, the number of comparisons is ½ n(n-1) ≈ ½ n². The number of assignments is also ½ n(n-1) ≈ ½ n².

Thus, the number of comparisons made by insertion sort ranges from n-1 (best) to ¼ n² (average) to ½ n² (worst). The number of assignments is always the same as the number of comparisons.

As with selection sort, insertion sort does not require extra array storage for its implementation.

As an exercise, modify the programming code so that it counts the number of comparisons and assignments made in sorting a list using insertion sort.

1.3 Inserting an Element in Place

Insertion sort uses the idea of adding a new element to an already sorted list so that the list remains sorted. We can treat this as a problem in its own right (nothing to do with insertion sort). Specifically, given a sorted list of items from list[m] to list[n], we want to add a new item (newItem, say) to the list so that list[m] to list[n+1] are sorted.

Adding a new item increases the size of the list by 1. We assume that the array has room to hold the new item. We write the function insertInPlace to solve this problem.

```
public static void insertInPlace(int newItem, int list[], int m, int n) {
//list[m] to list[n] are sorted
//insert newItem so that list[m] to list[n+1] are sorted
   int k = n;
   while (k >= m && newItem < list[k]) {
      list[k + 1] = list[k];
      --k;
   }
   list[k + 1] = newItem;
} //end insertInPlace
```

Using insertInPlace, we can rewrite insertionSort (calling it insertionSort2) as follows:

```
public static void insertionSort2(int list[], int lo, int hi) {
//sort list[lo] to list[hi] in ascending order
   for (int h = lo + 1; h <= hi; h++)
      insertInPlace(list[h], list, lo, h - 1);
} //end insertionSort2
```

We can test insertionSort2 with Program P1.2b.

Program P1.2b

```
import java.util.*;
public class InsertSort2Test {
   final static int MaxNumbers = 10;
   public static void main(String[] args) {
      Scanner in = new Scanner(System.in);
      int[] num = new int[MaxNumbers];
      System.out.printf("Type up to %d numbers followed by 0\n", MaxNumbers);
      int n = 0;
      int v = in.nextInt();
      while (v != 0 && n < MaxNumbers) {
         num[n++] = v;
         v = in.nextInt();
      }
      if (v != 0) {
         System.out.printf("\nMore than %d numbers entered\n", MaxNumbers);
         System.out.printf("First %d used\n", MaxNumbers);
      }
      if (n == 0) {
         System.out.printf("\nNo numbers supplied\n");
         System.exit(1);
      }
```

```
    //n numbers are stored from num[0] to num[n-1]
    insertionSort2(num, 0, n-1);
    System.out.printf("\nThe sorted numbers are\n");
    for (v = 0; v < n; v++) System.out.printf("%d ", num[v]);
        System.out.printf("\n");
} //end main

public static void insertionSort2(int list[], int lo, int hi) {
//sort list[lo] to list[hi] in ascending order
    for (int h = lo + 1; h <= hi; h++)
        insertInPlace(list[h], list, lo, h - 1);
} //end insertionSort2

public static void insertInPlace(int newItem, int list[], int m, int n) {
//list[m] to list[n] are sorted
//insert newItem so that list[m] to list[n+1] are sorted
    int k = n;
    while (k >= m && newItem < list[k]) {
        list[k + 1] = list[k];
        --k;
    }
    list[k + 1] = newItem;
} //end insertInPlace

} //end class InsertSort2Test
```

1.4 Sorting a String Array

Consider the problem of sorting a list of names in alphabetical order. In Java, a name is stored in a String variable, and we'll need a String array to store the list. For the most part, we can work with String as if it were a primitive type, but it is sometimes useful to remember that, strictly speaking, it is a class. Where necessary, we will point out the distinction.

One difference that concerns us here is that we cannot use the relational operators (==, <, >, and so on) to compare strings. We must use functions from the String class (or write our own). Common functions include equals, equalsIgnoreCase, compareTo, and compareToIgnoreCase. We write a function to sort an array of strings using insertion sort. We call it insertionSort3.

```
public static void insertionSort3(String[] list, int lo, int hi) {
//sort list[lo] to list[hi] in ascending order
    for (int h = lo + 1; h <= hi; h++) {
        String key = list[h];
        int k = h - 1; //start comparing with previous item
        while (k >= lo && key.compareToIgnoreCase(list[k]) < 0) {
            list[k + 1] = list[k];
            --k;
        }
        list[k + 1] = key;
    } //end for
} //end insertionSort3
```

The function is pretty much the same as the previous ones except for the declaration of list and the use of compareToIgnoreCase to compare two strings. If case matters, you can use compareTo.

We test insertionSort3 with Program P1.3.

Program P1.3

```
import java.util.*;
public class SortStrings {
    final static int MaxNames = 8;
    public static void main(String[] args) {
        String name[] = {"Graham, Ariel", "Perrott, Chloe",
                "Charles, Kandice", "Seecharan, Anella", "Reyes, Aaliyah",
                "Graham, Ashleigh", "Reyes, Ayanna", "Greaves, Sherrelle" };

        insertionSort3(name, 0, MaxNames - 1);

        System.out.printf("\nThe sorted names are\n\n");
        for (int h = 0; h < MaxNames; h++)
           System.out.printf("%s\n", name[h]);
    } //end main

    // insertionSort3 goes here

} //end class SortStrings
```

When run, Program P1.3 produced the following output:

```
The sorted names are

Charles, Kandice
Graham, Ariel
Graham, Ashleigh
Greaves, Sherrelle
Perrott, Chloe
Reyes, Aaliyah
Reyes, Ayanna
Seecharan, Anella
```

1.5 Sorting Parallel Arrays

It is quite common to have related information in different arrays. For example, suppose, in addition to name, we have an integer array id such that id[h] is an identification number associated with name[h], as shown in Figure 1-1.

	name	id
0	Graham, Ariel	3050
1	Perrott, Chloe	2795
2	Charles, Kandice	4455
3	Seecharan, Anella	7824
4	Reyes, Aaliyah	6669
5	Graham, Ashleigh	5000
6	Reyes, Ayanna	5464
7	Greaves, Sherrelle	6050

Figure 1-1. *Two arrays with related information*

Consider the problem of sorting the names in alphabetical order. At the end, we would want each name to have its correct ID number. So, for example, after the sorting is done, name[0] should contain "Charles, Kandice" and id[0] should contain 4455.

To achieve this, each time a name is moved during the sorting process, the corresponding ID number must also be moved. Since the name and ID number must be moved "in parallel," we say we are doing a "parallel sort" or we are sorting "parallel arrays."

We rewrite insertionSort3 to illustrate how to sort parallel arrays. We simply add the code to move an ID whenever a name is moved. We call it parallelSort.

```
public static void parallelSort(String[] list, int id[], int lo, int hi) {
//Sort the names in list[lo] to list[hi] in alphabetical order,
//ensuring that each name remains with its original id number.
    for (int h = lo + 1; h <= hi; h++) {
        String key = list[h];
        int m = id[h];  // extract the id number
        int k = h - 1; //start comparing with previous item
        while (k >= lo && key.compareToIgnoreCase(list[k]) < 0) {
            list[k + 1] = list[k];
            id[k+ 1] = id[k];  //move up id number when we move a name
            --k;
        }
        list[k + 1] = key;
        id[k + 1] = m; //store the id number in the same position as the name
    } //end for
} //end parallelSort
```

We test parallelSort by writing Program P1.4.

Program P1.4

```
import java.util.*;
public class ParallelSort {
    final static int MaxNames = 8;
    public static void main(String[] args) {
        String name[] = {"Graham, Ariel", "Perrott, Chloe",
                "Charles, Kandice", "Seecharan, Anella", "Reyes, Aaliyah",
                "Graham, Ashleigh", "Reyes, Ayanna", "Greaves, Sherrelle" };
        int id[] = {3050,2795,4455,7824,6669,5000,5464,6050};

        parallelSort(name, id, 0, MaxNames - 1);
```

```
            System.out.printf("\nThe sorted names and IDs are\n\n");
            for (int h = 0; h < MaxNames; h++)
               System.out.printf("%-20s %d\n", name[h], id[h]);
         } //end main

         // parallelSort goes here

      } //end class ParallelSort
```

When Program P1.4 was run, it produced the following output:

```
The sorted names and IDs are

Charles, Kandice    4455
Graham, Ariel       3050
Graham, Ashleigh    5000
Greaves, Sherrelle  6050
Perrott, Chloe      2795
Reyes, Aaliyah      6669
Reyes, Ayanna       5464
Seecharan, Anella   7824
```

We note, in passing, that if we have several sets of related items to process, storing each set in a separate array would not be the best way to proceed. It would be better to group the items in a class and work with the group as we would a single item. We'll show you how to do this in Section 2.14.

1.6 Binary Search

Binary search is a fast method for searching a list of items for a given one, *providing the list is sorted* (either ascending or descending). To illustrate the method, consider a list of 13 numbers, sorted in ascending order and stored in an array num[0..12].

num

17	24	31	39	44	49	56	66	72	78	83	89	96
0	1	2	3	4	5	6	7	8	9	10	11	12

Suppose we want to search for 66. The search proceeds as follows:

1. We find the middle item in the list. This is 56 in position 6. We compare 66 with 56. Since 66 is bigger, we know that if 66 is in the list at all, it *must* be *after* position 6, since the numbers are in ascending order. In our next step, we confine our search to locations 7 to 12.

2. We find the middle item from locations 7 to 12. In this case, we can choose either item 9 or item 10. The algorithm we will write will choose item 9, that is, 78.

3. We compare 66 with 78. Since 66 is smaller, we know that if 66 is in the list at all, it *must* be *before* position 9, since the numbers are in ascending order. In our next step, we confine our search to locations 7 to 8.

4. We find the middle item from locations 7 to 8. In this case, we can choose either item 7 or item 8. The algorithm we will write will choose item 7, that is, 66.

5. We compare 66 with 66. Since they are the same, our search ends successfully, finding the required item in position 7.

Suppose we were searching for 70. The search will proceed as described above until we compare 70 with 66 (in location 7).

- Since 70 is bigger, we know that if 70 is in the list at all, it *must* be *after* position 7, since the numbers are in ascending order. In our next step, we confine our search to locations 8 to 8. This is just one location.

- We compare 70 with item 8, that is, 72. Since 70 is smaller, we know that if 70 is in the list at all, it *must* be *before* position 8. Since it can't be after position 7 *and* before position 8, we conclude that it is not in the list.

At each stage of the search, we confine our search to some portion of the list. Let us use the variables lo and hi as the subscripts that define this portion. In other words, our search will be confined to num[lo] to num[hi].

Initially, we want to search the entire list so that we will set lo to 0 and hi to 12, in this example.

How do we find the subscript of the middle item? We will use the following calculation:

```
mid = (lo + hi) / 2;
```

Since integer division will be performed, the fraction, if any, is discarded. For example, when lo is 0 and hi is 12, mid becomes 6; when lo is 7 and hi is 12, mid becomes 9; and when lo is 7 and hi is 8, mid becomes 7.

As long as lo is less than or equal to hi, they define a nonempty portion of the list to be searched. When lo is equal to hi, they define a single item to be searched. If lo ever gets bigger than hi, it means we have searched the entire list and the item was not found.

Based on these ideas, we can now write a function binarySearch. To be more general, we will write it so that the calling routine can specify which portion of the array it wants the search to look for the item.

Thus, the function must be given the item to be searched for (key), the array (list), the start position of the search (lo), and the end position of the search (hi). For example, to search for the number 66 in the array num, above, we can issue the call binarySearch(66, num, 0, 12).

The function must tell us the result of the search. If the item is found, the function will return its location. If not found, it will return -1.

```
public static int binarySearch(int key, int[] list, int lo, int hi) {
//search for key from list[lo] to list[hi]
//if found, return its location; otherwise, return -1
   while (lo <= hi) {
      int mid = (lo + hi) / 2;
      if (key == list[mid]) return mid; // found
      if (key < list[mid]) hi = mid - 1;
      else lo = mid + 1;
   }
   return -1; //lo and hi have crossed; key not found
}
```

If item contains a number to be searched for, we can write code as follows:

```
int ans = binarySearch(item, num, 0, 12);
if (ans == -1) System.out.printf("%d not found\n", item);
else System.out.printf("%d found in location %d\n", item, ans);
```

If we want to search for item from locations i to j, we can write the following:

```
int ans = binarySearch(item, num, i, j);
```

We can test binarySearch with Program P1.5.

Program P1.5

```java
public class BinarySearchTest {
   public static void main(String[] args) {
      int[] num = {17, 24, 31, 39, 44, 49, 56, 66, 72, 78, 83, 89, 96};
      int n = binarySearch(66, num, 0, 12);
      System.out.printf("%d\n", n);    //will print 7; 66 in pos. 7
      n = binarySearch(66, num, 0, 6);
      System.out.printf("%d\n", n);    //will print -1; 66 not in 0 to 6
      n = binarySearch(70, num, 0, 12);
      System.out.printf("%d\n", n);    //will print -1; 70 not in list
      n = binarySearch(89, num, 5, 12);
      System.out.printf("%d\n", n);    //will print 11; 89 in pos. 11
   } //end main

   // binarySearch goes here
} //end class BinarySearchTest
```

When run, the program will print the following:

```
7
-1
-1
11
```

1.7 Searching an Array of Strings

We can search a sorted array of strings (names in alphabetical order, say) using the same technique we used for searching an integer array. The major differences are in the declaration of the array and the use of the String function compareTo, rather than == or <, to compare two strings. The following is the string version of binarySearch:

```java
public static int binarySearch(String key, String[] list, int lo, int hi) {
//search for key from list[lo] to list[hi]
//if found, return its location; otherwise, return -1
   while (lo <= hi) {
      int mid = (lo + hi) / 2;
      int cmp = key.compareTo(list[mid]);
      if (cmp == 0) return mid;   // search succeeds
      if (cmp < 0) hi = mid -1;   // key is 'less than' list[mid]
      else lo = mid + 1;          // key is 'greater than' list[mid]
   }
   return -1; //lo and hi have crossed; key not found
} //end binarySearch
```

Since we need to know whether one string is equal to, or less than, another, it is best to use the compareTo method.

Note that we call compareTo only once. The value returned (cmp) tells us all we need to know. If we are comparing words or names and we want the case of the letters to be ignored in the comparison, we can use compareToIgnoreCase.

The function can be tested with Program P1.6.

Program P1.6

```java
import java.util.*;
public class BinarySearchString {
    final static int MaxNames = 8;
    public static void main(String[] args) {
        String name[] = {"Charles, Kandice", "Graham, Ariel",
                "Graham, Ashleigh", "Greaves, Sherrelle", "Perrott, Chloe",
                "Reyes, Aaliyah", "Reyes, Ayanna", "Seecharan, Anella"};

        int n = binarySearch("Charles, Kandice", name, 0, MaxNames - 1);
        System.out.printf("%d\n", n);
                //will print 0, location of Charles, Kandice

        n = binarySearch("Reyes, Ayanna", name, 0, MaxNames - 1);
        System.out.printf("%d\n", n);
                //will print 6, location of Reyes, Ayanna

        n = binarySearch("Perrott, Chloe", name, 0, MaxNames - 1);
        System.out.printf("%d\n", n);
                //will print 4, location of Perrott, Chloe

        n = binarySearch("Graham, Ariel", name, 4, MaxNames - 1);
        System.out.printf("%d\n", n);
                //will print -1, since Graham, Ariel is not in locations 4 to 7

        n = binarySearch("Cato, Brittney", name, 0, MaxNames - 1);
        System.out.printf("%d\n", n);
                //will print -1 since Cato, Brittney is not in the list

    } //end main

    // binarySearch goes here

} //end class BinarySearchString
```

This sets up the array name with the names in alphabetical order. It then calls binarySearch with various names and prints the result of each search.

One may wonder what might happen with a call like this:

```java
n = binarySearch("Perrott, Chloe", name, 5, 10);
```

Here, we are telling binarySearch to look for "Perrott, Chloe" in locations 5 to 10 of the given array. However, locations 8 to 10 do not exist in the array. The result of the search will be unpredictable. The program may crash or return an incorrect result. The onus is on the calling program to ensure that binarySearch (or any other function) is called with valid arguments.

1.8 Example: Word Frequency Count

Let's write a program to read an English passage and count the number of times each word appears. Output consists of an alphabetical listing of the words and their frequencies.

We can use the following outline to develop our program:

```
while there is input
   get a word
   search for word
   if word is in the table
      add 1 to its count
   else
      add word to the table
      set its count to 1
   endif
endwhile
print table
```

This is a typical "search and insert" situation. We search for the next word among the words stored so far. If the search succeeds, the only thing to do is increment its count. If the search fails, the word is put in the table and its count set to 1.

A major design decision here is how to search the table, which, in turn, will depend on where and how a new word is inserted in the table. The following are two possibilities:

1. A new word is inserted in the next free position in the table. This implies that a sequential search must be used to look for an incoming word since the words would not be in any particular order. This method has the advantages of simplicity and easy insertion, but searching takes longer as more words are put in the table.

2. A new word is inserted in the table in such a way that the words are always in alphabetical order. This may entail moving words that have already been stored so that the new word may be slotted in the right place. However, since the table is in order, a binary search can be used to search for an incoming word.

For (2), searching is faster, but insertion is slower than in (1). Since, in general, searching is done more frequently than inserting, (2) might be preferable.

Another advantage of (2) is that, at the end, the words will already be in alphabetical order and no sorting will be required. If (1) is used, the words will need to be sorted to obtain the alphabetical order.

We will write our program using the approach in (2). The complete program is shown as Program P1.7.

Program P1.7

```java
import java.io.*;
import java.util.*;
public class WordFrequency {
   final static int MaxWords = 50;
   public static void main(String[] args) throws IOException {
      String[] wordList = new String[MaxWords];
      int[] frequency = new int[MaxWords];
      FileReader in = new FileReader("passage.txt");
      PrintWriter out = new PrintWriter(new FileWriter("output.txt"));

      for (int h = 0; h < MaxWords; h++) {
         frequency[h] = 0;
         wordList[h] = "";
      }
```

```java
    int numWords = 0;
    String word = getWord(in).toLowerCase();
    while (!word.equals("")) {
        int loc = binarySearch(word, wordList, 0, numWords-1);
        if (word.compareTo(wordList[loc]) == 0) ++frequency[loc]; //word found
        else //this is a new word
            if (numWords < MaxWords) { //if table is not full
                addToList(word, wordList, frequency, loc, numWords-1);
                ++numWords;
            }
            else out.printf("'%s' not added to table\n", word);
        word = getWord(in).toLowerCase();
    }
    printResults(out, wordList, frequency, numWords);
    in.close();
    out.close();
} // end main

public static int binarySearch(String key, String[] list, int lo, int hi){
//search for key from list[lo] to list[hi]
//if found, return its location;
//if not found, return the location in which it should be inserted
//the calling program will check the location to determine if found
    while (lo <= hi) {
        int mid = (lo + hi) / 2;
        int cmp = key.compareTo(list[mid]);
        if (cmp == 0) return mid;    // search succeeds
        if (cmp < 0) hi = mid -1;    // key is 'less than' list[mid]
        else lo = mid + 1;           // key is 'greater than' list[mid]
    }
    return lo; //key must be inserted in location lo
} //end binarySearch

public static void addToList(String item, String[] list, int[] freq, int p, int n) {
//adds item in position list[p]; sets freq[p] to 1
//shifts list[n] down to list[p] to the right
    for (int h = n; h >= p; h--) {
        list[h + 1] = list[h];
        freq[h + 1] = freq[h];
    }
    list[p] = item;
    freq[p] = 1;
} //end addToList

public static void printResults(PrintWriter out, String[] list, int freq[], int n) {
    out.printf("\nWords            Frequency\n\n");
    for (int h = 0; h < n; h++)
        out.printf("%-20s %2d\n", list[h], freq[h]);
} //end printResults
```

```
        public static String getWord(FileReader in) throws IOException {
        //returns the next word found
            final int MaxLen = 255;
            int c, n = 0;
            char[] word = new char[MaxLen];
            // read over non-letters
            while (!Character.isLetter((char) (c = in.read())) && (c != -1)) ;
            //empty while body
            if (c == -1) return ""; //no letter found
            word[n++] = (char) c;
            while (Character.isLetter(c = in.read()))
                if (n < MaxLen) word[n++] = (char) c;
            return new String(word, 0, n);
        } // end getWord

} //end class WordFrequency
```

Suppose the following data is stored in passage.txt:

```
Be more concerned with your character than your reputation,
because your character is what you really are,
while your reputation is merely what others think you are.
Our character is what we do when we think no one is looking.
```

When Program P1.7 is run, it stores its output in output.txt. Here is the output:

Words	Frequency
are	2
be	1
because	1
character	3
concerned	1
do	1
is	4
looking	1
merely	1
more	1
no	1
one	1
others	1
our	1
really	1
reputation	2
than	1
think	2
we	2
what	3
when	1
while	1
with	1
you	2
your	4

Here are some comments on Program P1.7:

- For our purposes, we assume that a word begins with a letter and consists of letters only. If you want to include other characters (such as a hyphen or apostrophe), you need only change the getWord function.

- MaxWords denotes the maximum number of distinct words catered for. For testing the program, we have used 50 for this value. If the number of distinct words in the passage exceeds MaxWords (50, say), any words after the 50th will be read but not stored, and a message to that effect will be printed. However, the count for a word already stored will be incremented if it is encountered again.

- main initializes the frequency counts to 0 and the items in the String array to the empty string. It then processes the words in the passage based on the outline shown at the start of Section 1.8.

- getWord reads the input file and returns the next word found.

- All words are converted to lowercase so that, for instance, The and the are counted as the same word.

- binarySearch is written so that if the word is found, its location is returned. If the word is not found, then the location in which it *should* be inserted is returned. The function addToList is given the location in which to insert a new word. Words to the right of, and including, this location, are shifted one position to make room for the new word.

1.9 Merging Ordered Lists

Merging is the process by which two or more ordered lists are combined into one ordered list. For example, given two lists of numbers, A and B, as follows:

```
A: 21 28 35 40 61 75
B: 16 25 47 54
```

they can be combined into one ordered list, C:

```
C: 16 21 25 28 35 40 47 54 61 75
```

The list C contains all the numbers from lists A and B. How can the merge be performed?

One way to think about it is to imagine that the numbers in the given lists are stored on cards, one per card, and the cards are placed face up on a table, with the smallest at the top. We can imagine the lists A and B as follows:

```
21    16
28    25
35    47
40    54
61
75
```

We look at the top two cards, 21 and 16. The smaller, 16, is removed and placed in C. This exposes the number 25.

The top two cards are now 21 and 25. The smaller, 21, is removed and added to C, which now contains 16 21. This exposes the number 28.

The top two cards are now 28 and 25. The smaller, 25, is removed and added to C, which now contains 16 21 25. This exposes the number 47.

The top two cards are now 28 and 47. The smaller, 28, is removed and added to C, which now contains 16 21 25 28. This exposes the number 35.

The top two cards are now 35 and 47. The smaller, 35, is removed and added to C, which now contains 16 21 25 28 35. This exposes the number 40.

The top two cards are now 40 and 47. The smaller, 40, is removed and added to C, which now contains 16 21 25 28 35 40. This exposes the number 61.

The top two cards are now 61 and 47. The smaller, 47, is removed and added to C, which now contains 16 21 25 28 35 40 47. This exposes the number 54.

The top two cards are now 61 and 54. The smaller, 54, is removed and added to C, which now contains 16 21 25 28 35 40 47 54. The list B has no more numbers.

We copy the remaining elements (61 75) of A to C, which now contains the following:

16 21 25 28 35 40 47 54 61 75

The merge is completed.

At each step of the merge, we compare the smallest remaining number of A with the smallest remaining number of B. The smaller of these is added to C. If the smaller comes from A, we move on to the next number in A; if the smaller comes from B, we move on to the next number in B.

This is repeated until all the numbers in either A or B have been used. If all the numbers in A have been used, we add the remaining numbers from B to C. If all the numbers in B have been used, we add the remaining numbers from A to C.

We can express the logic of the merge as follows:

```
while (at least one number remains in both A and B) {
    if (smallest in A < smallest in B)
        add smallest in A to C
        move on to next number in A
    else
        add smallest in B to C
        move on to next number in B
    endif
}
if (A has ended) add remaining numbers in B to C
else add remaining numbers in A to C
```

1.9.1 Implementing the Merge

Assume that an array A contains m numbers stored in A[0] to A[m-1] and an array B contains n numbers stored in B[0] to B[n-1]. Assume that the numbers are stored in ascending order. We want to merge the numbers in A and B into another array C such that C[0] to C[m+n-1] contains all the numbers in A and B sorted in ascending order.

We will use integer variables i, j, and k to subscript the arrays A, B, and C, respectively. "Moving on to the next position" in an array can be done by adding 1 to the subscript variable. We can implement the merge with this function:

```
public static int merge(int[] A, int m, int[] B, int n, int[] C) {
    int i = 0;  //i points to the first (smallest) number in A
    int j = 0;  //j points to the first (smallest) number in B
    int k = -1; //k will be incremented before storing a number in C[k]
    while (i < m && j < n) {
        if (A[i] < B[j]) C[++k] = A[i++];
        else C[++k] = B[j++];
    }
    if (i == m) ///copy B[j] to B[n-1] to C
        for ( ; j < n; j++) C[++k] = B[j];
```

```
            else // j == n, copy A[i] to A[m-1] to C
                for ( ; i < m; i++) C[++k] = A[i];
            return m + n;
        } //end merge
```

The function takes the arguments A, m, B, n, and C, performs the merge, and returns the number of elements, m + n, in C.

Program P1.8 shows a simple main function that tests the logic of merge. It sets up arrays A and B, calls merge, and prints C. When run, the program prints the following:

```
16 21 25 28 35 40 47 54 61 75
```

Program P1.8

```
public class MergeTest {
    public static void main(String[] args) {
        int[] A = {21, 28, 35, 40, 61, 75};   //size 6
        int[] B = {16, 25, 47, 54};       //size 4
        int[] C = new int[20];   //enough to hold all the elements
        int n = merge(A, 6, B, 4, C);
        for (int j = 0; j < n; j++) System.out.printf("%d ", C[j]);
        System.out.printf("\n");
    } //end main

    // merge goes here

} //end class MergeTest
```

As a matter of interest, we can also implement merge as follows:

```
public static int merge(int[] A, int m, int[] B, int n, int[] C) {
    int i = 0;  //i points to the first (smallest) number in A
    int j = 0;  //j points to the first (smallest) number in B
    int k = -1; //k will be incremented before storing a number in C[k]
    while (i < m || j < n) {
        if (i == m) C[++k] = B[j++];
        else if (j == n) C[++k] = A[i++];
        else if (A[i] < B[j]) C[++k] = A[i++];
        else C[++k] = B[j++];
    }
    return m + n;
}
```

The while loop expresses the following logic: as long as there is at least one element to process in either A *or* B, we enter the loop. If we are finished with A (i == m), copy an element from B to C. If we are finished with B (j == n), copy an element from A to C. Otherwise, copy the smaller of A[i] and B[j] to C. Each time we copy an element from an array, we add 1 to the subscript for that array.

While the previous version implements the merge in a straightforward way, it seems reasonable to say that this version is a bit neater.

EXERCISES 1

1. A survey of 10 pop artists is made. Each person votes for an artist by specifying the number of the artist (a value from 1 to 10). Each voter is allowed one vote for the artist of their choice. The vote is recorded as a number from 1 to 10. The number of voters is unknown beforehand, but the votes are terminated by a vote of 0. Any vote that is not a number from 1 to 10 is a spoiled vote. A file, votes.txt, contains the names of the candidates. The first name is considered as candidate 1, the second as candidate 2, and so on. The names are followed by the votes. Write a program to read the data and evaluate the results of the survey.

   Print the results in alphabetical order by artist name and in order by votes received (most votes first). Print all output to the file, results.txt.

2. Write a program to read names and phone numbers into two arrays. Request a name and print the person's phone number. Use binary search to look up the name.

3. Write a program to read English words and their equivalent Spanish words into two arrays. Request the user to type several English words. For each, print the equivalent Spanish word. Choose a suitable end-of-data marker. Search for the typed words using binary search. Modify the program so that the user types Spanish words instead.

4. The *median* of a set of *n* numbers (not necessarily distinct) is obtained by arranging the numbers in order and taking the number in the middle. If *n* is odd, there is a unique middle number. If *n* is even, then the average of the two middle values is the median. Write a program to read a set of *n* positive integers (assume $n < 100$) and print their median; *n* is not given, but 0 indicates the end of the data.

5. The *mode* of a set of *n* numbers is the number that appears most frequently. For example, the mode of 7 3 8 5 7 3 1 3 4 8 9 is 3. Write a program to read a set of *n* positive integers (assume $n < 100$) and print their mode; *n* is not given, but 0 indicates the end of the data.

6. An array chosen contains n distinct integers arranged in no particular order. Another array called winners contains m distinct integers arranged in *ascending* order. Write code to determine how many of the numbers in chosen appear in winners.

7. A multiple-choice examination consists of 20 questions. Each question has five choices, labeled A, B, C, D, and E. The first line of data contains the correct answers to the 20 questions in the first 20 *consecutive* character positions, for example:

   BECDCBAADEBACBAEDDBE

   Each subsequent line contains the answers for a candidate. Data on a line consists of a candidate number (an integer), followed by one or more spaces, followed by the 20 answers given by the candidate in the next 20 *consecutive* character positions. An X is used if a candidate did not answer a particular question. You may assume all data is valid and stored in a file exam.dat. A sample line is as follows:

   4325 BECDCBAXDEBACCAEDXBE

   There are at most 100 candidates. A line containing a "candidate number" 0 only indicates the end of the data.

Points for a question are awarded as follows—correct answer: 4 points; wrong answer: -1 point; no answer: 0 points.

Write a program to process the data and print a report consisting of candidate number and the total points obtained by the candidate, *in ascending order by candidate number*. At the end, print the average number of points gained by the candidates.

8. A is an array sorted in descending order. B is an array sorted in descending order. Merge A and B into C so that C is in *descending* order.

9. A is an array sorted in descending order. B is an array sorted in descending order. Merge A and B into C so that C is in *ascending* order.

10. A is an array sorted in ascending order. B is an array sorted in descending order. Merge A and B into C so that C is in *ascending* order.

11. An array A contains integers that first increase in value and then decrease in value. Here's an example:

17	24	31	39	44	49	36	29	20	18	13
0	1	2	3	4	5	6	7	8	9	75

It is unknown at which point the numbers start to decrease. Write efficient code to code to copy the numbers in A to another array B so that B is sorted in ascending order. Your code must take advantage of the way the numbers are arranged in A.

12. Two words are anagrams if one word can be formed by rearranging all the letters of the other word, for example: section, notices. Write a program to read two words and determine whether they are anagrams.

Write another program to read a list of words and find all sets of words such that words within a set are anagrams of each other.

CHAPTER 2

■ ■ ■

Introduction to Objects

In this chapter, we will explain the following:

- What is a class, an object, a field, and a method

- That an object variable does not hold an object but, rather, a pointer (or reference) to where the object is actually located

- The distinction between a class variable (also called a static variable) and an instance variable (also called a non-static variable)

- The distinction between a class method (also called a static method) and an instance method (also called a non-static method)

- What the access modifiers public, private, and protected mean

- What is meant by information hiding

- How to refer to class and instance variables

- How to initialize class and instance variables

- What is a constructor and how to write one

- What is meant by overloading

- What is meant by data encapsulation

- How to write accessor and mutator methods

- How to print an object's data in various ways

- Why the `tostring()` method is special in Java

- What happens when we assign an object variable to another

- What it means to compare one object variable with another

- How to compare the contents of two objects

- How a function can return more than one value using an object

2.1 Objects

Java is considered an *object-oriented* programming language. The designers created it such that objects become the center of attention. Java programs create and manipulate objects in an attempt to model how the real world operates. For our purposes, an object is an entity that has a *state* and *methods* to manipulate that state. The state of an object is determined by its *attributes*.

For example, we can think of a person as an object. A person has attributes such as name, age, gender, height, color of hair, color of eyes, and so on. Within a program, each attribute is represented by an appropriate variable; for instance, a String variable can represent *name*, an int variable can represent *age*, a char variable can represent *gender*, a double variable can represent *height*, and so on.

We normally use the term *field names* (or, simply, *fields*) to refer to these variables. Thus, the *state* of an object is defined by the *values* in its *fields*. In addition, we will need methods to set and/or change the values of the fields as well as to retrieve their values. For example, if we are interested in a person's height, we would need a method to "look into" the object and return the value of the *height* field.

A car is another common example of an object. It has attributes such as manufacturer, model, seating capacity, fuel capacity, actual fuel in the tank, mileage, type of music equipment, and speed. A book object has attributes such as author, title, price, number of pages, type of binding (hardcover, paperback, spiral), and if it is in stock. A person, a car, and a book are examples of concrete objects. Note, however, that an object could also represent an abstract concept such as a department in a company or a faculty in a university.

In the previous example, we did not speak of a *specific* person. Rather, we spoke of a general category "person" such that everyone in the category has the attributes mentioned. (Similar remarks apply to car and book.) In Java terminology, "person" is a *class*. We think of a class as a general category (a template) from which we can create specific objects.

An object, then, is an *instance* of a class; in this example, a Person object would refer to a specific person. To work with two Person objects, we would need to create two objects from the class definition of Person. Each object would have its own copy of the field variables (also called *instance* variables); the values of the variables in one object could be different from the values of the variables in the other object.

2.2 Defining Classes and Creating Objects

The simplest Java programs consist of a single class. Within the class, we write one or more methods/functions to perform some task. Program P2.1 shows an example.

Program P2.1

```java
//prompt for two numbers and find their sum
import java.util.*;
public class Sum {
    public static void main(String[] args) {
        Scanner in = new Scanner(System.in);
        System.out.printf("Enter first number: ");
        int a = in.nextInt();
        System.out.printf("Enter second number: ");
        int b = in.nextInt();
        System.out.printf("%d + %d = %d\n", a, b, a + b);
    }
} //end class Sum
```

The program consists of one class (ProgramP1_1) and one method (main) within the class. The class is used simply as the framework within which to write the logic of the program. We will now show how to define and use a class to create (we say *instantiate*) objects.

In Java, every object belongs to some class and can be created from the class definition only. Consider the following (partial) definition of the class Book:

```
public class Book {
    private static double Discount = 0.25;    //class variable
    private static int MinBooks = 5;          //class variable

    private String author;     // instance variable
    private String title;      // instance variable
    private double price;      // instance variable
    private int pages;         // instance variable
    private char binding;      // instance variable
    private boolean inStock;   // instance variable

    // methods to manipulate book data go here
} //end class Book
```

The class header (the first line) consists of the following:

- An optional *access modifier*; public is used in the example and will be used for most of our classes. Essentially it means that the class is available for use by any other class; it can also be *extended* to create subclasses. Other access modifiers are abstract and final; we won't deal with those in this book.

- The keyword class.

- A user identifier for the name of the class; Book is used in the example.

The braces enclose the *body* of the class. In general, the body will include the declaration of the following:

- Static variables (class variables); there will be one copy for the entire class—all objects will share that one copy. A class variable is declared using the word static. If we omit the word static, the variable is *instance*.

- Non-static variables (instance variables); each object created will have its own copy. It's the instance variables that comprise the data for an object.

- Static methods (class methods); these are loaded once when the class is loaded and can be used without creating any objects. It makes no sense for a static method to access non-static variables (which belong to objects), so Java forbids it.

- Non-static methods (instance methods); these can be used *only* via an object created from the class. It's the non-static methods that manipulate the data (the non-static fields) in objects.

- The String class is predefined in Java. If word is String (a String object, to be precise) and we write word.toLowerCase(), we are asking that the instance method toLowerCase of the String class be applied to the String object, word. This method converts uppercase letters to lowercase in the (String) object used to invoke it.

- Similarly, if in is a Scanner object (created when we say new Scanner...), the expression in.nextInt() applies the instance method nextInt to the object in; here, it reads the next integer from the input stream associated with in.

In the Book class, we declare two class variables (Discount and MinBooks, declared with static) and six instance variables; they are *instance* by default (the word static is omitted).

2.2.1 Access to Class and Instance Variables

In addition to static, a field can be declared using the optional access modifiers private, public, or protected. In the Book class, we declared all our instance variables using private. The keyword private indicates that the variable is "known" only inside the class and can be manipulated *directly* only by methods within the class. In other words, no method from outside the class has direct access to a private variable. However, as we will see shortly, we can provide public methods that other classes can use to set and access the values of private variables. This way, we ensure that class data can be changed only by methods within the class.

Declaring a variable public means that it can be accessed directly from outside the class. Hence, other classes can "do as they please" with a public variable. For example, if Discount is declared as public, then any other class can access it using Book.Discount and change it in any way it pleases. This is not normally encouraged since a class then loses control over its data.

For the most part, we will declare a class's fields using private. Doing so is the first step in implementing the concept of *information hiding*, which is part of the philosophy of object-oriented programming. The idea is that users of an object must not be able to deal directly with the object's data; they should do so via the object's methods.

Declaring a variable protected means that it can be accessed directly from the class and any of its subclasses, as well as other classes in the same package. We will not use protected variables in this introduction.

If no access modifier is specified, then the variable can be accessed directly by other classes in the same package only.

A method *within* a class can refer to *any* variable (static or non-static, public or private) in the class simply by using its name. (An exception is that a *static* method cannot access non-static variables.) If a *static* variable is known outside the class (that is, not private), it is referenced by qualifying the variable with the class name, as in Book.Discount and Book.MinBooks.

From outside the class, a nonprivate *instance* variable can be referenced only via the object to which it belongs; this is illustrated in the next Section. However, as indicated, good programming practice dictates that, most of the time, our variables will be declared private, so the notion of direct access from outside the class does not arise.

2.2.2 Initializing Class and Instance Variables

When the Book class is loaded, storage is immediately allocated to the class variables Discount and MinBooks; they are then assigned initial values of 0.25 and 5, respectively. The meaning behind these variables is that if five or more copies of a book are sold, then a 25 percent discount is given. Since these values apply to all books, it would be a waste of storage to store them with each book's data, hence their declaration as static variables. All book objects will have access to the single copy of these variables. (Note, however, that if we wanted to vary these values from book to book, then they become attributes of a specific book and would have to be declared non-static.)

When the class is first loaded, no storage is allocated to the instance (non-static) variables. At this time, we have only a specification of the instance variables, but none actually exists as yet. They will come into existence when an object is created from the class. The data for an object is determined by the instance variables. When an object is "created," storage is allocated for all the instance variables defined in the class; each object created has its *own copy* of the instance variables. To create an object, we use the keyword new as in the following:

```
Book b;
b = new Book();
```

The first statement declares b as a variable of type Book. From this, we see that a class name is considered to be a type (similar to int or char) and can be used to declare variables. We say that b is an *object variable* of type Book.

The declaration of b does *not* create an object; it simply creates a variable whose value will eventually be a *pointer* to an object. When declared as shown, its value is undefined.

The second statement finds some available memory where a Book object can be stored, creates the object, and stores the *address* of the object in b. (Think of the address as the first memory location occupied by the object. If the object occupies locations 2575 to 2599, its address is 2575.) We say that b contains a *reference* or *pointer* to the object. Thus, the *value* of an object variable is a *memory address*, not an object. This is illustrated as shown in Figure 2-1.

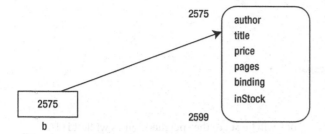

Figure 2-1. *An instance of a Book object*

As a shortcut, we can declare b and create a book object in one statement, like this:

```
Book b = new Book();
```

It is a common error to think that the Book variable b can hold a Book object. It cannot; it can hold only a *reference* to a Book object. (In a similar manner, we should be familiar with the idea that a String variable does not hold a string but, rather, the *address* of where the string is stored.) However, where the distinction (between an object and a reference to the object) does not matter, we will speak as if b holds a Book object.

Once an object b is created, we can refer to its instance fields like this:

```
b.author       b.title        b.price
b.pages        b.binding      b.inStock
```

However, we can do so from *outside* the class only if the fields are declared public. We will see later how to access the fields indirectly when they are declared private.

When an object is created, unless we say otherwise, its instance fields are initialized as follows:

- Numeric fields are set to 0.

- Character fields are set to '\0' (Unicode '\u0000', to be precise).

- Boolean fields are set to false.

- Object fields are set to null. (A variable with the value null means that it does not reference or point to anything.)

In our example, the following happens:

- b.author (of type String) is set to null; remember that String is an object type.

- b.title (of type String) is set to null.

- b.price (of type double) is set to 0.0.

- b.pages (of type int) is set to 0.

- b.binding (of type char) is set to '\0'.

- b.inStock (of type boolean) is set to false.

We could specify an initial value when we declare an instance variable. Consider this code:

```
public class Book {
    private static double Discount = 0.25;
    private static int MinBooks = 5;
```

```
        private String author = "No Author";
        private String title;
        private double price;
        private int pages;
        private char binding = 'P'; // for paperback
        private boolean inStock = true;
    }
```

Now, when an object is created, author, binding, and inStock will be set to the specified values while title, price, and pages will assume the default values. A variable is given a default value only if no explicit value is assigned to it. Suppose we create an object b with this:

```
    Book b = new Book();
```

The fields will be initialized as follows:

- author is set to "No Author".   // specified in the declaration

- title is set to null.   // default for (String) object type

- price is set to 0.0.   // default for numeric type

- pages is set to 0.   // default for numeric type

- binding is set to 'P'.   // specified in the declaration

- inStock is set to true.   // specified in the declaration

2.3 Constructors

Constructors provide more flexible ways of initializing the state of an object when it is created. In the following statement, Book() is termed a *constructor*:

```
    Book b = new Book();
```

It is similar to a method call. But, you might say, we did not write any such method in our class definition. True, but in such cases, Java provides a *default constructor*—one with no arguments (also called a *no-arg* constructor). The default constructor is quite simplistic; it just sets the values of the instance variables to their default initial values. Later, we could assign more meaningful values to the object's fields, as in the following:

```
    b.author = "Noel Kalicharan";
    b.title = "DigitalMath";
    b.price = 29.95;
    b.pages = 200;
    b.binding = 'P';   //for paperback
    b.inStock = true;   //stock is available
```

Now suppose that when we create a book object, we want Java to assign the author and title automatically. We want to be able to use statements such as the following for creating new book objects:

```
    Book b = new Book("Noel Kalicharan", "DigitalMath");
```

We can do this, but we must first write an appropriate constructor, one defined with two String parameters. The following shows how it can be done:

```
public Book(String a, String t) {
   author = a;
   title = t;
}
```

Here are some important points to note:

- A constructor for a class has the *same name* as the class. Our class is called Book; therefore, the constructor must be called Book. Since a constructor is meant to be used by other classes, it is declared public.

- A constructor can have zero or more parameters. When called, the constructor must be given the appropriate number and type of arguments. In our example, the constructor is declared with two String parameters, a and t. When calling the constructor, two String arguments must be supplied.

- The body of the constructor contains the code that would be executed when the constructor is called. Our example sets the instance variable author to the first argument and title to the second argument. In general, we can have statements other than those that set the values of instance variables. We can, for instance, validate a supplied value before assigning it to a field. We will see an example of this in the next section.

- A constructor does not have a return type, not even void.

- If initial values are provided for instance variables in their declaration, those values are stored *before* the constructor is called.

For example, suppose the class Book is now declared as follows:

```
public class Book {
   private static double Discount = 0.25;
   private static int MinBooks = 5;

   private String author = "No Author";
   private String title;
   private double price;
   private int pages;
   private char binding = 'P'; // for paperback
   private boolean inStock = true;

   public Book(String a, String t) {
      author = a;
      title = t;
   }
} //end class Book
```

The statement

```
Book b = new Book("Noel Kalicharan", "DigitalMath");
```

will be executed as follows:

1. Storage is found for a Book object, and the address of the storage is stored in b.

2. The fields are set as follows:

```
author is set to "No Author";    // specified in the declaration
title is set to null;            // default for (String) object type
price is set to 0.0;             // default for numeric type
pages is set to 0;               // default for numeric type
binding is set to 'P';           // specified in the declaration
inStock is set to true.          // specified in the declaration
```

3. The constructor is called with arguments "Noel Kalicharan" and "DigitalMath"; this sets author to "Noel Kalicharan" and title to "DigitalMath", leaving the other fields untouched. When the constructor is finished, the fields will have the following values:

```
author     "Noel Kalicharan"
title      "DigitalMath"
price      0.0
pages      0
binding    'P'
inStock    true
```

2.3.1 Overloading a Constructor

Java allows us to have more than one constructor, provided each has a different *signature*. When several constructors can have the same name, this is referred to as *overloading the constructor*. Suppose we want to be able to use the no-arg constructor as well as the one with author and title arguments. We can include both in the class declaration like this:

```java
public class Book {
    private static double Discount = 0.25;
    private static int MinBooks = 5;

    private String author = "No Author";
    private String title;
    private double price;
    private int pages;
    private char binding = 'P'; // for paperback
    private boolean inStock = true;

    public Book() { }

    public Book(String a, String t) {
        author = a;
        title = t;
    }
} //end class Book
```

Observe that the body of the no-arg constructor consists of an empty block. When the following statement is executed, the instance variables are set to their initial values (specified or default), and the constructor is executed. In this case, nothing further happens.

```
Book b = new Book();
```

Be warned that when we provide a constructor, the *default* no-arg constructor is no longer available. If we want to use a no-arg constructor as well, we must write it explicitly, as in the previous example. We are free, of course, to write whatever we want in the body, including nothing.

As a final example, we provide a constructor that lets us set all the fields explicitly when an object is created. Here it is:

```
public Book(String a, String t, double p, int g, char b, boolean s) {
    author = a;
    title = t;
    price = p;
    pages = g;
    binding = b;
    inStock = s;
}
```

If b is a variable of type Book, a sample call is as follows:

```
b = new Book("Noel Kalicharan", "DigitalMath", 29.95, 200, 'P', true);
```

The fields will be given the following values:

```
author     "Noel Kalicharan"
title      "DigitalMath"
price      29.95
pages      200
binding    'P'
inStock    true
```

2.4 Data Encapsulation, Accessor, and Mutator Methods

We will use the term *user class* to denote a class whose methods need to access the fields and methods of another class.

When a class's field is declared public, any other class can access the field directly, by name. Consider the following class:

```
public class Part {
    public static int NumParts = 0;    // class variable
    public String name;                // instance variable
    public double price;               // instance variable
}
```

Here, we define one static (or class) variable and two instance variables as public. *Any* user class can access the static variable using Part.NumParts and can include statements such as this:

```
Part.NumParts = 25;
```

This may not be desirable. Suppose NumParts is meant to count the number of objects created from Part. Any outside class can set it to any value it pleases, so the writer of the class Part cannot guarantee that it will always reflect the number of objects created.

An instance variable, as always, can be accessed via an object only. When a user class creates an object p of type Part, it can use p.price (or p.name) to refer directly to the instance variable and can change it, if desired, with a simple assignment statement. There is nothing to stop the user class from setting the variable to an unreasonable value. For instance, suppose that all prices are in the range 0.00 to 99.99. A user class can contain the following statement, compromising the integrity of the price data:

```
p.price = 199.99;
```

To solve these problems, we must make the data fields private; we say we must *hide* the data. We then provide public methods for others to set and retrieve the values in the fields. Private data and public methods are the essence of *data encapsulation*. Methods that set or change a field's value are called *mutator* methods. Methods that retrieve the value in a field are called *accessor* methods.

Let's show how the two problems mentioned can be solved. First, we redefine the fields as private:

```
public class Part {
    private static int NumParts = 0;    // class variable
    private String name;    // instance variable
    private double price;    // instance variable
}
```

Now that they are private, no other class has access to them. If we want NumParts to reflect the number of objects created from the class, we would need to increment it each time a constructor is called. We could, for example, write a no-arg constructor as follows:

```
public Part() {
    name = "NO PART";
    price = -1.0;    // we use -1 since 0 might be a valid price
    NumParts++;
}
```

Whenever a user class executes a statement such as the following, a new Part object is created *and* 1 is added to NumParts:

```
Part p = new Part();
```

Hence, the value of NumParts will always be the number of Part objects created. Further, this is the *only* way to change its value; the writer of the class Part can guarantee that the value of NumParts will always be the number of objects created.

Of course, a user class may need to know the value of NumParts at any given time. Since it has no access to NumParts, we must provide a *public accessor method* (GetNumParts, say; we use uppercase G for a static accessor, since it provides a quick way to distinguish between static and non-static), which returns the value. Here is the method:

```
public static int GetNumParts() {
    return NumParts;
}
```

The method is declared static since it operates only on a static variable and does not need an object to be invoked. It can be called with Part.GetNumParts(). If p is a Part object, Java allows you to call it with p.GetNumParts(). However, this tends to imply that GetNumParts is an instance method (one that is called via an object and operates on instance variables), so it could be misleading. We recommend that class (static) methods be called via the class name rather than via an object from the class.

As an exercise, add a field to the Book class to count the number of book objects created and update the constructors to increment this field.

2.4.1 An Improved Constructor

Instead of a no-arg constructor, we could take a more realistic approach and write a constructor that lets the user assign a name and price when an object is created, as in the following:

```
Part af = new Part("Air Filter", 8.75);
```

We could write the constructor as:

```
public Part(String n, double p) {
    name = n;
    price = p;
    NumParts++;
}
```

This will work except that a user can still set an invalid price for a part. There is nothing to stop the user from writing this statement:

```
Part af = new Part("Air Filter", 199.99);
```

The constructor will dutifully set price to the invalid value 199.99. However, we can do more in a constructor than merely assign values to variables. We can test a value and reject it, if necessary. We will take the view that if an invalid price is supplied, the object will still be created but a message will be printed and the price will be set to -1.0. Here is the new version of the constructor:

```
public Part(String n, double p) {
    name = n;
    if (p < 0.0 || p > 99.99) {
        System.out.printf("Part: %s\n", name);
        System.out.printf("Invalid price: %3.2f. Set to -1.0.\n", p);
        price = -1.0;
    }
    else price = p;
    NumParts++;
} //end constructor Part
```

As a matter of good programming style, we should declare the price limits (0.00 and 99.99) and the "null" price (-1.0) as class constants. We could use the following:

```
private static final double MinPrice = 0.0;
private static final double MaxPrice = 99.99;
private static final double NullPrice = -1.0;
```

These identifiers can now be used in the constructor.

2.4.2 Accessor Methods

Since a user class may need to know the name or price of an item, we must provide public accessor methods for name and price. An accessor method simply returns the value in a particular field. By convention, we preface the name of these methods with the word get. The methods are as follows:

```
public String getName() {   // accessor
    return name;
}

public double getPrice() {  // accessor
    return price;
}
```

Note that the return type of an accessor is the same as the type of the field. For example, the return type of getName is String since name is of type String.

Since an accessor method returns the value in an instance field, it makes sense to call it only in relation to a specific object (since each object has its own instance fields). If p is an object of type Part, then p.getName() returns the value in the name field of p and p.getPrice() returns the value in the price field of p.

As an exercise, write accessor methods for all the fields of the Book class.

These accessors are examples of non-static or instance methods (the word static is not used in their declaration). We can think of each object as having its own copy of the instance methods in a class. In practice, though, the methods are merely *available* to an object. There will be one copy of a method, and the method will be *bound to* a specific object when the method is invoked on the object.

Assuming that a Part object p is stored at location 725, we can picture the object as shown in Figure 2-2.

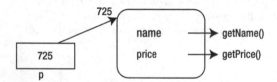

Figure 2-2. *A Part object with its fields and accessors*

Think of the fields name and price as locked inside a box, and the only way the outside world can see them is via the methods getName and getPrice.

2.4.3 Mutator Methods

As the writer of the class, we have to decide whether we will let a user change the name or price of an object after it has been created. It is reasonable to assume that the user may not want to change the name. However, prices change, so we should provide a method (or methods) for changing the price. As an example, we write a *public mutator method* (setPrice, say) that user classes can call, as in the following:

```
p.setPrice(24.95);
```

This sets the price of Part object p to 24.95. As before, the method will not allow an invalid price to be set. It will validate the supplied price and print an appropriate message, if necessary. Using the constants declared in Section 2.4.1, here is setPrice:

```
public void setPrice(double p) {
   if (p < MinPrice || p > MaxPrice) {
      System.out.printf("Part: %s\n", name);
      System.out.printf("Invalid price: %3.2f; Set to %3.2f\n", p, NullPrice);
      price = NullPrice;
   }
   else price = p;
} //end setPrice
```

With this addition, we can think of Part p as shown in Figure 2-3.

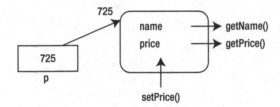

Figure 2-3. *Part object with setPrice() added*

Observe the direction of the arrow for setPrice; a value is being sent from the outside world to the private field of the object.

Again, we emphasize the superiority of declaring a field private and providing mutator/accessor methods for it as opposed to declaring the field public and letting a user class access it directly.

We could also provide methods to increase or decrease the price by a given amount or by a given percentage. These are left as exercises.

As another exercise, write mutator methods for the price and inStock fields of the Book class.

2.5 Printing an Object's Data

To verify that our parts are being given the correct values, we would need some way of printing the values in an object's fields.

2.5.1 Using an Instance Method (the Preferred Way)

One way of doing this is to write an instance method (printPart, say), which, when invoked on an object, will print *that* object's data. To print the data for Part p, we will write this:

```
p.printPart();
```

Here is the method:

```
public void printPart() {
   System.out.printf("\nName of part: %s\n", name);
   System.out.printf("Price: $%3.2f\n", price);
} //end printPart
```

Suppose we create a part with this:

```
Part af = new Part("Air Filter", 8.75);
```

The expression af.printPart() would display the following:

```
Name of part: Air Filter
Price: $8.75
```

When printPart is called via af, the references in printPart to the fields name and price become references to the fields of af. This is illustrated in Figure 2-4.

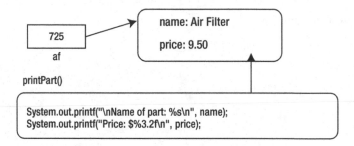

Figure 2-4. name *and* price *refer to the fields of* af

2.5.2 Using a Static Method

We could, if we want, write printPart as a static method, which will be called with p as an *argument* in order to print its fields. In this case, we will write the following:

```
public static void printPart(Part p) {
    System.out.printf("\nName of part: %s\n", p.name);
    System.out.printf("Price: $%3.2f\n", p.price);
}
```

The field names have to be qualified with the object variable p. Without p, we would have the case of a static method referring to a non-static field, which is forbidden by Java.

If c is a Part object created in a user class, we will have to use the following to print its fields:

```
Part.printPart(c);
```

This is slightly more cumbersome than using the instance method, shown previously. By comparison, you can use, for instance, Character.isDigit(ch) to access the static method isDigit in the standard Java class Character.

2.5.3 Using the toString() Method

The toString method returns a String and is special in Java. If we use an object variable in a context where a string is needed, then Java will attempt to invoke toString from the class to which the object belongs. For example, suppose we write the following, where p is a Part variable:

```
System.out.printf("%s", p);
```

Since it is not clear what it means to print an arbitrary object, Java will look for guidance in the class itself. Presumably, the class will know how to print its objects. If it provides a `toString` method, Java will use it. (If it doesn't, Java will print something generic like the name of the class and the address, in hexadecimal, of the object, for instance: Part@72e15c32.) In our example, we could add the following to the class Part:

```java
public String toString() {
    return "\nName of part: " + name + "\nPrice: $" + price + "\n";
}
```

If af is the Air Filter part, then the following statement would invoke the call af.toString():

```java
System.out.printf("%s", af);
```

In effect, the printf becomes this:

```java
System.out.printf("%s", af.toString());
```

af.toString() will return this:

```
"\nName of part: Air Filter \nPrice: $8.75\n"
```

The result is that printf will print this:

```
Name of part: Air Filter
Price: $8.75
```

2.6 The Class Part

Putting all the changes together, the class Part now looks like this:

```java
public class Part {
    // class constants
    private static final double MinPrice = 0.0;
    private static final double MaxPrice = 99.99;
    private static final double NullPrice = -1.0;
    private static int NumParts = 0;    // class variable

    private String name;     // instance variable
    private double price;    // instance variable

    public Part(String n, double p) {    // constructor
        name = n;
        if (p < MinPrice || p > MaxPrice) {
            System.out.printf("Part: %s\n", name);
            System.out.printf("Invalid price: %3.2f; Set to %3.2f\n", p, NullPrice);
            price = NullPrice;
        }
        else price = p;
        NumParts++;
    } //end constructor Part
```

```
        public static int GetNumParts() {    // accessor
            return NumParts;
        }

        public String getName() {    // accessor
            return name;
        }

        public double getPrice() {    // accessor
            return price;
        }

        public void setPrice(double p) {    // mutator
            if (p < MinPrice || p > MaxPrice) {
                System.out.printf("Part: %s\n", name);
                System.out.printf("Invalid price: %3.2f; Set to %3.2f\n", p, NullPrice);
                price = NullPrice;
            }
            else price = p;
        } //end setPrice

        public void printPart() {
            System.out.printf("\nName of part: %s\n", name);
            System.out.printf("Price: $%3.2f\n", price);
        }

        public String toString() {
            return "\nName of part: " + name + "\nPrice: $" + price + "\n";
        }
    } // end class Part
```

2.6.1 Testing the Class Part

When we write a class, we must test it to ensure it is working as it should. For the class Part, we must check that the constructor is working properly, in other words, that the accessor methods return the correct values and the mutator method sets the (new) price correctly.

We must also check that the class handles invalid prices properly. In Program P2.2, we create three part objects (one with an invalid price) and print their name/price information. We then print the number of parts created by calling GetNumParts. *Before* we run the test program, we should work out the expected output so we can *predict* what a correct program should output. If the output matches our prediction, fine; if not, there is a problem that must be addressed.

Program P2.2

```
        public class PartTest{
            // a program for testing the class Part

            public static void main(String[] args) {
                Part a, b, c; // declare 3 Part variables

                // create 3 Part objects
                a = new Part("Air Filter", 8.75);
```

```
        b = new Part("Ball Joint", 29.95);
        c = new Part("Headlamp", 199.99); // invalid price

        a.printPart(); // should print Air Filter, $8.75
        b.printPart(); // should print Ball Joint, $29.95
        c.printPart(); // should print Headlamp, $-1.0

        c.setPrice(36.99);
        c.printPart(); // should print Headlamp, $36.99

        // print the number of parts; should print 3
        System.out.printf("\nNumber of parts: %d\n", Part.GetNumParts());
    } //end main
} // end class PartTest
```

When Program P2.2 is run, the following output is produced:

```
Part: Headlamp
Invalid price: 199.99; Set to -1.0

Name of part: Air Filter
Price: $8.75

Name of part: Ball Joint
Price: $29.95

Name of part: Headlamp
Price: $-1.0

Name of part: Headlamp
Price: $36.99

Number of parts: 3
```

This is the expected output, so we are assured that the class is working as it should.

Here's a final word on the Part class. If, for some strange reason, the class Part did not provide a printPart or a toString method, a user class can write its own method to print a part's fields. However, it would have to use the accessor methods of Part to get at an object's data since it cannot reference the private fields directly. The following shows how to do this:

```
    public static void printPart(Part p) {
    // a method in a user class
        System.out.printf("\nName of part: %s\n", p.getName());
        System.out.printf("Price: $%3.2f\n", p.getPrice());
    }
```

From the user class, we can write this:

```
    Part af = new Part("Air Filter", 8.75);
    printPart(af);
```

The following will be printed:

```
Name of part: Air Filter
Price: $8.75
```

2.7 How to Name Your Java Files

If our program consists of a single public class, Java requires us to store such a class in a file called *name of class*.
java. So if the class is Palindrome, we must call the file Palindrome.java.

In the Part example, we must store the Part class in a file called Part.java, and we must store the PartTest class in a file called PartTest.java. We could compile these classes with the following commands:

```
javac Part.java
javac PartTest.java
```

We could then run the test with this command:

```
java PartTest
```

Recall that this will execute main from the class PartTest. Note that it makes no sense to attempt something like this:

```
java Part
```

If we do, Java will simply complain that there is no main method in the class Part.

We could, if we want, put both classes in one file. However, only one of the classes can be designated as public. So, for example, we could leave class PartTest as it is and simply remove the word public from public class Part. We could now put both classes in one file, which *must* be named PartTest.java since PartTest is the public class.

When we compile PartTest.java, Java will produce two files—PartTest.class and Part.class. We can then run the test with this:

```
java PartTest
```

2.8 Working with Objects

So far, we have seen how to define a class and create objects from the class using a constructor. We have also seen how to retrieve data from an object using accessor methods and how to change data in an object using mutator methods. We now look at some issues that arise in working with objects.

2.8.1 Assigning an Object Variable to Another

An object variable (p, say) is declared using a class name (Part, say), like this:

```
Part p;
```

We emphasize again that p cannot hold an object but rather a pointer (or reference) to an object. The value of p is a memory address—the location at which a Part object is stored. Consider the following:

```
Part a = new Part("Air Filter", 8.75);
Part b = new Part("Ball Joint", 29.95);
```

Suppose the Air Filter object is stored at location 3472 and the Ball Joint object is stored at location 5768. Then the value of a would be 3472, and the value of b would be 5768. After the two objects have been created, we have the situation shown in Figure 2-5.

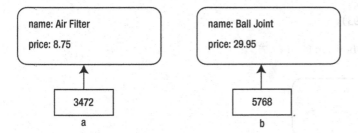

Figure 2-5. *After creation of two Part objects*

Suppose we then assign a to c, like this:

```
Part c = a; // assign 3472 to c
```

This assigns the value 3472 to c; in effect, c (as well as a) now points to the Air Filter object. We can use either variable to access the object. For instance, the following sets the price of the Air Filter object to 9.50:

```
c.setPrice(9.50);
```

We have the situation shown in Figure 2-6.

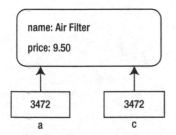

Figure 2-6. *After assigning a to c*

If we now retrieve the price of object a with the following, the (new) price of Air Filter would be returned:

```
a.getPrice(); // returns the price 9.50
```

Suppose we write this statement:

```
c = b; // assign 5768 to c
```

c is assigned 5768 and now points to the Ball Joint object. It no longer points to Air Filter. We can use b or c to access Ball Joint data. If we have the *address* of an object, we have all the information we need to manipulate the object.

2.8.2 Losing Access to an Object

Consider the following:

```
Part a = new Part("Air Filter", 8.75);
Part b = new Part("Ball Joint", 29.95);
```

Assume these statements create the situation shown in Figure 2-7.

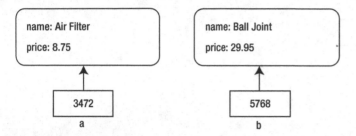

Figure 2-7. *After creation of two Part objects*

Suppose we execute this statement:

```
a = b;
```

The situation changes to that shown in Figure 2-8.

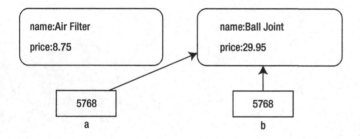

Figure 2-8. *After assigning b to a*

Both a and b now have the same value, 5768. They both point to the Ball Joint object. In effect, when we change the value of a, we lose access to the Air Filter object. When no variable points to an object, the object is inaccessible and cannot be used. The storage occupied by the object will be garbage collected by the system and returned to the pool of available storage. This takes place automatically without any action on the part of the program.

However, suppose we had written this:

```
c = a;    // c holds 3472, address of "Air Filter"
a = b;    // a, b hold 5768, address of "Ball Joint"
```

Now, we would still have access to Air Filter via c.

2.8.3 Comparing Object Variables

Consider the following that creates two identical, but separate, objects and stores their addresses in a and b:

```
Part a = new Part("Air Filter", 8.75);
Part b = new Part("Air Filter", 8.75);
```

Assume these statements create the situation shown in Figure 2-9.

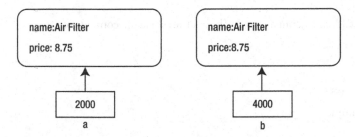

Figure 2-9. *After creation of two identical objects*

Since the objects are identical, it may come as a surprise that the following condition is false:

```
a == b
```

However, if you remember that a and b contain *addresses* and not objects, then we are comparing the address in a (2000) with the address in b (4000). Since these are different, the comparison is false.

Two object variables would compare equal only when they contain the *same address* (in which case they point to the same object). This could happen, for instance, when we assign one object variable to another.

We would, of course, need to know whether two *objects* are the same. That is, if a and b point to two objects, are the *contents* of these objects the same? To do this, we must write our own method that compares the fields, one by one.

Using the class Part as an example, we write a method equals, which returns true if one object is identical to another and false otherwise. The method can be used as follows to compare Part objects pointed to by a and b:

```
if (a.equals(b)) ...
```

The method simply checks whether the name fields and the price fields of the two objects are the same. Since the name fields are String objects, we call the equals method of the String class to compare them.[1]

```
public boolean equals(Part p) {
    return name.equals(p.name) && (price == p.price);
}
```

In the method, the variables name and price (without being qualified) refer to the fields of the object via which the method is invoked. Suppose we had used the following expression:

```
a.equals(b)
```

The variables refer to the fields a.name and a.price. Of course, p.name and p.price refer to the fields of the argument to equals (b, in the example). In effect, the return statement becomes this:

```
return a.name.equals(b.name) && (a.price == b.price);
```

Now, suppose we have these statements:

```
Part a = new Part("Air Filter", 8.75);
Part b = new Part("Air Filter", 8.75);
```

(a == b) is false (since a and b hold different addresses), but a.equals(b) is true (since the contents of the objects they point to are the same).

2.9 The `null` Pointer

An object variable is declared as in the following example:

```
Part p;
```

Initially, it is undefined (just like variables of the primitive types). The most common way to give p a value is to create a Part object and store its address in p using the new operator, like this:

```
p = new Part("Air Filter", 8.75);
```

Java also provides a special pointer value, denoted by null, which can be assigned to any object variable. We could write the following to assign null to the Part variable, p:

```
Part p = null;
```

In effect, this says that p has a defined value, but it does not point to anything. If p has the value null, it is an error to attempt to reference an object pointed to by p. Put another way, if p is null, it makes no sense to talk about p.name or p.price since p is not pointing to anything.

If two object variables p and q are both null, we can compare them with ==, and the result will be true. On the other hand, if p points to some object and q is null, then, as expected, the comparison is false.

Null pointers are useful when we need to initialize a list of object variables. We also use them when we are creating data structures such as linked lists or binary trees and we need a special value to indicate the end of a list. We will see how to use null pointers in the next chapter.

2.10 Passing an Object as an Argument

An object variable holds an address—the address of an actual object. When we use an object variable as an argument to a method, it's an address that is passed to the method. Since arguments in Java are passed "by value," a temporary location containing the value of the variable is what is actually passed. In Section 2.6.1, we met the static method printPart in the class Part for printing a part. Here it is:

```
public static void printPart(Part p) {
    System.out.printf("\nName of part: %s\n", p.name);
    System.out.printf("Price: $%3.2f\n", p.price);
}
```

Further, suppose a user class contains these statements:

```
Part af = new Part("Air Filter", 8.75);
printPart(af);
```

and suppose the first statement assigns the address 4000, say, to af. When printPart is called, 4000 is copied to a temporary location and this location is passed to printPart where it becomes known as p, the name of the formal parameter. Since the value of p is 4000, in effect it has access to the original object. In this example, the method simply prints the values of the instance variables. But it could also change them, if it wanted.

Consider the following method in the class Part, which adds amount to the price of a part:

```
public static void changePrice(Part p, double amount) {
    p.price += amount;
}
```

The user class can add 1.50 to the price of the Air Filter with this call:

```
Part.changePrice(af, 1.50);
```

As indicated earlier, the parameter p has access to the original object. Any change made to the object pointed to by p is, in fact, a change to the original object.

We emphasize that the method *cannot* change the *value* of the actual argument af (since it has no access to it), but it *can* change the *object pointed to* by af.

In passing, note that we have used this example mainly for illustrative purposes. In practice, it would probably be better to write an instance method to change the price of a Part object.

2.11 Array of Objects

In Java, a String is an object. Therefore, an array of Strings is, in fact, an array of objects. However, a String is a special kind of object in Java and, in some ways, is treated differently from other objects. For one thing, a String is *immutable*; we cannot change its value. For another, we think of a String as having one field—the characters in the string—whereas a typical object will have several. For these reasons, we take a look at arrays of objects other than Strings.

Consider the class Part defined previously. The class contains two instance variables defined as follows:

```
public class Part {
    private String name;   // instance variable
    private double price;  // instance variable

    // methods and static variables
} //end class Part
```

It is helpful to recall what happens when we declare a Part variable p as in the following:

```
Part p;
```

First, remember that p can hold the *address* of a Part object, not an object itself. The declaration simply allocates storage *for p* but leaves it undefined. We can assign the null value to p, with this:

```
p = null;
```

We can also create a Part object and assign its address to p with this statement:

```
p = new Part("Air Filter", 8.75);
```

Now consider the following declaration:

```
Part[] part = new Part[5];
```

This declares an array called part with 5 elements. Since they are object variables, these elements are guaranteed by Java to be set to null. As yet, no Part objects have been created. We can create objects and assign them individually to each element of part, as follows:

```
part[0] = new Part("Air Filter", 8.75);
part[1] = new Part("Ball Joint", 29.95);
part[2] = new Part("Headlamp", 36.99);
part[3] = new Part("Spark Plug", 5.00);
part[4] = new Part("Disc Pads", 24.95);
```

The array part can now be pictured as shown in Figure 2-10.

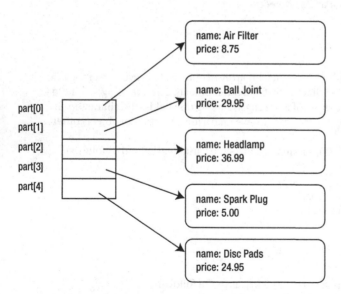

Figure 2-10. *An array of* Part *objects*

Each element of part contains the address of the corresponding object.

Remember that, in general, each element of an array can be treated in the same way as a simple variable of the array type. For instance, part[2] can be treated in the same way as p, above. And just as we can write p.setPrice(40.00), we can write part[2].setPrice(40.00) to change the price of Headlamp to 40.00.

How do we refer to the fields of a Part object? As usual, it depends on whether the code is being written inside the class Part or outside of it. If inside, the code can access the instance variables name and price directly, for example, part[2].name. If outside, it must use the accessor and mutator methods to get and set the values in the fields, for example, part[2].getName().

If we have to deal with hundreds of parts, it would be better to store the parts' data in a file (parts.dat, say) and read them into the array using a for or while loop. Suppose the data above was stored in the file like this (we write the part name as one word so it can be read with next from the Scanner class):

```
AirFilter   8.75
BallJoint   29.95
Headlamp    36.99
Spark Plug  5.00
DiscPads    24.95
```

We can set up the part array with the following code:

```
Scanner in = new Scanner(new FileReader("parts.dat"));
Part[] part = new Part[5];
for (int h = 0; h < part.length; h++)
    part[h] = new Part(in.next(), in.nextDouble());
```

This code is much better and more flexible. To read 1,000 parts, we just need to change the declaration of part and supply the data in the file. The code above remains unchanged. As usual, we don't *have* to fill the entire array with parts data. We can read data until some end-of-data marker (End, say) is reached.

If we need to print the parts' data, we could use the following:

```
for (int h = 0; h <  part.length; h++) part[h].printPart();
```

Suppose we want to interchange two parts in the array, for example, part[2] with part[4]. We do it the same way we would interchange the values of any two variables of the same type, like this:

```
Part p = part[2];
part[2] = part[4];
part[4] = p;
```

It is useful to note that the actual objects remain where they were originally stored. All we do here is exchange the addresses stored in part[2] and part[4]. In Figure 2-10, think of the arrows as being interchanged.

2.11.1 Finding the Part with the Lowest Price

Suppose we want to find the part with the lowest price (in one sense, we want to find the "smallest" object). Assuming we are writing this code outside the class Part, we can write getLowestPrice to return the position of the part with the lowest price as follows:

```
public static int getLowestPrice(Part[]  part, int lo, int hi) {
// return the position of the part with the lowest price
// from  part[lo] to  part[hi], inclusive

   int small = lo;
   for (int h = lo + 1; h <= hi; h++)
```

```
            if (part[h].getPrice() <  part[small].getPrice()) small = h;
        return small;
    } //end getLowestPrice
```

If we were writing inside the class Part, we could leave the method as it is. But since we now have direct access to the instance variables, we could replace the if statement with this one:

```
if (part[h].price < part[small].price) small = h;
```

To print the name of the part with the lowest price, we could write this:

```
System.out.printf("\nPart with lowest price: %s\n",
    part[getLowestPrice(part, 0,  part.length-1)].getName());
```

As an exercise, write a function to return the item with the highest price.

2.12 Searching an Array of Objects

We assume you know how to search for an item in an array of primitive types or an array of strings. Here, we consider how to search an array of objects (more precisely, references to objects) with more than one field. For example, suppose we had a Person class defined (partially) by the following:

```
public class Person {
    String name;
    int age;
    char gender;

    // constructors, static fields and other methods
} //end class Person
```

We want to search an array person containing objects of type Person for one with a given name, key. In the case of searching for a primitive type or string, the type of the search key is the same as the type of elements in the array. In the case of searching an array of objects with more than one field, the type of the search key is the same as *one of the fields* of the object.

Our search method must compare key with the correct field. In this example, we compare key with person[h].name. The following method searches for a given name in an array of Person. We use equalsIgnoreCase so that case differences in the key and the array would not matter; Mary would be the same as mary.

```
// search for key in the first n elements of the array person;
// if found, return the position, else return -1
public static int sequentialSearch(String key, Person[] person, int n) {
    for (int h = 0; h < n; h++)
        if (key.equalsIgnoreCase(person[h].name)) return h;
    return -1;
}
```

If we want to search for someone with a given age, we just need to declare key as int and change the if statement to this:

```
if (key == person[h].age) return h;
```

Note that this would return the first person it finds with the given age. We write Program P2.3 to test this function.

Program P2.3

```java
import java.util.*;
public class SearchTest {
    public static void main(String[] args) {
        // set up an array with 7 persons
        Person[] person = new Person[7];
        person[0] = new Person("Gary", 25, 'M');
        person[1] = new Person("Inga", 21, 'F');
        person[2] = new Person("Abel", 30, 'M');
        person[3] = new Person("Olga", 36, 'F');
        person[4] = new Person("Nora", 19, 'F');
        person[5] = new Person("Mary", 27, 'F');
        person[6] = new Person("Bert", 32, 'M');

        Scanner in = new Scanner(System.in);
        String s;
        System.out.printf("Enter names, one at a time, and I'll tell you\n");
        System.out.printf("their age and gender. To end, press Enter\n\n");
        while (!(s = in.nextLine()).equals("")) {
            int n = sequentialSearch(s, person, person.length);
            if (n >= 0)
                System.out.printf("%d %c\n\n", person[n].age, person[n].gender);
            else System.out.printf("Not found\n\n");
        }
    } // end main

    // search for key in the first n elements of the array person ;
    // if found, return the position, else return -1
    public static int sequentialSearch(String key, Person[] person, int n) {
        for (int h = 0; h < n; h++)
            if (key.equalsIgnoreCase(person[h].name)) return h;
        return -1;
    } // end sequentialSearch

} // end class SearchTest

class Person {
    String name;
    int age;
    char gender;
    Person(String n, int a, char g) {
        name = n;
        age = a;
        gender = g;
    }
} //end class Person
```

The main method sets up an array called person with data for seven people. It then requests the user to enter names. For each name, sequentialSearch is called; it returns a value n, say. If found (n >= 0), the age and gender of the person is printed. If not, the message Not found is printed. The following is a sample run:

```
Enter names, one at a time, and I'll tell you
their age and gender. To end, press Enter

Olga
36  F

Bart
Not found

bert
32  M

INGA
21  F
```

Note how we define the class Person. We omit the word public so we can put it in the same file as SearchTest. For variety, we use no access modifier (public or private) on the field names—name, age, gender. When we do this, other classes in the same *file* can refer to the field names directly; for example, in main, we refer to person[n].age and person[n].gender.

We can also use a binary search on an array of objects, provided the objects are sorted based on the field we want to search. For example, we can binary-search the person array for a name provided the objects are arranged in order by name. Here is the function:

```
// search for a person with name key in the first n elements of the
// array person ; if found, return the position, else return -1
public static int binarySearch(String key, Person[] person, int n) {
    int lo = 0, hi = n - 1;
    while (lo <= hi) {   // as long as more elements remain to consider
        int mid = (lo + hi) / 2;
        int cmp = key.compareToIgnoreCase(person[mid].name);
        if (cmp == 0) return mid;     // search succeeds
        if (cmp < 0) hi = mid - 1;    // key is 'less than' person[mid].name
        else lo = mid + 1;            // key is 'greater than' person[mid].name
    }
    return -1;          // key is not in the array
} // end binarySearch
```

As an exercise, write a program similar to Program P2.3 to test binarySearch.

2.13 Sorting an Array of Objects

We assume you know how to sort an array of strings or primitive types using selection and insertion sort. The following shows how to sort an *object* array, Person, in ascending order by name using selection sort:

```
public static void selectionSort(Person[] list, int lo, int hi) {
// sort list[lo] to list[hi] using selection sort
    for (int h = lo; h <= hi; h++)
```

```
        swap(list, h, getSmallest(list, h, hi));
    } //end selectionSort

    public static int getSmallest(Person[] list, int lo, int hi) {
    // return the position of the 'smallest' name from list[lo] to list[hi]
        int small = lo;
        for (int h = lo + 1; h <= hi; h++)
            if (list[h].name.compareToIgnoreCase(list[small].name) < 0) small = h;
        return small;
    } //end getSmallest

    public static void swap(Person[] list, int h, int k) {
    // swaps list[h] with list[k]
        Person hold = list[h];
        list[h] = list[k];
        list[k] = hold;
    } //end swap
```

In getSmallest, we compare the name field of one array element with the name field of another array element. We could sort the array person from Program P2.1 with the following call:

```
    selectionSort(person, 0, person.length - 1);
```

We could then print the array person with this:

```
    for (int h = 0; h < person.length; h++) person[h].printPerson();
```

where printPerson is defined in class Person as follows:

```
    void printPerson() {
        System.out.printf("%s %d %c\n", name, age, gender);
    }
```

For the array in Program P2.3, this will print the following output:

```
Abel 30 M
Bert 32 M
Gary 25 M
Inga 21 F
Mary 27 F
Nora 19 F
Olga 36 F
```

We can also sort an array of Person objects using insertion sort as follows:

```
    public static void insertionSort(Person[] list, int lo, int hi) {
    //sort list[lo] to list[hi] in ascending order by name
        for (int h = lo + 1; h <= hi; h++) {
```

```
            Person hold = list[h];
            int k = h - 1; //start comparing with previous item
            while (k >= 0 && hold.name.compareToIgnoreCase(list[k].name) < 0) {
               list[k + 1] = list[k];
               --k;
            }
            list[k + 1] = hold;
         } //end for
      } //end insertionSort
```

We could sort, by name, the array person from Program P2.3 with the following call:

```
insertionSort(person, 0, person.length - 1);
```

In the while condition, we compare the name field of the person being processed (the one in position h) with the name field of an array element.

2.14 Using a Class to Group Data: Word Frequency Count

In Section 1.8, we wrote a program (Program P1.7) to do a frequency count of the words in a passage. There, we used a String array (wordlist) to hold the words and an int array (frequency) to hold the frequencies. The code was written such that frequency[i] held the count for the word in wordlist[i]. We now show how to solve the same problem in a slightly different way by using a class.

We can think of each word in the passage as an object with two attributes—the letters in the word and the number of times it appears. We will define a class, WordInfo, from which we will create "word objects."

```
class WordInfo {
    String word;
    int freq = 0;

    WordInfo(String w, int f) {
        word = w;
        freq = f;
    }

    void incrFreq() {
        freq++;
    }
} //end class WordInfo
```

The class has two fields: word and freq. It has a constructor to initialize a WordInfo object to a given word and frequency. It also has a method to add 1 to the frequency of a word. Suppose wo is a WordInfo object created with this statement:

```
WordInfo wo = new WordInfo(aWord, 1); //String aWord
```

wo.word refers to the word, and wo.freq is its frequency. And we can add 1 to its frequency with wo.incrFreq(). Next, we will define a WordInfo array; each element will hold information about one word.

```
WordInfo[] wordTable = new WordInfo[MaxWords + 1];
```

MaxWords denotes the maximum number of distinct words catered for. For testing the program, we have used 50 for this value. If the number of distinct words in the passage exceeds MaxWords (50, say), any words after the 50th will be read but not stored, and a message to that effect will be printed. However, the count for a word already stored will be incremented if it is encountered again.

These ideas are implemented as shown in Program P2.4.

Program P2.4

```java
import java.io.*;
import java.util.*;
public class P2_4WordFrequency {
    final static int MaxWords = 50;

    public static void main(String[] args) throws IOException {
        WordInfo[] wordTable = new WordInfo[MaxWords];

        FileReader in = new FileReader("passage.txt");
        PrintWriter out = new PrintWriter(new FileWriter("output.txt"));

        for (int h = 0; h < MaxWords; h++) wordTable[h] = new WordInfo("", 0);
        int numWords = 0;

        String word = getWord(in).toLowerCase();
        while (!word.equals("")) {
            int loc = binarySearch(word, wordTable, 0, numWords-1);
            if (word.compareTo(wordTable[loc].word) == 0) wordTable[loc].incrFreq();
            else //this is a new word
                if (numWords < MaxWords) { //if table is not full
                    addToList(word, wordTable, loc, numWords-1);
                    ++numWords;
                }
                else out.printf("'%s' not added to table\n", word);
            word = getWord(in).toLowerCase();
        }

        printResults(out, wordTable, numWords);
        in.close();
        out.close();
    } //end main

    public static int binarySearch(String key, WordInfo[] list, int lo, int hi) {
    //search for key from list[lo] to list[hi]
    //if found, return its location;
    //if not found, return the location in which it should be inserted
    //the calling program will check the location to determine if found
        while (lo <= hi) {
            int mid = (lo + hi) / 2;
            int cmp = key.compareTo(list[mid].word);
            if (cmp == 0) return mid;   // search succeeds
            if (cmp < 0) hi = mid -1;   // key is 'less than' list[mid].word
            else lo = mid + 1;       // key is 'greater than' list[mid].word
        }
```

```
        return lo; //key must be inserted in location lo
    } //end binarySearch

    public static void addToList(String item, WordInfo[] list, int p, int n) {
    //sets list[p].word to item; sets list[p].freq to 1
    //shifts list[n] down to list[p] to the right
        for (int h = n; h >= p; h--) list[h + 1] = list[h];
        list[p] = new WordInfo(item, 1);
    } //end addToList

    public static void printResults(PrintWriter out, WordInfo[] list, int n) {
        out.printf("\nWords            Frequency\n\n");
        for (int h = 0; h < n; h++)
            out.printf("%-20s %2d\n", list[h].word, list[h].freq);
    } //end printResults

    public static String getWord(FileReader in) throws IOException {
    //returns the next word found
        final int MaxLen = 255;
        int c, n = 0;
        char[] word = new char[MaxLen];
        // read over non-letters
        while (!Character.isLetter((char) (c = in.read())) && (c != -1)) ;
        //empty while body
        if (c == -1) return ""; //no letter found

        word[n++] = (char) c;
        while (Character.isLetter(c = in.read()))
            if (n < MaxLen) word[n++] = (char) c;
        return new String(word, 0, n);
    } //end getWord

} //end class P2_4WordFrequency

class WordInfo {
    String word;
    int freq = 0;

    WordInfo(String w, int f) {
        word = w;
        freq = f;
    }

    void incrFreq() {
        freq++;
    }
} //end class WordInfo
```

Suppose the file passage.txt contains the following data:

```
Strive not to be a success, but rather to be of value.
Whatever the mind can conceive and believe, it can achieve.
There is only one way to avoid criticism: do nothing, say nothing,
and be nothing.
```

When run, Program P2.4 stores its output in the file output.txt. Here is the output:

Words	Frequency
a	1
achieve	1
and	2
avoid	1
be	3
believe	1
but	1
can	2
conceive	1
criticism	1
do	1
is	1
it	1
mind	1
not	1
nothing	3
of	1
one	1
only	1
rather	1
say	1
strive	1
success	1
the	1
there	1
to	3
value	1
way	1
whatever	1

2.15 How to Return More Than One Value: Voting

This example will be used to illustrate several issues concerning the use of classes and objects. We will again use a class to group data, and we will show how a function can return more than one value using an object.

- **Problem**: In an election, there are seven candidates. Each voter is allowed one vote for the candidate of their choice. The vote is recorded as a number from 1 to 7. The number of voters is unknown beforehand, but the votes are terminated by a vote of 0. Any vote that is not a number from 1 to 7 is an invalid (spoiled) vote.

- A file, votes.txt, contains the names of the candidates. The first name is considered as candidate 1, the second as candidate 2, and so on. The names are followed by the votes. Write a program to read the data and evaluate the results of the election. Print all output to the file results.txt.

- Your output should specify the total number of votes, the number of valid votes, and the number of spoiled votes. This is followed by the votes obtained by each candidate and the winner(s) of the election.

Given this data in votes.txt:

```
Nirvan Singh
Denise Duncan
Avasa Tawari
Torrique Granger
Saskia Kalicharan
Dawren Greenidge
Jordon Cato

3 1 6 5 4 3 5 3 5 3 2 8 1 6 7 7 3 5
6 9 3 4 7 1 2 4 5 5 1 4 0
```

your program should send the following output to results.txt:

```
Invalid vote: 8
Invalid vote: 9

Number of voters: 30
Number of valid votes: 28
Number of spoilt votes: 2

Candidate           Score

Nirvan Singh         4
Denise Duncan        2
Avasa Tawari         6
Torrique Granger     4
Saskia Kalicharan    6
Dawren Greenidge     3
Jordon Cato          3

The winner(s)
Avasa Tawari
Saskia Kalicharan
```

We will use the following outline for solving this problem:

```
get the names and set the scores to 0
process the votes
print the results
```

We need to store the names of the seven candidates and the score obtained by each. We *could* use a String array for the names and an int array for the scores. But what if we needed to store many more attributes of a candidate? For each attribute, we would need to add another array of the appropriate type. To cater for this possibility and to make our program more flexible, we will create a class Person and use an array of Person.

What will this Person class look like? For our problem, it will have two instance fields, name and numVotes, say. We define it as follows:

```
class Person {
    String name;
    int numVotes;

    Person(String s, int n) {
        name = s;
        numVotes = n;
    }
} //end class Person
```

To cater for seven candidates, we set the symbolic constant MaxCandidates to 7 and declare the Person array candidate as follows:

```
Person[] candidate = new Person[MaxCandidates+1];
```

We will use candidate[h] to store information for candidate h, h = 1, 7; we will not use candidate[0]. This will enable us to process the votes more naturally than if we had used candidate[0]. For example, if there is a vote for candidate 4, we want to increment the vote count for candidate[4]. If we had used candidate[0] to store information for the first candidate, we would have had to increment the count for candidate[3], given a vote of 4. This can be misleading and disconcerting.

Suppose in is declared as follows:

```
Scanner in = new Scanner(new FileReader("votes.txt"));
```

We will read the names and set the scores to 0 with the following code:

```
for (int h = 1; h <= MaxCandidates; h++)
    candidate[h] = new Person(in.nextLine(), 0);
```

When this code is executed, we can picture candidate as shown in Figure 2-11. Remember, we are not using candidate[0].

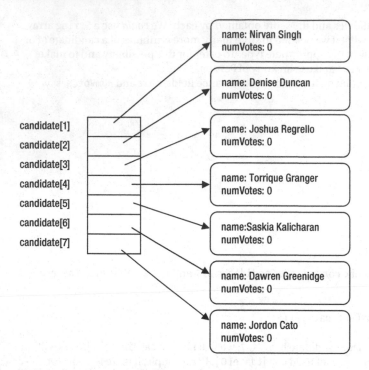

Figure 2-11. *Array candidate after reading the names and setting the scores to 0*

Next, we must process the votes. We will delegate this to the function processVotes. This will read each vote and add 1 to the score for the appropriate candidate. Thus, if the vote is 5, it must add 1 to the score for candidate 5.

Another task of this function is to count the number of valid and spoiled votes and return these values to main. But how does a function return more than one value? Well, it can return *one* value—an object—and this object can contain many fields.

In this example, we can declare a class (VoteCount, say) with two fields and a constructor, like this:

```
class VoteCount {
    int valid, spoilt;

    VoteCount(int v, int s) {
        valid = v;
        spoilt = s;
    }
}
```

The following statement will create an object called votes and set votes.valid and votes.spoilt to 0.

```
VoteCount votes = new VoteCount(0, 0);
```

We could also have dispensed with the constructor and created the object with this statement:

```
VoteCount votes = new VoteCount();
```

This *would* initialize the fields to 0, but it is better to do so explicitly, like this:

```
votes.valid = votes.spoilt = 0;
```

When we read a valid vote, ++votes.valid adds 1 to votes.valid, and when we read an invalid vote, ++votes.spoilt adds 1 to votes.spoilt. At the end, the function will return votes— an object containing the two counts.

Finally, we must write printResults, which prints the results in the format specified earlier. First we print the total number of votes broken down into valid and spoiled votes. Then, using a for loop, we print the individual scores.

Next, it determines the winning score by calling getLargest to find the candidate whose numVotes field is the largest. This is accomplished by these statements:

```
int win = getLargest(list, 1, MaxCandidates);
int winningVote = list[win].numVotes;
```

Here, list is the Person array. Using winningVote, it then makes another pass through the array looking for candidates with this score. This ensures that if there are ties for the winner, all will be printed. Program P2.5 is the complete solution for solving this voting problem.

Program P2.5

```java
import java.util.*;
import java.io.*;
public class Voting {
    final static int MaxCandidates = 7;

    public static void main(String[] args) throws IOException {
        Scanner in = new Scanner(new FileReader("votes.txt"));
        PrintWriter out = new PrintWriter(new FileWriter("results.txt"));
        Person[] candidate = new Person[MaxCandidates+1];

        //get the names and set the scores to 0
        for (int h = 1; h <= MaxCandidates; h++)
            candidate[h] = new Person(in.nextLine(), 0);

        VoteCount count = processVotes(candidate, MaxCandidates, in, out);
        printResults(out, candidate, MaxCandidates, count);
        in.close();
        out.close();
    } //end main

    public static VoteCount processVotes(Person[] list, int max, Scanner in, PrintWriter out) {
        VoteCount votes = new VoteCount(0, 0); //set valid, spoilt counts to 0
        int v = in.nextInt();
        while (v != 0) {
            if (v < 1 || v > max) {
                out.printf("Invalid vote: %d\n", v);
                ++votes.spoilt;
            }
            else {
                ++list[v].numVotes;
                ++votes.valid;
            }
```

```
            v = in.nextInt();
         } //end while
         return votes;
      } //end processVotes

      public static void printResults(PrintWriter out, Person[] list, int max, VoteCount votes) {
         out.printf("\nNumber of voters: %d\n", votes.valid + votes.spoilt);
         out.printf("Number of valid votes: %d\n", votes.valid);
         out.printf("Number of spoilt votes: %d\n", votes.spoilt);
         out.printf("\nCandidate          Score\n\n");

         for (int h = 1; h <= MaxCandidates; h++)
            out.printf("%-18s %3d\n", list[h].name, list[h].numVotes);

         out.printf("\nThe winner(s)\n");
         int win = getLargest(list, 1, MaxCandidates);
         int winningVote = list[win].numVotes;
         for (int h = 1; h <= MaxCandidates; h++)
            if (list[h].numVotes == winningVote) out.printf("%s\n", list[h].name);
      } //end printResults

      public static int getLargest(Person[] list, int lo, int hi) {
         int big = lo;
         for (int h = lo + 1; h <= hi; h++)
            if (list[h].numVotes > list[big].numVotes) big = h;
         return big;
      } //end getLargest
} //end class Voting

class Person {
   String name;
   int numVotes;

   Person(String s, int n) {
      name = s;
      numVotes = n;
   }
} //end class Person

class VoteCount {
   int valid, spoilt;

   VoteCount(int v, int s) {
      valid = v;
      spoilt = s;
   }
} //end class VoteCount
```

If we wanted to print the results in alphabetical order, we could do so by calling selectionSort (Section 2.13) with this statement:

```
selectionSort(candidate, 1, MaxCandidates);
```

We could achieve the same result by calling insertionSort (Section 2.13) like this:

```
insertionSort(candidate, 1, MaxCandidates);
```

But suppose we wanted to print the names of the candidates in *descending* order by number of votes received, that is, with the winning candidate(s) first. To do this, the object array candidate must be sorted in descending order using the numVotes field to control the sorting. This could be done by the following call where sortByVote uses an insertion sort (*any* sort will do) and is written using the formal parameter list:

```
sortByVote(candidate, 1, MaxCandidates);
```

We can write sortByVote as follows:

```
public static void sortByVote(Person[] list, int lo, int hi) {
//sort list[lo] to list[hi] in descending order by numVotes
   for (int h = lo + 1; h <= hi; h++) {
      Person hold = list[h];
      int k = h - 1; //start comparing with previous item
      while (k >= lo && hold.numVotes > list[k].numVotes) {
         list[k + 1] = list[k];
         --k;
      }
      list[k + 1] = hold;
   } //end for
} //end sortByVote
```

Suppose we add sortByVote to Program P2.5, and we insert this statement:

```
sortByVote(candidate, 1, MaxCandidates);
```

just before this one:

```
printResults(out, candidate, MaxCandidates, count);
```

If we run the program with the same data as before, it will produce the following output. The candidates are printed with the highest score first and the lowest score last.

```
Invalid vote: 8
Invalid vote: 9

Number of voters: 30
Number of valid votes: 28
Number of spoilt votes: 2

Candidate          Score ·

Avasa Tawari         6
Saskia Kalicharan    6
Nirvan Singh         4
Torrique Granger     4
Dawren Greenidge     3
Jordon Cato          3
Denise Duncan        2

The winner(s)
Avasa Tawari
Saskia Kalicharan
```

EXERCISES 2

1. What is meant by the *state* of an object? What determines the state of an object?

2. Distinguish between a class and an object.

3. Distinguish between a class variable and an instance variable.

4. Distinguish between a class method and an instance method.

5. Distinguish between a public variable and a private variable.

6. Explain what happens when the statement String S = new String("Hi") is executed.

7. To what values are instance fields initialized when an object is created?

8. What is a *no-arg* constructor? How does it become available to a class?

9. You have written a constructor for a class. What do you need to do to use the no-arg constructor?

10. What is meant by the term *data encapsulation*?

11. "An object variable does not hold an object." Explain.

12. Explain the role of the toString() method in Java.

13. Write a program to read names and phone numbers into an array of objects. Request a name and print the person's phone number.

14. Write a program to read English words and their equivalent Spanish words into an object array. Request the user to type several English words. For each, print the equivalent Spanish word. Choose a suitable end-of-data marker. Search for the typed words using binary search.

15. A date consists of day, month, and year. Write a class to create date objects and manipulate dates. For example, write a function that, given two dates, d1 and d2, returns -1 if d1 comes before d2, 0 if d1 is the same as d2, and 1 if d1 comes after d2. Also, write a function that returns the number of days that d2 is ahead of d1. If d2 comes before d1, return a negative value. And write a method to print a date in the format of your choice.

16. A time in 24-hour clock format is represented by two numbers; for example, 16 45 means the time 16:45, that is, 4:45 p.m. Using an object to represent a time, write a function that given two time objects, t1 and t2, returns the number of minutes from t1 to t2. For example, if the two given times are 16 45 and 23 25, your function should return 400.

17. Consider the problem of working with fractions, where a fraction is represented by two integer values—one for the numerator and the other for the denominator. For example, 5/9 is represented by the two numbers 5 and 9. Write a class to manipulate fractions. For example, write methods to add, subtract, multiply, and divide fractions. Also, write a method to reduce a fraction to its lowest terms; you will need to find the HCF of two integers.

18. A bookseller needs to store information about books. For each book, he wants to store the author, title, price, and quantity in stock. He also needs to know, at any time, how many book objects have been created. Write Java code for the class Book based on the following:

   - Write a no-arg constructor, which sets the author to No Author, the title to No Title, and the price and the quantity in stock to 0.

   - Write a constructor that, given four arguments—author, title, price and quantity—creates a Book object with the given values. The price must be at least $5 and the quantity cannot be negative. If any of these conditions is violated, the price and quantity are both set to 0.

   - Write accessor methods for the author and price fields.

   - Write a method that sets the price of a book to a given value. If the given price is not at least $5, the price should remain unchanged.

   - Write a method that reduces the quantity in stock by a given amount. If doing so makes the quantity negative, a message should be printed and the quantity left unchanged.

   - Write an instance method that prints the data for a book, one field per line.

   - Write a toString() method that returns a string that, if printed, will print the data for a book, one field per line.

   - Write an equals method that returns true if the *contents* of two Book objects are the same and false otherwise.

   - Write a Test class that creates three Book objects of your choice, prints their data, and prints the number of Book objects created.

19. A multiple-choice examination consists of 20 questions. Each question has five choices, labeled A, B, C, D, and E. The first line of data contains the correct answers to the 20 questions in the first 20 *consecutive* character positions. Here's an example:

BECDCBAADEBACBAEDDBE

Each subsequent line contains the answers for a candidate. Data on a line consists of a candidate number (an integer), followed by one or more spaces, followed by the 20 answers given by the candidate in the next 20 *consecutive* character positions. An X is used if a candidate did not answer a particular question. You may assume all data is valid and stored in a file called exam.dat. A sample line is as follows:

    4325   BECDCBAXDEBACCAEDXBE

There are at most 100 candidates. A line containing a "candidate number" 0 indicates only the end of the data.

Points for a question are awarded as follows: correct answer: 4 points; wrong answer: -1 point; no answer: 0 points.

Write a program to process the data and print a report consisting of candidate number and the total points obtained by the candidate, *in ascending order by candidate number*. (This question is in chapter 1 as well, but this time you'll solve it using objects).

20. A data file contains registration information for six courses—CS20A, CS21A, CS29A, CS30A, CS35A, and CS36A. Each line of data consists of a seven-digit student registration number followed by six (ordered) values, each of which is 0 or 1. A value of 1 indicates that the student is registered for the corresponding course; 0 means the student is not. Thus, 1 0 1 0 1 1 means that the student is registered for CS20A, CS29A, CS35A, and CS36A, but not for CS21A and CS30A. You may assume that there are no more than 100 students and a registration number 0 ends the data. Write a program to read the data and produce a class list for each course. Each list begins on a new page and consists of the registration numbers of those students taking the course.1 There is no conflict in using the same name equals to compare Parts and Strings. If equals is invoked via a Part object, then the equals method from the Part class is used. If equals is invoked via a String object, then the equals method from the String class is used.

CHAPTER 3

■ ■ ■

Linked Lists

In this chapter, we will explain the following:

- The notion of a linked list
- How to write declarations for working with a linked list
- How to count the nodes in a linked list
- How to search for an item in a linked list
- How to find the last node in a linked list
- The difference between static storage and dynamic storage allocation
- How to build a linked list by adding a new item at the end of the list
- How to insert a node into a linked list
- How to build a linked list by adding a new item at the head of the list
- How to delete items from a linked list
- How to build a linked list by adding a new item in such a way that the list is always sorted
- How to organize your Java files
- How to use linked lists to determine whether a phrase is a palindrome
- How to save a linked list
- The differences between using linked lists and arrays for storing a list of items
- How to represent a linked list using arrays
- How to merge two sorted linked lists
- The concept of a circular list and a doubly linked list

3.1 Defining Linked Lists

When values are stored in a one-dimensional array ($x[0]$ to $x[n]$, say), they can be thought of as being organized as a "linear list." Consider each item in the array as a *node*. A linear list means that the nodes are arranged in a linear order such that the following holds:

$x[1]$ is the first node
$x[n]$ is the last node
if $1 < k <= n$, then $x[k]$ is preceded by $x[k - 1]$
if $1 <= k < n$ then $x[k\ ]$ is followed by $x[k + 1]$

Thus, given a node, the "next" node is assumed to be in the next location, if any, in the array. The order of the nodes is the order in which they appear in the array, starting from the first. Consider the problem of inserting a new node between two existing nodes, $x[k]$ and $x[k + 1]$.

This can be done only if $x[k + 1]$ and the nodes after it are moved to make room for the new node. Similarly, the deletion of $x[k]$ involves the movement of the nodes $x[k +1]$, $x[k + 2]$, and so on. Accessing any given node is easy; all we have to do is provide the appropriate subscript.

In many situations, we use an array for representing a linear list. But we can also represent such a list by using an organization in which each node in the list points *explicitly* to the next node. This new organization is referred to as a *linked list*.

In a (singly) linked list, each node contains a pointer that points to the next node in the list. We can think of each node as a cell with two components, like this:

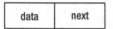

The data item can actually be one or more fields (depending on what needs to be stored in a node), and next "points to" the next node of the list. (You can use any names you want, instead of data and next.)

Since the next field of the *last* node does not point to anything, we must set it to a special value called the *null pointer*. In Java, the null pointer value is denoted by null.

In addition to the cells of the list, we need an object variable (top, say) that "points to" the first item in the list. If the list is empty, the value of top is null.

Pictorially, we represent a linked list as shown in Figure 3-1.

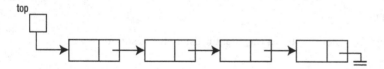

Figure 3-1. *A linked list*

The electrical earth symbol is used to represent the null pointer.

Traversing a linked list is like going on a treasure hunt. You are told where the first item is. This is what top does. When you get to the first item, it directs you to where the second item is (this is the purpose of next). When you get to the second item, it tells you where the third item is (via next), and so on. When you get to the last item, its null pointer tells you that that is the end of the hunt (the end of the list).

How can we represent a linked list in a Java program? Since each node consists of at least two fields, we will need to use a class to define the format of a node. The data component can consist of one or more fields (each of which can itself be an object with many fields). The *type* of these fields will depend on what kind of data needs to be stored.

But what is the type of the next field? We know it's a pointer but a pointer to what? It's a pointer to an object that is just like the one being defined! This is usually called a *self-referencing* structure. As an example, suppose the data at each node is a positive integer. We can define the class from which nodes will be created as follows (using num instead of data):

```
class Node {
    int num;
    Node next;
}
```

The variable top can now be declared as a Node variable, using this:

```
Node top;
```

As explained, the declaration of top allocates storage for top but does not allocate storage for any nodes. The *value* of top can be the address of a Node object, but, so far, there are no nodes in the list. As we know, we can create a Node object and assign its address to top with this statement:

```
top = new Node();
```

This will create the following:

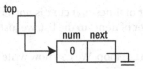

Recall that when an object is created, unless specified otherwise, Java will set a numeric field to 0 and an object field to null.

We will see how to create linked lists a little later, but first we look at some basic operations that may be performed on a linked list.

3.2 Basic Operations on a Linked List

For illustrative purposes, we assume that we have a linked list of integers. We ignore, for the moment, *how* the list might be built.

3.2.1 Counting the Nodes in a Linked List

Perhaps the simplest operation is to count the number of nodes in a list. To illustrate, we write a function that, given a pointer to a linked list, returns the number of nodes in the list.

Before we write the function, let's see how we can traverse the items in the list, starting from the first one. Suppose top points to the head of the list. Consider the following code:

```
Node curr = top;
while (curr != null) curr = curr.next;
```

Initially, curr points to the first item, if any, in the list. If it is not null, the following statement is executed:

```
curr = curr.next;
```

This sets curr to point to "whatever the current node is pointing to," in effect, the next node. For example, consider the following list:

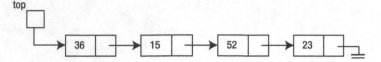

- Initially, curr points to (the node containing) 36. Since curr is not null, it is set to point to whatever 36 is pointing to, that is, (the node containing) 15.

- The while condition is tested again. Since curr is not null, curr = curr.next is executed, setting curr to point to whatever 15 is pointing to, that is, 52.

- The while condition is tested again. Since curr is not null, curr = curr.next is executed, setting curr to point to whatever 52 is pointing to, that is, 23.

- The while condition is tested again. Since curr is not null, curr = curr.next is executed, setting curr to point to whatever 23 is pointing to, that is, null.

- The while condition is tested again. Since curr *is* null, the while loop is no longer executed.

Note that each time curr is not null, we enter the while loop. But the number of times that curr is *not* null is exactly the same as the number of items in the list. So, in order to count the number of items in the list, we just have to count how many times the while body is executed.

To do this, we use a counter initialized to 0 and increment it by 1 inside the while loop. We can now write the function as follows (we call it length):

```
public static int length(Node top) {
    int n = 0;
    Node curr = top;
    while (curr != null) {
        n++;
        curr = curr.next;
    }
    return n;
}
```

Note that if the list is empty, curr will be null the first time, and the while loop will not be executed. The function will return 0, the correct result.

Strictly speaking, the variable curr is not necessary. The function will work fine if we omit curr and replace curr by top in the function. At the end of the execution of the function, top will be null.

You may be worried that you have lost access to the list, but do not be. Remember that top in length is a *copy* of whatever variable (head, say) is pointing to the list in the calling function. Changing top has no effect whatsoever on head. When length returns, head is still pointing to the first item in the list.

3.2.2 Searching a Linked List

Another common operation is to search a linked list for a given item. For example, given the following list, we may want to search for the number 52:

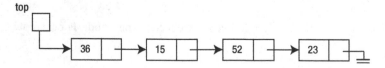

Our search should be able to tell us that 52 is in the list. On the other hand, if we search for 25, our search should report that 25 is not in the list.

Suppose the number we are searching for is stored in the variable key. The search proceeds by comparing key with each number in the list, starting from the first one. If key matches with any item, we have found it. If we get to the end of the list and key does not match any item, we can conclude that key is not in the list.

We must write the logic so that the search ends if we find a match *or* we reach the end of the list. Put another way, the search continues if we have not reached the end of the list *and* we do not have a match. If curr points to some item in the list, we can express this logic as follows:

```
while (curr != null && key != curr.num) curr = curr.next;
```

Java guarantees that the operands of && are evaluated from left to right and evaluation ceases as soon as the truth value of the expression is known, in this case, as soon as one operand evaluates to false or the entire expression has been evaluated. We take advantage of this by writing the condition curr != null first. If curr *is* null, the && is immediately false, and the second condition key != curr.num is not evaluated.

If we wrote the following and curr happens to be null, our program will crash when it tries to retrieve curr.num:

```
while (key != curr.num && curr != null) curr = curr.next; //wrong
```

In effect, this asks for the number pointed to by curr, but if curr is null, it does not point to anything. We say we are trying to "dereference a null pointer," which is an error.

Let's write the search as a function that, given a pointer to the list and key, returns the node containing key if it is found. If it's not found, the function returns null.

We assume the Node declaration from the previous section. Our function will return a value of type Node. Here it is:

```
public static Node search(Node top, int key) {
    while (top != null && key != top.num)
        top = top.next;
    return top;
}
```

If key is not in the list, top will become null, and null will be returned. If key is in the list, the while loop is exited when key is equal to top.num; at this stage, top is pointing to the node containing key, and *this* value of top is returned.

3.2.3 Finding the Last Node in a Linked List

Sometimes, we need to find the pointer to the last node in a list. Recall that the last node in the list is distinguished by *its* next pointer being null. Here is a function that returns a pointer to the last node in a given list. If the list is empty, the function returns null.

```
public static Node getLast(Node top) {
    if (top == null) return null;
    while (top.next != null)
        top = top.next;
    return top;
}
```

We get to the while statement if top is not null. It therefore makes sense to ask about top.next. If *this* is not null, the loop is entered, and top is set to this non-null value. This ensures that the while condition is defined the next time it is executed. When top.next is null, top is pointing at the last node, and *this* value of top is returned.

3.3 Building a Linked List: Adding a New Item at the Tail

Consider the problem of building a linked list of positive integers in the order in which they are given. Say the incoming numbers are as follows (0 terminates the data):

```
36 15 52 23 0
```

We want to build the following linked list:

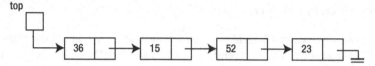

One question that arises is, how many nodes will there be in the list? This, of course, depends on how many numbers are supplied. One disadvantage of using an array for storing a linear list is that the size of the array must be specified beforehand. If, when the program is run, it finds that it needs to store more items than this size allows, it may have to be aborted.

With the linked list approach, whenever a new node must be added to the list, storage is allocated for the node, and the appropriate pointers are set. Thus, we allocate just the right amount of storage for the list—no more, no less.

We do use extra storage for the pointers, but this is more than compensated for by more efficient use of storage as well as easy insertions and deletions. Allocating storage "as needed" is usually referred to as *dynamic storage allocation*. (On the other hand, array storage is referred to as *static* storage.)

In our solution to building the list as described earlier, we start with an empty list. Our program will reflect this with the following statement:

```
top = null;
```

When we read a new number, we must do the following:

- Allocate storage for a node

- Put the number in the new node

- Make the new node the last one in the list

Using our Node class from Section 3.1, let's write a constructor which, given an integer argument, sets num to the integer and sets next to null.

```
public Node(int n) {
    num = n;
    next = null;
}
```

Consider the following statement:

```
Node p = new Node(36);
```

First, storage for a new node is allocated. Assuming an int occupies 4 bytes and a pointer occupies 4 bytes, the size of Node is 8 bytes. So, 8 bytes are allocated starting at address 4000, say. 36 is stored in the num field, and null is stored in the next field, like this:

The value 4000 is then assigned to p; in effect, p is pointing at the object just created. Since the actual address 4000 is not normally important, we usually depict this as follows:

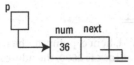

In other words, p is pointing to the object wherever it happens to be.

When we read the first number, we must create a node for it and set top to point to the new node. In our example, when we read 36, we must create the following:

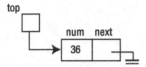

If n contains the new number, this can be accomplished with this:

```
if (top == null) top = new Node(n);
```

There are no arrows inside the computer, but the effect is achieved with the following (assuming the new node is stored at location 4000):

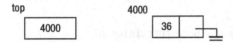

For each subsequent number, we must set the next field of the current last node to point to the new node. The new node becomes the last node. Suppose the new number is 15. We must create this:

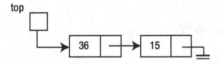

But how do we find the last node of the existing list? One method is to start at the top of the list and follow the next pointers until we encounter null. This is time-consuming if we have to do it for each new number. A better approach is to keep a pointer (last, say) to the last node of the list. This pointer is updated as new nodes are added. The code for this could be written like this:

```
np = new Node(n);            //create a new node
if (top == null) top = np;   //set top if first node
else last.next = np;         //set last.next for other nodes
last = np;                   //update last to  new node
```

Suppose there is just one node in the list; this is also the last node. In our example, the value of last will be 4000. Suppose the node containing 15 is stored at location 2000. We have the following situation:

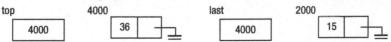

The code above will set the next field at location 4000 to 2000 and set last to 2000. The following is the result:

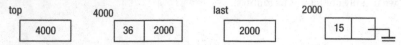

Now top (4000) points to the node containing 36; this node's next field is 2000 and, hence, points to the node containing 15. This node's next field is null, indicating the end of the list. The value of last is 2000, the address of the last node in the list.

Program P3.1 reads the numbers and creates the linked list as discussed. To verify that the list has been built correctly, we should print its contents. The function printList traverses the list from the first node to the last, printing the number at each node.

Program P3.1

```java
import java.util.*;
public class BuildList1 {

    public static void main(String[] args) {
        Scanner in = new Scanner(System.in);
        Node top, np, last = null;

        top = null;
        System.out.printf("Enter some integers ending with 0\n");
        int n = in.nextInt();
        while (n != 0) {
            np = new Node(n);           //create a new node containing n
            if (top == null) top = np;  //set top if first node
            else last.next = np;        //set last.next for other nodes
            last = np;                  //update last to  new node
            n = in.nextInt();
        }
        System.out.printf("\nThe items in the list are\n");
        printList(top);
    } //end main

    public static void printList(Node top) {
        while (top != null) {  //as long as there's a node
            System.out.printf("%d ", top.num);
            top = top.next;     //go on to the next node
        }
        System.out.printf("\n");
    } //end printList

} //end class BuildList1

class Node {
    int num;
    Node next;
```

```
    public Node(int n) {
        num = n;
        next = null;
    }
} //end class Node
```

To verify that the list has been built correctly, we should print its contents. The method `printList` traverses the list from the first node to the last, printing the number at each node. The following is a sample run of Program P3.1:

```
Enter some integers ending with 0
9 1 8 2 7 3 6 4 5 0

The items in the list are
9 1 8 2 7 3 6 4 5
```

3.4 Insertion Into a Linked List

A list with one pointer in each node is called a *one-way*, or *singly*, *linked list*. One important characteristic of such a list is that access to the nodes is via the "top of list" pointer and the pointer field in each node. (However, other explicit pointers may point to specific nodes in the list, for example, the pointer `last`, shown earlier, which pointed to the last node in the list.) This means that access is restricted to being sequential.

The only way to get to node 4, say, is via nodes 1, 2, and 3. Since we can't access the *k*th node directly, we will not be able, for instance, to perform a binary search on a linked list. The great advantage of a linked list is that it allows for easy insertions and deletions anywhere in the list.

Suppose we want to insert a new node between the second and third nodes. We can view this simply as insertion after the second node. For example, suppose `prev` points to the second node and `np` points to the new node, as shown in Figure 3-2.

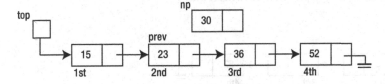

Figure 3-2. *Inserting a new node in a linked list*

We can insert the new node by setting its `next` field to point to the third node and the `next` field of the second node to point to the new node. Note that all we need to do the insertion is the second node; its `next` field will give us the third node. The insertion can be done with this:

```
np.next = prev.next;
prev.next = np;
```

The first statement says, "Let the new node point to whatever the second node is pointing at, in other words, the third node." The second statement says, "Let the second node point to the new node." The net effect is that the new node is inserted between the second and the third. The new node becomes the third node, and the original third node becomes the fourth node. This changes Figure 3-2 into Figure 3-3.

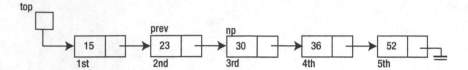

Figure 3-3. *After insertion of new node*

Does this code work if prev were pointing at the last node so that we are, in fact, inserting after the last node? Yes. If prev is the last node, then prev.next is null. Therefore, the following statement sets np.next to null so that the new node becomes the last node:

```
np.next = prev.next;
```

As before, prev.next is set to point to the new node. This is illustrated by changing this:

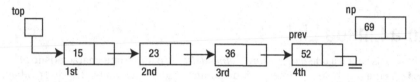

to this:

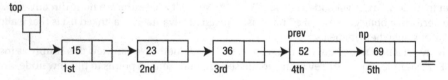

In many situations, it is required to insert a new node at the head of the list. That is, we want to make the new node the first node. Assuming that np points to the new node, we want to convert this:

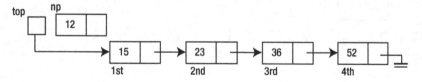

to this:

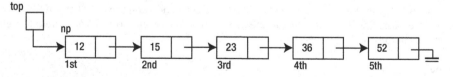

This can be done with the following code:

```
np.next = top;
top = np;
```

The first statement sets the new node to point to whatever top is pointing at (that is, the first node), and the second statement updates top to point to the new node.

You should observe that the code works even if the list is initially empty (that is, if top is null). In this case, it converts this:

to this:

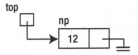

3.5 Building a Linked List: Adding a New Item at the Head

Consider again the problem of building a linked list of positive integers but, this time, we insert each new number at the head of the list rather than at the end. The resulting list will have the numbers in reverse order to how they are given. Suppose the incoming numbers are as follows (0 terminates the data):

36 15 52 23 0

We would like to build the following linked list:

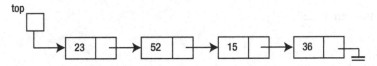

The program to build the list in reverse order is actually simpler than the previous one. It is almost identical to Program P3.1. The only changes are in the while loop. As each new number is read, we set its link to point to the first node, and we set top to point to the new node, making it the (new) first node. These changes are incorporated into Program P3.2, written as class BuildList2.

Program P3.2

```java
import java.util.*;
public class BuildList2 {

    public static void main(String[] args) {
        Scanner in = new Scanner(System.in);
        Node top, np, last = null;

        top = null;
        System.out.printf("Enter some integers ending with 0\n");
        int n = in.nextInt();
        while (n != 0) {
            np = new Node(n);      //create a new node containing n
            np.next = top;         //set it to point to first node
            top = np;              //update top to point to new node
            n = in.nextInt();
        }
```

```
            System.out.printf("\nThe items in the list are\n");
            printList(top);
        } //end main

        public static void printList(Node top) {
            while (top != null) {  //as long as there's a node
                System.out.printf("%d ", top.num);
                top = top.next;  //go on to the next node
            }
            System.out.printf("\n");
        } //end printList

    } //end class BuildList2

    class Node {
        int num;
        Node next;

        public Node(int n) {
            num = n;
            next = null;
        }
    } //end class Node
```

The following is a sample run of Program P3.2:

```
Enter some integers ending with 0
9 1 8 2 7 3 6 4 5 0

The items in the list are
5 4 6 3 7 2 8 1 9
```

Program P3.1 inserts incoming numbers at the tail of the list. This is an example of adding an item to a queue. A *queue* is a linear list in which insertions occur at one end and deletions (see the next section) occur at the other end.

Program P3.2 inserts incoming numbers at the head of the list. This is an example of adding an item to a stack. A *stack* is a linear list in which insertions and deletions occur *at the same end*. In stack terminology, when we add an item, we say the item is *pushed* onto the stack. Deleting an item from a stack is referred to as *popping* the stack.

We will treat with stacks and queues more fully in Chapter 4.

3.6 Deletion from a Linked List

Deleting a node from the top of a linked list is accomplished by this statement:

```
    top = top.next;
```

This says let top point to whatever the first node was pointing at (that is, the second node, if any). Since top is now pointing at the second node, effectively the first node has been deleted from the list. The statement changes the following:

to this:

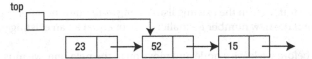

Of course, before we delete, we should check that there *is* something to delete, in other words, that top is not null. If there is only one node in the list, deleting it will result in the empty list; top will become null.

Deleting an arbitrary node from a linked list requires more information. Suppose curr (for "current") points to the node to be deleted. Deleting this node requires that we change the next field of the *previous* node. This means we must know the pointer to the previous node; suppose it is prev (for "previous"). Then deletion of node curr can be accomplished by this statement:

```
prev.next = curr.next;
```

This changes the following:

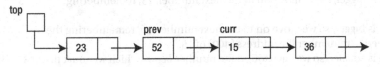

to this:

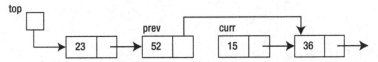

Effectively, the node pointed to by curr is no longer in the list—it has been deleted.

One may wonder what happens to nodes that have been deleted. In our discussion, *deletion* meant "logical deletion." That is, as far as processing the list is concerned, the deleted nodes are not present. But the nodes are still in memory, occupying storage, even though we may have lost the pointers to them.

If we have a large list in which many deletions have occurred, then there will be a lot of "deleted" nodes scattered all over memory. These nodes occupy storage even though they will never, and cannot, be processed.

Java's solution to this problem is *automatic garbage collection*. From time to time, Java checks for these "unreachable" nodes and removes them, reclaiming the storage they occupy. The programmer never has to worry about these "deleted" nodes.

3.7 Building a Sorted Linked List

As a third possibility, suppose we want to build the list so that the numbers are always sorted in ascending order. Suppose the incoming numbers are as follows (0 terminates the data):

```
36 15 52 23 0
```

We would like to build the following linked list:

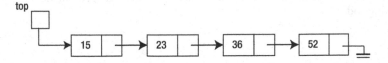

When a new number is read, it is inserted in the existing list (which is initially empty) in its proper place. The first number is simply added to the empty list.

Each subsequent number is compared with the numbers in the existing list. As long as the new number is greater than a number in the list, we move down the list until the new number is smaller than, or equal to, an existing number or we come to the end of the list.

To facilitate the insertion of the new number, before we leave a node and move on to the next one, we must save the pointer to it in case the new number must be inserted after this node. However, we can know this only when we compare the new number with the number in the next node.

To illustrate these ideas, consider the following sorted list, and suppose we want to add a new number (30, say) to the list so that it remains sorted:

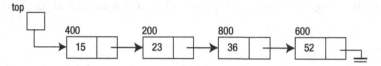

Assume the number above a node is the address of the node. Thus, the value of top is 400.

First, we compare 30 with 15. It is bigger, so we move on to the next number, 23, remembering the address (400) of 15.

Next, we compare 30 with 23. It is bigger, so we move on to the next number, 36, remembering the address (200) of 23. We no longer need to remember the address (400) of 15.

Next, we compare 30 with 36. It is smaller, so we have found the number *before* which we must insert 30. This is the same as inserting 30 *after* 23. Since we have remembered the address of 23, we can now perform the insertion.

We will use the following code to process the new number, n:

```
prev = null;
curr = top;
while (curr != null && n > curr.num) {
    prev = curr;
    curr = curr.next;
}
```

Initially, prev is null and curr is 400. The insertion of 30 proceeds as follows:

- 30 is compared with curr.num, 15. It is bigger, so we set prev to curr (400) and set curr to curr.next, 200; curr is not null.

- 30 is compared with curr.num, 23. It is bigger, so we set prev to curr (200) and set curr to curr.next, 800; curr is not null.

- 30 is compared with curr.num, 36. It is smaller, so we exit the while loop with prev being 200 and curr being 800.

We have the following situation:

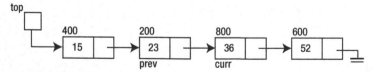

If the new number is stored in a node pointed to by np, we can now add it to the list (except at the head; see the next section) with the following code:

```
np.next = curr;  //we could also use prev.next for curr
prev.next = np;
```

This will change the following:

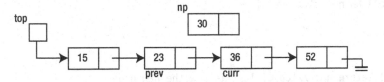

to this:

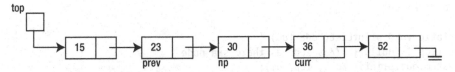

As an exercise, verify that this code will work if the number to be added is bigger than all the numbers in the list. Hint: when will the while loop exit?

If the number to be added is *smaller* than all the numbers in the list, it must be added at the head of the list and becomes the new first node in the list. This means that the value of top has to be changed to the new node.

The while loop shown earlier will work in this case as well. The while condition will be false on the very first test (since n will be smaller than curr.num). On exit, we simply test whether prev is *still* null; if it is, the new node must be inserted at the top of the list.

If the list were initially empty, the while loop will exit immediately (since curr will be null). In this case also, the new node must be inserted at the top of the list, becoming the only node in the list.

Program P3.3 contains all the details. The insertion of a new node in its proper position in the list is delegated to the function addInPlace. This function returns a pointer to the top of the modified list.

Program P3.3

```
import java.util.*;
public class BuildList3 {

    public static void main(String[] args) {
        Scanner in = new Scanner(System.in);
        Node top, np, last = null;

        top = null;
        System.out.printf("Enter some integers ending with 0\n");
        int n = in.nextInt();
        while (n != 0) {
            top = addInPlace(top, n);
            n = in.nextInt();
        }
        printList(top);
    } //end main

    public static Node addInPlace(Node top, int n) {
    // This functions inserts n in its ordered position in a (possibly empty)
    // list pointed to by top, and returns a pointer to the new list
```

```
                Node np, curr, prev;

                np = new Node(n);
                prev = null;
                curr = top;
                while (curr != null && n > curr.num) {
                    prev = curr;
                    curr = curr.next;
                }
                np.next = curr;
                if (prev == null) return np; //top of list is now the new node
                prev.next = np;
                return top; //the top of the list has not changed
            } //end addInPlace

            public static void printList(Node top) {
                while (top != null) {  //as long as there's a node
                    System.out.printf("%d ", top.num);
                    top = top.next;  //go on to the next node
                }
                System.out.printf("\n");
            } //end printList

        } //end class BuildList3

        class Node {
            int num;
            Node next;

            public Node(int n) {
                num = n;
                next = null;
            }
        } //end class Node
```

When run, Program P3.3 builds a sorted linked list from the numbers provided and then prints the numbers in the order that they appear in the list. The following shows some sample output:

```
    Enter some integers ending with 0
    9 1 8 2 7 3 6 4 5 0
    1 2 3 4 5 6 7 8 9
```

3.8 A Linked List Class

We have discussed many of the basic ideas involved in the processing of linked lists, and we have seen how to implement common operations on linked lists. We used static methods (printList, addInPlace) and passed the "head node" of the list as an argument.

Let's now change our viewpoint slightly. Our goal is to write a "linked list class" from which we can create "linked list objects," which we can use for working with linked lists.

The first question to answer is, "What defines a linked list?" That's easy. It's the (object) variable, essentially a pointer, which points to the first node in the list. So, our class will begin as follows:

```
public class LinkedList {
   Node head = null;
      .
      .
      .
} //end class LinkedList
```

We will use head as our "top of list" variable. Java will initialize head to null when we use a statement like the following, but we do so explicitly to draw attention to its initial value:

```
LinkedList LL = new LinkedList();
```

How do we define Node? Well, it depends on the kind of items (the "data") that we want to store in the list. If we want a list of integers, we can use this:

```
class Node {
   int num;
   Node next;
}
```

If we want a list of characters, we can use this:

```
class Node {
   char ch;
   Node next;
}
```

And if we want a list of parts, we can use this:

```
class Node {
   Part part;
   Node next;
}
```

As you can see, we would need to change the definition of Node each time we wanted a different kind of linked list. But we would also need to change a method if its code depends on the kind of item in the list. Consider, for example, a method that adds a new node at the head of a list of integers.

```
public void addHead(int n) {
   Node p = new Node(n); //assume Node has the appropriate constructor
   p.next = head;
   head = p;
}
```

This can be used, for instance, as follows (LL is a LinkedList):

```
LL.addHead(25);
```

This will add a node containing 25 at the head of the list, LL.

But if we need a list of characters, we would need to change the heading to this:

```
public void addHead(char c)
```

and, for a list of Part objects, to this:

```
public void addHead(Part p)
```

If there are many methods in the class, these changes could become quite tedious every time we need to change the kind of data stored in our list.

We will use an approach that will minimize the changes required in LinkedList.

Let's define the class Node as follows:

```
class Node {
    NodeData data;
    Node next;

    public Node(NodeData nd) {
        data = nd;
        next = null;
    }
} //end class Node
```

We write the class in terms of an unspecified, as yet, data type, NodeData. There are two fields, data and next. Without knowing anything more about NodeData, we can write addHead as follows:

```
public void addHead(NodeData nd) {
    Node p = new Node(nd);
    p.next = head;
    head = p;
}
```

A class (TestList, say) that wants to use LinkedList must provide a definition of NodeData that is available to LinkedList. Suppose we want a linked list of integers. We can define NodeData as follows (we will explain the need for toString shortly):

```
public class NodeData {
    int num;

    public NodeData(int n) {
        num = n;
    }

    public String toString() {
        return num + " ";
        //" " needed to convert num to a string; may also use "" (empty string)
    }
} //end class NodeData
```

And we can build a linked list in reverse order with code such as the following:

```
LinkedList LL = new LinkedList();
System.out.printf("Enter some integers ending with 0\n");
int n = in.nextInt();
while (n != 0) {
   LL.addHead(new NodeData(n)); //NodeData argument required
   n = in.nextInt();
}
```

Note that since addHead requires a NodeData argument, we must create a NodeData object with the integer n; this object is passed to addHead.

How can we print the items in a list? Presumably, we would like a method (printList, say) in the LinkedList class, which does the job. But since LinkedList does not know what NodeData might contain (and it could vary from one run to the next), how can it print the data in a node?

The trick is to let NodeData print itself using the toString method. Here is one way to write printList:

```
public void printList() {
   Node curr = head;
   while (curr != null) {
      System.out.printf("%s", curr.data); //invokes curr.data.toString()
      curr = curr.next;
   }
   System.out.printf("\n");
} //end printList
```

Recall that curr.data is a NodeData object. Since we use it in a context where a string is required, Java will look in the NodeData class for a toString method. Since it finds one, it will use it to print curr.data. The printf statement could also have been written as follows where we call toString explicitly:

```
System.out.printf("%s ", curr.data.toString());
```

If LL is a LinkedList, the list can be printed with this statement:

```
LL.printList();
```

So far, our LinkedList class consists of the following:

```
public class LinkedList {
   Node head = null;

   public void addHead(NodeData nd) {
      Node p = new Node(nd);
      p.next = head;
      head = p;
   }

   public void printList() {
      Node curr = head;
      while (curr != null) {
         System.out.printf("%s", curr.data); //invokes curr.data.toString()
         curr = curr.next;
      }
```

```
        System.out.printf("\n");
    } //end printList

} //end class LinkedList
```

We could add a method to check whether a linked list is empty.

```
public boolean empty() {
    return head == null;
}
```

If LL is a LinkedList, we can use empty as follows:

```
while (!LL.empty()) { ...
```

Now suppose we want to add a method that will build a linked list in "sorted order." Again, since LinkedList does not know what NodeData might contain, how do we define "sorted order" in LinkedList? Once more, the solution is to let NodeData tell us when one NodeData item is less than, equal to, or greater than another NodeData item.

We can do this by writing an instance method (we'll call it compareTo) in NodeData. Here it is:

```
public int compareTo(NodeData nd) {
    if (this.num == nd.num) return 0;
    if (this.num < nd.num) return -1;
    return 1;
}
```

Here, we use the Java keyword this for the first time. If a and b are two NodeData objects, remember that we can call the method with a.compareTo(b). In the method, this refers to the object used to call it. Thus, this.num refers to a.num. We note that the method will work just the same without this because num, by itself, does refer to a.num.

Since the NodeData class we are using has one integer field, num, compareTo reduces to comparing two integers. The expression a.compareTo(b) returns 0 if a.num is equal to b.num, -1 if a.num is less than b.num, and 1 if a.num is greater than b.num.

Using compareTo, we can write addInPlace as follows:

```
public void addInPlace(NodeData nd) {
    Node np, curr, prev;

    np = new Node(nd);
    prev = null;
    curr = head;
    while (curr != null && nd.compareTo(curr.data) > 0) { //new value is bigger
        prev = curr;
        curr = curr.next;
    }
    np.next = curr;
    if (prev == null) head = np;
    else prev.next = np;
} //end addInPlace
```

If LL is a LinkedList, we can use it as follows:

```
LL.addInPlace(new NodeData(25));
```

This will create a Node with a NodeData object containing 25 and insert this node in the list so that the list is in ascending order.

Program P3.4 reads integers, builds a linked list in ascending order, and prints the sorted list. You will observe that we have dropped the word public from the classes NodeData, Node, and LinkedList. This is merely to allow us to store the entire program in one file, which must be called LinkedListTest.java since the name of the public class is LinkedListTest. Recall that Java requires that a file contain only one public class. We will elaborate on this in Section 3.9.

Program P3.4

```java
import java.util.*;
public class LinkedListTest {
    public static void main(String[] args) {
        Scanner in = new Scanner(System.in);
        LinkedList LL = new LinkedList();
        System.out.printf("Enter some integers ending with 0\n");
        int n = in.nextInt();
        while (n != 0) {
            LL.addInPlace(new NodeData(n));
            n = in.nextInt();
        }
        LL.printList();
    } //end main
} //end LinkedListTest

class NodeData {
    int num;

    public NodeData(int n) {
        num = n;
    }

    public int compareTo(NodeData nd) {
        if (this.num == nd.num) return 0;
        if (this.num < nd.num) return -1;
        return 1;
    } //end compareTo

    public String toString() {
        return num + " ";
        //" " needed to convert num to a string; may also use "" (empty string)
    }
} //end class NodeData

class Node {
    NodeData data;
    Node next;
```

```java
        public Node(NodeData nd) {
            data = nd;
            next = null;
        }
    } //end class Node

    class LinkedList {
        Node head = null;

        public boolean empty() {
            return head == null;
        }

        public void addHead(NodeData nd) {
            Node p = new Node(nd);
            p.next = head;
            head = p;
        }

        public void addInPlace(NodeData nd) {
            Node np, curr, prev;

            np = new Node(nd);
            prev = null;
            curr = head;
            while (curr != null && nd.compareTo(curr.data) > 0) { //new value is bigger
                prev = curr;
                curr = curr.next;
            }
            np.next = curr;
            if (prev == null) head = np;
            else prev.next = np;
        } //end addInPlace

        public void printList() {
            Node curr = head;
            while (curr != null) {
                System.out.printf("%s", curr.data); //invokes curr.data.toString()
                curr = curr.next;
            }
            System.out.printf("\n");
        } //end printList

    } //end class LinkedList
```

The following is a sample run of Program P3.4.

```
Enter some integers ending with 0
9 1 8 2 7 3 6 4 5 0
1 2 3 4 5 6 7 8 9
```

3.9 How to Organize Java Files

In the previous section, we dealt with four classes—LinkedList, Node, NodeData, and LinkedListTest—and noted that in order to store them in one file (as Program P3.4) we had to drop the word public from all but LinkedListTest. Here, we recap some of our previous comments and explain how each class may be stored in its own file.

We can store the LinkedListTest class in a file, which must be called LinkedListTest.java. Remember that a public class x must be stored in a file called x.java. We can store the other classes in the *same* file provided we write the class header as class xxx rather than public class xxx.

However, in order for these classes to be usable by other classes, we will organize them differently. We will declare the NodeData class as public and store it in a file by itself. The file must be called NodeData.java and, so far, will contain the following:

```java
public class NodeData {
    int num;

    public NodeData(int n) {
        num = n;
    }

    public int compareTo(NodeData nd) {
        if (this.num == nd.num) return 0;
        if (this.num < nd.num) return -1;
        return 1;
    }

    public String toString() {
        return num + " ";
        //" " needed to convert num to a string; may also use "" (empty string)
    }
} //end class NodeData
```

We will declare the LinkedList class as public and store it in a file called LinkedList.java. Since the Node class is used only by the LinkedList class, we will omit the word public and store it in the same file, which, so far, will contain the following:

```java
public class LinkedList {
    Node head = null;

    public boolean empty() {
        return head == null;
    }

    public void addHead(NodeData nd) {
        Node p = new Node(nd);
        p.next = head;
        head = p;
    }
```

```java
    public void addInPlace(NodeData nd) {
        Node np, curr, prev;

        np = new Node(nd);
        prev = null;
        curr = head;
        while (curr != null && nd.compareTo(curr.data) > 0) { //nd is bigger
            prev = curr;
            curr = curr.next;
        }
        np.next = curr;
        if (prev == null) head = np;
        else prev.next = np;
    } //end addInPlace

    public void printList() {
        Node curr = head;
        while (curr != null) {
            System.out.printf("%s", curr.data); //invokes curr.data.toString()
            curr = curr.next;
        }
        System.out.printf("\n");
    } //end printList

} //end class LinkedList

class Node {
    NodeData data;
    Node next;

    public Node(NodeData d) {
        data = d;
        next = null;
    }
} //end class Node
```

We note that if the Node class were needed by another class, it would be best to declare it `public` and put it in a file called `Node.java`.

3.10 Expanding the LinkedList Class

To prepare for the next example, we will expand the `LinkedList` class with the following methods. The function `getHeadData` returns the data field of the first node, if any, in the list.

```java
    public NodeData getHeadData() {
        if (head == null) return null;
        return head.data;
    }
```

The method `deleteHead` removes the first node, if any, in the list.

```
public void deleteHead() {
    if (head != null) head = head.next;
}
```

The method addTail adds a new node at the end of the list. It finds the last node (for which next is null) and sets it to point to the new node.

```
public void addTail(NodeData nd) {
    Node p = new Node(nd);
    if (head == null) head = p;
    else {
        Node curr = head;
        while (curr.next != null) curr = curr.next;
        curr.next = p;
    }
} //end addTail
```

The function copyList makes a copy of the list used to call it and returns the copy.

```
public LinkedList copyList() {
    LinkedList temp = new LinkedList();
    Node curr = this.head;
    while (curr != null) {
        temp.addTail(curr.data);
        curr = curr.next;
    }
    return temp;
} //end copyList
```

The method reverseList reverses the order of the nodes in the given list. It works on the original list, not a copy.

```
public void reverseList() {
    Node p1, p2, p3;
    if (head == null || head.next == null) return;
    p1 = head;
    p2 = p1.next;
    p1.next = null;
    while (p2 != null) {
        p3 = p2.next;
        p2.next = p1;
        p1 = p2;
        p2 = p3;
    }
    head = p1;
} //end reverseList
```

The function equals compares two linked lists. If L1 and L2 are two linked lists, the expression L1.equals(L2) is true if they contain identical elements in the same order and false otherwise.

```
public boolean equals(LinkedList LL) {
    Node t1 = this.head;
    Node t2 = LL.head;
```

```
    while (t1 != null && t2 != null) {
        if (t1.data.compareTo(t2.data) != 0) return false;
        t1 = t1.next;
        t2 = t2.next;
    }
    if (t1 != null || t2 != null) return false; //if one ended but not the other
    return true;
} //end equals
```

3.11 Example: Palindrome

Consider the problem of determining whether a given string is a *palindrome* (the same when spelled forward or backward). The following are examples of palindromes (ignoring case, punctuation, and spaces):

```
civic
Racecar
Madam, I'm Adam.
A man, a plan, a canal, Panama.
```

If all the letters were of the same case (upper or lower) and the string (word, say) contained no spaces or punctuation marks, we *could* solve the problem as follows:

```
compare the first and last letters
if they are different, the string is not a palindrome
if they are the same, compare the second and second to last letters
if they are different, the string is not a palindrome
if they are the same, compare the third and third to last letters
```

We continue until we find a nonmatching pair (and it's not a palindrome) or there are no more pairs to compare (and it is a palindrome).

This method is efficient, but it requires us to be able to access any letter in the word directly. This is possible if the word is stored in an array and we use a subscript to access any letter. However, if the letters of the word are stored in a linked list, we cannot use this method since we can access the letters only sequentially.

To illustrate how linked lists may be manipulated, we will use linked lists to solve the problem using the following idea:

1. Store the original phrase in a linked list, one character per node.

2. Create another list containing the letters only of the phrase, all converted to lowercase; call this list1.

3. Reverse list1 to get list2.

4. Compare list1 with list2, node by node, until we get a mismatch (the phrase is not a palindrome) or we come to the end of the lists (the phrase is a palindrome).

Consider the phrase Damn Mad!; this will be stored as follows:

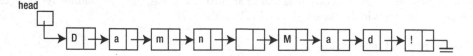

Step 2 will convert it to this:

list1

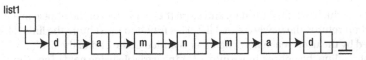

Step 3 will reverse this list to get the following:

list2

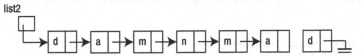

Comparing list1 and list2 will reveal that Damn Mad! is a palindrome.

We will write a program that prompts the user to type a phrase and tells her whether it is a palindrome. It then prompts for another phrase. To stop, the user must press the Enter key. The following is a sample run:

```
Type a phrase. (To stop, press "Enter" only): Damn Mad!
is a palindrome
Type a phrase. (To stop, press "Enter" only): So Many Dynamos!
is a palindrome
Type a phrase. (To stop, press "Enter" only): Rise to vote, sir.
is a palindrome
Type a phrase. (To stop, press "Enter" only): Thermostat
is not a palindrome
Type a phrase. (To stop, press "Enter" only): A Toyota's a Toyota.
is a palindrome
Type a phrase. (To stop, press "Enter" only):
```

Previously, we worked with a linked list of integers. But, now, we need a linked list of characters. If we did things right, we should need to make changes in the NodeData class only. We should not have to change *anything* in the LinkedList class, and we won't. Here is what NodeData should look like:

```java
public class NodeData {
    char ch;

    public NodeData(char c) {
        ch = c;
    }

    public char getData() {return ch;}

    public int compareTo(NodeData nd) {
        if (this.ch == nd.ch) return 0;
        if (this.ch < nd.ch) return -1;
        return 1;
    }

    public String toString() {
        return ch + "";
    }
} //end class NodeData
```

We have added an accessor, getData, to return the value in the only data field, ch. The other changes essentially involve changing int to char.

We will write a function, getPhrase, which will read the data and store the characters of the phrase in a linked list, one character per node. The function returns the newly created list. This function must build the linked list in the order in which the characters are typed by the user—each new character is added at the end of the list.

The function achieves this by first reading the entire phrase into a String variable using nextLine. Then, starting at the last character and going backward, it inserts each new character at the *head* of the linked list. (We could also start at the first character and add each new character at the *tail* of the list, but this requires more work.) Here is the function:

```
public static LinkedList getPhrase(Scanner in) {
    LinkedList phrase = new LinkedList();
    String str = in.nextLine();
    for (int h = str.length() - 1; h >= 0; h--)
        phrase.addHead(new NodeData(str.charAt(h)));
    return phrase;
} //end getPhrase
```

Next, we write a function, lettersLower, which, given a linked list of characters, creates another list containing the letters only, all converted to lowercase. As each letter is encountered, it is converted to lowercase and added to the *tail* of the new list using addTail. Here is lettersLower:

```
public static LinkedList lettersLower(LinkedList phrase) {
    LinkedList word = new LinkedList();

    while (!phrase.empty()) {
        char ch = phrase.getHeadData().getData();
        if (Character.isLetter(ch)) word.addTail(new NodeData(Character.toLowerCase(ch)));
        phrase.deleteHead();
    }
    return word;
} //end lettersLower
```

The expression phrase.getHeadData() returns the data field (of type NodeData) of the first node in the list. The accessor, getData, in the NodeData class returns the character stored in the node.

We now have everything we need to write Program P3.5, which solves the palindrome problem. It assumes that the NodeData and LinkedList classes are declared public and stored in separate files.

Program P3.5

```
import java.util.*;
public class P3_5Palindrome {
    public static void main(String[] args) {
        Scanner in = new Scanner(System.in);
        System.out.printf("Type a phrase. (To stop, press 'Enter' only): ");
        LinkedList aPhrase = getPhrase(in);
        while (!aPhrase.empty()) {
            LinkedList w1 = lettersLower(aPhrase);
            System.out.printf("Converted to: ");
            w1.printList();
            LinkedList w2 = w1.copyList();
            w2.reverseList();
```

```
            if (w1.equals(w2)) System.out.printf("is a palindrome\n");
            else System.out.printf("is not a palindrome\n");
            System.out.printf("Type a phrase. (To stop, press 'Enter' only): ");
            aPhrase = getPhrase(in);
        }
    } //end main

    public static LinkedList getPhrase(Scanner in) {
        LinkedList phrase = new LinkedList();
        String str = in.nextLine();
        for (int h = str.length() - 1; h >= 0; h--)
            phrase.addHead(new NodeData(str.charAt(h)));
        return phrase;
    }

    public static LinkedList lettersLower(LinkedList phrase) {
        LinkedList word = new LinkedList();

        while (!phrase.empty()) {
            char ch = phrase.getHeadData().getData();
            if (Character.isLetter(ch)) word.addTail(new NodeData(Character.toLowerCase(ch)));
            phrase.deleteHead();
        }
        return word;
    }

} //end class P3_5Palindrome
```

■ **Note**   The solution presented was used mainly to show how linked lists can be manipulated. The problem can be solved more efficiently using character arrays or strings where we would have direct access to any character of the given phrase. For instance, we would be able to compare the first and last letters directly. Even in the solution presented here, we could clean up the phrase as it is being input by retaining letters only and converting them to lowercase. As an exercise, write a program to solve the problem using arrays.

3.12 Saving a Linked List

When we create a linked list, the actual "pointer" value in a node is determined at run time depending on where, in memory, storage for the node is allocated. Each time the program is run, the pointer values will change. So, what do we do if, having created a linked list, we need to save it for later use?

Since it would be useless to save the pointer values, we must save the contents of the nodes in such a way that we would be able to re-create the list when needed. The simplest way to do this is to write the items to a file (see Chapter 8) in the order that they appear in the linked list. Later, we can read the file and re-create the list as each item is read.

Sometimes, we may want to compact a linked list into an array. One reason might be that the linked list is sorted and we want to search it quickly. Since we are restricted to a sequential search on a linked list, we can transfer the items to an array where we can use a binary search.

For example, suppose we have a linked list of at most 50 integers pointed to by top. If num and next are the fields of a node, we can store the integers in an array saveLL with the following code:

```
int saveLL[50], n = 0;
while (top != null & n < 50) {
    saveLL[n++] = top.num;
    top = top.next;
}
```

On completion, the value of n will indicate how many numbers were saved. They will be stored in saveLL[0..n-1].

3.13 Arrays vs. Linked Lists

Arrays and linked lists are the two common ways to store a linear list, and each has its advantages and disadvantages.

The big difference between the two is that we have direct access to any element of an array by using a subscript, whereas to get to any element of a linked list, we have to traverse the list starting from the top.

If the list of items is unsorted, we must search the list using a sequential search whether the items are stored in an array or a linked list. If the list is sorted, it is possible to search the array using a binary search. Since binary search requires direct access to an element, we cannot perform a binary search on a linked list. The only way to search a linked list is sequential.

Inserting an item at the tail of a list stored in an array is easy (assuming there is room), but inserting an item at the head requires that all the other items be moved to make room for the new one. Inserting an item in the middle would require about half of the items to be moved to make room for the new one. Inserting an item anywhere in a linked list is easy since it requires setting/changing just a couple links.

Similarly, deleting an item from a linked list is easy regardless of where the item is located (head, tail, middle). Deleting an item from an array is easy only if it is the last one; deleting any other item would require other items to be moved to "close the space" previously occupied by the deleted item.

Maintaining an array in sorted order (when new items are added) is cumbersome since each new item has to be inserted "in place," and, as we've seen, this would normally require that other items be moved. However, finding the location in which to insert the item can be done quickly using a binary search.

Finding the *position* at which to insert a new item in a sorted linked list must be done using a sequential search. However, once the position is found, the item can be quickly inserted by setting/changing a couple links.

Table 3-1 summarizes the strengths and weaknesses of storing a list of items in an array versus storing the items in a linked list.

Table 3-1. *Storing List of Items in an Array vs. in Linked List*

Array	Linked List
Direct access to any element	Must traverse list to get to element
If unsorted, sequential search	If unsorted, sequential search
If sorted, binary search	If sorted, sequential search
Easy to insert item at the tail of the list	Easy to insert item anywhere in the list
Must move items to insert anywhere but the tail	Easy to insert item anywhere in the list
Deletion (except the last one) requires items to be moved	Deleting any item is easy
Need to move items when adding a new item to a sorted list	Adding a new item to a sorted linked list is easy
Can use binary search on a sorted list to find the position at which to insert new item	Must use sequential search to find the position at which to insert a new item in a sorted linked list

3.14 Storing a Linked List Using Arrays

We have seen how to create a linked list using dynamic storage allocation. When we need to add another node to a linked list, we request the storage for that node. If we need to delete a node from a linked list, we first delete it logically by changing pointers and then physically by freeing the storage occupied by the node.

It is also possible to represent a linked list using arrays. Consider, once again, the following linked list:

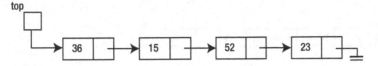

We can store this as follows:

top [5]

	data	next
0		
1	15	7
2		
3	23	-1
4		
5	36	1
6		
7	52	3
8		
9		

Here, the links (pointers) are merely array subscripts. Since an array subscript is just an integer, top is an int variable, and next is an int array. In this example, the data happens to be integers (so data is an int array), but it could be of any other type, even an object.

The value of top is 5, so this says that the first item in the list is found at array index 5; data[5] holds the data (36, in this case), and next[5] (1, in this case) tells us where to find the next (second) item in the list.

So, the second item is found at array index 1; data[1] holds the data (15), and next[1] (7) tells us where to find the next (third) item in the list.

The third item is found at array index 7; data[7] holds the data (52), and next[7] (3) tells us where to find the next (fourth) item in the list.

The fourth item is found at array index 3; data[3] holds the data (23), and next[3] (-1) tells us where to find the next item in the list. Here, we use -1 as the null pointer, so we've come to the end of the list. Any value that cannot be confused with a valid array subscript can be used to denote the null pointer, but -1 is commonly used.

All the operations described in this chapter for working with linked lists (for example, adding, deleting, and traversing) can be performed in a similar manner on linked lists stored using arrays. The main difference is that, previously, if curr points to the current node, curr.next points to the next node. Now, if curr points to the current node, next[curr] points to the next node.

One disadvantage of using arrays to store a linked list is that you must have some idea of how big the list is expected to be in order to declare the arrays. Another is that storage for deleted items cannot be freed or garbage-collected. However, the storage can be reused to store new items.

3.15 Merging Two Sorted Linked Lists

In Section 1.10, we considered the problem of merging two ordered lists. There, we showed how to solve the problem when the lists were stored in arrays. We now will show how to solve the same problem when the lists are stored as linked lists. We consider the problem of merging two ordered linked lists to produce one ordered list.

Suppose the given lists are as follows:

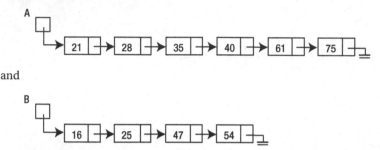

and

We want to create one linked list with all the numbers in ascending order, thus:

C

```
16 → 21 → 25 → 28 → 35 → 40 → 47 → 54 → 61 → 75
```

We will create the merged list by creating a new node for each number that we add to list C; we leave lists A and B untouched. We will use the same algorithm that we used in Section 1.10. Here it is for easy reference:

```
while (at least one number remains in both A and B) {
   if (smallest in A < smallest in B)
      add smallest in A to C
      move on to next number in A
   else
      add smallest in B to C
      move on to next number in B
   endif
}
//at this stage, at least one of the lists has ended
while (A has numbers) {
   add smallest in A to C
   move on to next number in A
}
while (B has numbers) {
   add smallest in B to C
   move on to next number in B
}
```

Since our lists contain integers, we will have to use the int version of NodeData.

If A and B are of type LinkedList, we will write an instance method, merge, in the LinkedList class such that A.merge(B) will return a LinkedList containing the merged elements of A and B. Here is merge:

```
public LinkedList merge(LinkedList LL) {
   Node A = this.head;
   Node B = LL.head;
```

```
        LinkedList C = new LinkedList();
        while (A != null && B != null) {
            if (A.data.compareTo(B.data) < 0) {
                C.addTail(A.data);
                A = A.next;
            }
            else {
                C.addTail(B.data);
                B = B.next;
            }
        }
        while (A != null) {
            C.addTail(A.data);
            A = A.next;
        }
        while (B != null) {
            C.addTail(B.data);
            B = B.next;
        }
        return C;
    } //end merge
```

As implemented, addTail has to traverse the entire list to find the end before adding each new node. This is inefficient. We *could* keep a pointer (tail, say) to the end of the list to facilitate adding a node at the end. But this would complicate the class unnecessarily at this stage.

Since adding a node at the head is a simple, efficient operation, it would be better to add a new node at the head and, when the merge is completed, reverse the list. We will modify merge by replacing addTail with addHead and, just before return C, we insert the statement C.reverseList();.

To test merge, we write Program P3.6. It requests the user to enter data for two lists. The data can be entered in any order. The lists will be built in sorted order by adding each new number "in place."

We remind you that this program requires the int version of the NodeData class, which is declared public and stored in the file NodeData.java. It also requires that the function merge be put in the LinkedList class, which is declared public and stored in the file LinkedList.java. Of course, Program P3.6 is stored in the file MergeLists.java.

Program P3.6

```
        import java.util.*;
        public class MergeLists {
            public static void main(String[] args) {
                Scanner in = new Scanner(System.in);
                LinkedList A = createSortedList(in);
                LinkedList B = createSortedList(in);
                System.out.printf("\nWhen we merge\n");
                A.printList();
                System.out.printf("with\n");
                B.printList();
                System.out.printf("we get\n");
                A.merge(B).printList();
            } //end main
```

```
    public static LinkedList createSortedList(Scanner in) {
        LinkedList LL = new LinkedList();
        System.out.printf("Enter some integers ending with 0\n");
        int n = in.nextInt();
        while (n != 0) {
            LL.addInPlace(new NodeData(n));
            n = in.nextInt();
        }
        return LL;
    } //end createSortedList

} //end MergeLists
```

The following is a sample run of Program P3.6:

```
Enter some integers ending with 0
8 4 12 6 10 2 0
Enter some integers ending with 0
5 7 15 1 3  0

When we merge
2 4 6 8 10 12
with
1 3 5 7 15
we get
1 2 3 4 5 6 7 8 10 12 15
```

3.16 Circular and Two-Way Linked Lists

So far, our discussion has been primarily about one-way (singly linked) lists. Each node contains one pointer that tells us the location of the next item. The last node has a null pointer, indicating the end of the list. While this is the most commonly used type of list, two common variations are the *circular* list and the *two-way* (or doubly linked) list.

3.16.1 Circular Lists

In a circular list, we let the last item point back to the first, as follows:

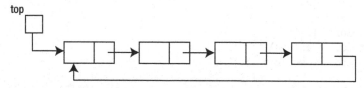

Now, there is no null pointer to tell us when we have reached the end of the list, so we must be careful in traversing that we do not end up in an infinite loop. In other words, say we were to write something like this:

```
Node curr = top;
while (curr != null) {
    //do something with node pointed to by curr
    curr = curr.next;
}
```

This loop will *never* terminate since curr never becomes null. To avoid this problem, we can save the pointer of our starting node and recognize when we have returned to this node. Here's an example:

```
Node curr = top;
do {
    //do something with node pointed to by curr
    curr = curr.next;
} while (curr != top) {
```

Alert readers will observe that since the body of a do...while loop is executed at least once, we should ensure that the list is not empty before going into the loop and trying to dereference a null pointer.

Circular lists are useful for representing situations that are, well, circular. For example, in a card or board game in which players take turns, we can represent the order of play using a circular list. If there are four players, they will play in the order 1, 2, 3, 4, 1, 2, 3, 4, 1, 2, and so on. After the last person plays, it's the turn of the first.

In the children's game *count-out*, the children are arranged in a circle and some variation of "eenie, meenie, mynie, mo; sorry, child, you've got to go" is used to eliminate one child at a time. The last remaining child wins the game.

We will write a program that uses a circular list to find the winner of the game described as follows:

The count-out game: n *children (numbered 1 to* n*) are arranged in a circle. A sentence consisting of* m *words is used to eliminate one child at a time until one child is left. Starting at child 1, the children are counted from 1 to* m *and the* mth *child is eliminated. Starting with the child after the one just eliminated, the children are again counted from 1 to* m *and the* mth *child is eliminated. This is repeated until one child is left. Counting is done circularly, and eliminated children are not counted. Write a program to read values for* n *and* m *(> 0), play the game as described, and print the number of the last remaining child.*

It is possible to use an array (child, say) to solve this problem. To declare the array, we would need to know the maximum number (max, say) of children to cater for. We could set child[1] to child[n] to 1 to indicate that all *n* children are initially in the game. When a child (h, say) is eliminated, we would set child[h] to 0 and start counting out from the next child still in the game.

As the game progresses, several entries in child will be set to 0, and when we count, we must ensure that 0s are not counted. In other words, even when a child has been eliminated, we must still inspect the array item and skip it if 0. As more children are eliminated, we will need to inspect and skip more zero entries. This is the main disadvantage of using an array to solve this problem.

We can write a more efficient solution using a circular linked list. First, we create the list with *n* nodes. The value at each node is the child's number. For *n* = 4, the list will look like the following, assuming curr points to the first child:

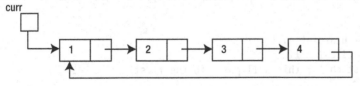

Suppose *m* = 5. We start counting from 1; when we reach 4, the count of 5 takes us back to child 1, which is eliminated. The list will look like this:

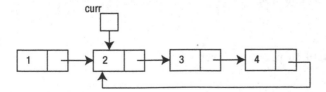

105

As shown, child 1 is no longer in the list; the storage for this node would be reclaimed eventually by Java. We count to 5 again, starting from child 2. The count ends at child 3, which is eliminated by setting child 2's pointer to point to child 4. The list will look like this:

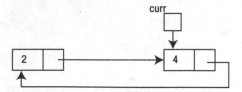

Finally, we count to 5 starting at child 4. The count ends at child 4, which is eliminated. Child 2 is the winner.

Note that this solution (as opposed to the array version) really does eliminate a child from the game by deleting its node. Eliminated children are neither inspected nor counted since they are gone! This is more in keeping with the way the game is played.

Program P3.7 plays the game and finds the winner using a linked list representation. We keep the solution simple and faithful to the description of the game. As such, we do not use the LinkedList class. Rather, we use a Node class with two fields: an int to hold the number of a child and a pointer to the next child.

After getting the number of children and the length of the count-out, the program calls linkCircular to create a circular linked list of the children and then playGame to eliminate all but one of the children.

Program P3.7

```
import java.util.*;
public class CountOut {
   public static void main(String[] args) {
      Scanner in = new Scanner(System.in);
      int m, n;
      do {
         System.out.printf("Enter number of children and length of count-out: ");
         n = in.nextInt();
         m = in.nextInt();
      } while (n < 1 || m < 1);

      Node last = linkCircular(n); //link children in a circular list
      Node winner = playGame(last, n-1, m); //eliminate n-1 children
      System.out.printf("The winning child: %d\n", winner.num);
   } //end main

   public static Node linkCircular(int n) {
      //link n children in a circular list;
      //return pointer to last child; this will point to the first
      Node first, np;

      first = np = new Node(1);       //first child
      for (int h = 2; h <= n; h++) { //link the others
         np.next = new Node(h);
         np = np.next;
      }
      np.next = first; //set last child to point to first
      return np;
   } //end linkCircular
```

```
    public static Node playGame(Node last, int x, int m) {
    //Eliminate x children with countout length of m;
    //last points to the last child which points to the first child
        Node prev = last, curr = last.next; //curr points to first child
        //eliminate x children
        for (int h = 1; h <= x; h++) {
            //curr is pointing at the first child to be counted;
            //count m-1 more to get to the mth child
            for (int c = 1; c < m; c++) {
                prev = curr;
                curr = curr.next;
            }
            //delete the mth child
            prev.next = curr.next;
            curr = prev.next; //set curr to the child after the one eliminated
        }
        return curr;
    } //end playGame

} //end class CountOut

class Node {
    int num;
    Node next;

    public Node(int n) {
        num = n;
        next = null;
    }
} //end class Node
```

The following is a sample run of Program P3.7:

```
Enter number of children and length of count-out: 9 10
The winning child: 8
```

3.16.2 Two-Way (Doubly Linked) Lists

As the name implies, each node will contain two pointers; one points to the next node, and the other points to the previous node. While this requires more work to implement and maintain, there are some advantages.

The obvious one is that it is now possible to traverse the list in both directions, starting from either end. If required, reversing the list is now a simple operation.

If we land at a node (the current node) in a singly linked list, there is no way to get to (or know) the previous node unless that information was kept as the list was traversed. With a doubly linked list, we have a direct pointer to the previous node so we can move in either direction.

One possible disadvantage is that more storage is required for the extra link. Another is that adding and deleting nodes is more complicated since more pointers have to be set.

EXERCISES 3

1. Write an instance method in the `LinkedList` class that returns `true` if the list is sorted in ascending order and `false` otherwise.

2. Write an instance method to reverse the nodes of a linked list by creating a new list. The method returns the newly created list.

3. Write a method to sort a linked list of integers as follows:

   (a) Find the largest value in the list.

   (b) Delete it from its position and insert it at the head of the list.

   (c) Starting from what is now the second element, repeat (a) and (b).

   (d) Starting from what is now the third element, repeat (a) and (b).

   Continue until the list is sorted.

4. Write a function that takes three arguments—a pointer to a linked list of integers and two integers n and j—and inserts n after the jth element of the list. If j is 0, n is inserted at the head of the list. If j is greater than the number of elements in the list, n is inserted after the last one.

5. The characters of a string are held on a linked list, one character per node.

   (a) Write a method that, given a pointer to a string and two characters, c1 and c2, replaces all occurrences of c1 with c2.

   (b) Write a function that, given a pointer to a string and a character, c, deletes all occurrences of c from the string. Return a pointer to the modified string.

   (c) Write a function that creates a new list consisting of the letters only in the given list, all converted to lowercase and stored in alphabetical order. Return a pointer to the new list.

   (d) Write a function that, given pointers to two strings, returns true if the first is a substring of the other and false otherwise.

6. Write a function that, given an integer n, converts n to binary and stores each bit in one node of a linked list with the *least* significant bit at the head of the list and the *most* significant bit at the tail. For example, given 13, the bits are stored in the order 1 0 1 1, from head to tail. Return a pointer to the head of the list.

7. Write a function that, given a pointer to a linked list of bits stored as in 6, *traverses the list once* and returns the decimal equivalent of the binary number.

8. You are given two pointers, b1 and b2. Each points to a binary number stored as in question 6. You must return a pointer to a newly created linked list representing the binary sum of the given numbers with the *least* significant bit at the head of the list and the *most* significant bit at the tail of the list. Write functions to do this in two ways:

   (i) Using the functions from 6 and 7

   (ii) Performing a "bit by bit" addition

9. Repeat exercises 6, 7, and 8 but, this time, store the bits with the *most* significant bit at the head of the list and the *least* significant bit at the tail.

10. Two words are anagrams if one word can be formed by rearranging all the letters of the other word, for example: *treason*, *senator*. A word is represented as a linked list with one letter per node of the list.

    Write a function that, given w1 and w2, with each pointing to a word of lowercase letters, returns 1 if the words are anagrams and 0 if they are not. Base your algorithm on the following: for each letter in w1, search w2 for it; if found, delete it and continue; otherwise, return 0.

11. Rewrite the count-out program, but, this time, store the children in an array. Your program should use the same logic as that of Program P3.7 except that you must use array storage to implement the circular list and the required operations.

12. The digits of an integer are held on a linked list in reverse order, one digit per node. Write a function that, given pointers to two integers, performs a digit-by-digit addition and returns a pointer to the digits of the sum stored in reverse order. Note: this idea can be used to add arbitrarily large integers.

CHAPTER 4

■ ■ ■

Stacks and Queues

In this chapter, we will explain the following:

- The notion of an abstract data type

- What a stack is

- How to implement a stack using an array

- How to implement a stack using a linked list

- How to create a header file for use by other programs

- How to implement a stack for a general data type

- How to convert an expression from infix to postfix

- How to evaluate an arithmetic expression

- What a queue is

- How to implement a queue using an array

- How to implement a queue using a linked list

4.1 Abstract Data Types

We are familiar with the notion of declaring variables of a given type (double, say) and then performing operations on those variables (for example, add, multiply, and assign) without needing to know *how* those variables are stored in the computer. In this scenario, the compiler designer can change the way a double variable is stored, and the programmer would not have to change any programs that use double variables. This is an example of an abstract data type.

An *abstract data type* is one that allows a user to manipulate the data type without any knowledge of how the data type is represented in the computer. In other words, as far as the user is concerned, all he needs to know are the operations that can be performed on the data type. The person who is implementing the data type is free to change its implementation without affecting the users.

In this chapter, we show how to implement stacks and queues as abstract data types.

4.2 Stacks

A *stack* as a linear list in which items are added at one end and deleted from the same end. The idea is illustrated by a "stack of plates" placed on a table, one on top of the other. When a plate is needed, it is taken from the top of the stack. When a plate is washed, it is added to the top of the stack. Note that if a plate is now needed, this "newest" plate is the one that is taken. A stack exhibits the "last in, first out" property.

To illustrate the stack idea, we will use a stack of integers. Our goal is to define a data type called Stack so that a user can declare variables of this type and manipulate them in various ways. What are some of these ways?

As indicated earlier, we will need to add an item to the stack; the term commonly used is *push*. We will also need to take an item off the stack; the term commonly used is *pop*.

Before we attempt to take something off the stack, it is a good idea to ensure that the stack has something on it, in other words, that it is not *empty*. We will need an operation that tests whether a stack is empty.

Given these three operations—*push*, *pop*, and *empty*—let's illustrate how they can be used to read some numbers and print them in reverse order. For example, say we have these numbers:

```
36 15 52 23
```

And say we want to print the following:

```
23 52 15 36
```

We can solve this problem by adding each new number to the top of a stack, S. After all the numbers have been placed on the stack, we can picture the stack as follows:

```
23      (top of stack)
52
15
36      (bottom of stack)
```

Next, we remove the numbers, one at a time, printing each as it is removed.

We will need a way of telling when all the numbers have been read. We will use 0 to end the data. The logic for solving this problem can be expressed as follows:

```
create an empty stack, S
read(num)
while (num != 0) {
    push num onto S
    read(num)
}
while (S is not empty) {
    pop S into num //store the number at the top of S in num
    print num
}
```

We now show how we can implement a stack of integers and its operations.

4.2.1 Implementing a Stack Using an Array

To simplify the presentation of the basic principles, we will work with a stack of integers. Later, we will see how to implement a stack for a general data type.

In the array implementation of a stack (of integers), we use an integer array (ST, say) for storing the numbers and an integer variable (top, say) that contains the subscript of the item at the top of the stack.

Since we are using an array, we will need to know its size in order to declare it. We will need to have some information about the problem to determine a reasonable size for the array. We will use the symbolic constant MaxStack. If we attempt to push more than MaxStack elements onto the stack, a *stack overflow* error will be reported.

We begin our definition of the class Stack as follows:

```
public class Stack {
    final static int MaxStack = 100;
    int top = -1;
    int[] ST = new int[MaxStack];

    //the rest of the class goes here
} //end class Stack
```

Valid values for top will range from 0 to MaxStack-1. When we initialize a stack, we will set top to the invalid subscript -1.

We can now declare a stack variable, S, with this statement:

```
Stack S = new Stack();
```

When this statement is executed, the situation in memory can be represented by that shown in Figure 4-1.

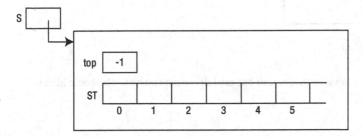

Figure 4-1. *Array representation of stack in memory*

This represents an empty stack. We will need a function that tells us whether a stack is empty. We can add the following instance method to the Stack class:

```
public boolean empty() {
    return top == -1;
}
```

This simply checks whether top has the value -1.

The major operations on a stack are *push* and *pop*. To push an item, n, onto a stack, we must store it in ST and update top to point to it. The basic idea is as follows:

```
add 1 to top
set ST[top] to n
```

However, we must guard against trying to add something to the stack when it is already full. The stack is full when top has the value MaxStack - 1, the subscript of the last element. In this case, we will report that the stack is full and halt the program. Here is the instance method, push, in the Stack class:

```
public void push(int n) {
    if (top == MaxStack - 1) {
        System.out.printf("\nStack Overflow\n");
        System.exit(1);
    }
    ++top;
    ST[top] = n;
} //end push
```

To illustrate, after the numbers 36, 15, 52, and 23 have been pushed onto S, our picture in memory looks like Figure 4-2.

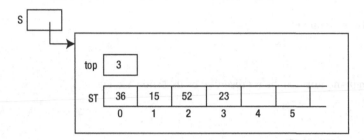

Figure 4-2. *Stack view after pushing 36, 15, 52, and 23*

Finally, to pop an item off the stack, we return the value in location top and decrease top by 1. The basic idea is as follows:

```
set hold to ST[top]
subtract 1 from top
return hold
```

Again, we must guard against trying to take something off an empty stack. What should we do if the stack is empty and pop is called? We could simply report an error and halt the program. However, it might be better to return some "rogue" value, indicating that the stack is empty. We take the latter approach in our function pop. Here is the instance method pop in the Stack class:

```
public int pop() {
    if (this.empty())return RogueValue; //a symbolic constant
    int hold = ST[top];
    --top;
    return hold;
}
```

Note that even though we have written pop to do something reasonable if it is called and the stack is empty, it is better if the programmer establishes that the stack is *not* empty (using the empty function) *before* calling pop.

Given the class Stack, we can now write Program P4.1, which reads some numbers, terminated by 0, and prints them in reverse order. Note that the word public is dropped from the class Stack in order to store the entire program in one file, StackTest.java.

Program P4.1

```java
import java.util.*;
public class StackTest {
   public static void main(String[] args) {
      Scanner in = new Scanner(System.in);
      Stack S = new Stack();
      System.out.printf("Enter some integers ending with 0\n");
      int n = in.nextInt();
      while (n != 0) {
         S.push(n);
         n = in.nextInt();
      }
      System.out.printf("\nNumbers in reverse order\n");
      while (!S.empty())
         System.out.printf("%d ", S.pop());
      System.out.printf("\n");
   } //end main
} //end StackTest

class Stack {
   final static int MaxStack = 100;
   final static int RogueValue = -999999;
   int top = -1;
   int[] ST = new int[MaxStack];

   public boolean empty() {
      return top == -1;
   }

   public void push(int n) {
      if (top == MaxStack - 1) {
         System.out.printf("\nStack Overflow\n");
         System.exit(1);
      }
      ++top;
      ST[top] = n;
   } //end push

   public int pop() {
      if (this.empty())return RogueValue; //a symbolic constant
      int hold = ST[top];
      --top;
      return hold;
   }

} //end class Stack
```

The following shows a sample run of Program P4.1:

```
Enter some integers ending with 0
1 2 3 4 5 6 7 8 9 0

Numbers in reverse order
9 8 7 6 5 4 3 2 1
```

It is important to observe that the code in main that uses the stack does so via the functions push, pop, and empty and makes *no* assumption about *how* the stack elements are stored. This is the hallmark of an abstract data type—it can be used without the user needing to know how it is implemented.

Next, we will implement the stack using a linked list, but main will remain the same for solving the problem of printing the numbers in reverse order.

4.2.2 Implementing a Stack Using a Linked List

The array implementation of a stack has the advantages of simplicity and efficiency. However, one major disadvantage is the need to know what size to declare the array. Some reasonable guess has to be made, but this may turn out to be too small (and the program has to halt) or too big (and storage is wasted).

To overcome this disadvantage, a linked list can be used. Now, we will allocate storage for an element only when it is needed.

The stack is implemented as a linked list with new items added at the head of the list. When we need to pop the stack, the item at the head is removed.

Again, we illustrate the principles using a stack of integers. First, we will need to define a Node class that will be used to create nodes for the list. We will use the following declarations:

```
class Node {
    int data;
    Node next;

    public Node(int d) {
        data = d;
        next = null;
    }
} //end class Node
```

Next, we will write the class, Stack, which begins as follows:

```
class Stack {
    Node top = null;

    public boolean empty() {
        return top == null;
    }
    ...
```

There is one instance variable—top of type Node. It is initialized to null to denote the empty stack. The function empty simply checks whether top is null. The empty stack, S, is depicted as in Figure 4-3.

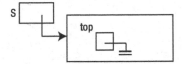

Figure 4-3. *Empty stack*

The method push simply adds an item at the head of the stack and can be written as follows:

```
public void push(int n) {
    Node p = new Node(n);
    p.next = top;
    top = p;
} //end push
```

After 36, 15, 52, and 23 (in that order) have been pushed onto a stack, S, we can picture it as shown in Figure 4-4. S is a pointer to top, which is a pointer to the linked list of stack elements.

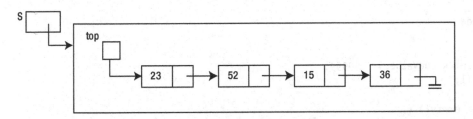

Figure 4-4. *Stack view after pushing 36, 15, 52, and 23*

To pop an item from the stack, we first check whether the stack is empty. If it is, a rogue value is returned. If not, the item at the head of the list is returned, and the node containing the item is deleted from the list. Here is pop:

```
public int pop() {
    if (this.empty()) return RogueValue; //a symbolic constant
    int hold = top.data;
    top = top.next;
    return hold;
} //end pop
```

We rewrite Program P4.1 as Program P4.2. The class StackTest remains the same as before, but the class Stack uses our new definitions of empty, push, and pop. We emphasize again that even though our *implementation* of the stack has changed from using an array to using a linked list, the code that uses the stack (main) remains the same.

Program P4.2

```
import java.util.*;
public class StackTest {
    public static void main(String[] args) {
        Scanner in = new Scanner(System.in);
        Stack S = new Stack();
        System.out.printf("Enter some integers ending with 0\n");
        int n = in.nextInt();
```

117

```
            while (n != 0) {
               S.push(n);
               n = in.nextInt();
            }
            System.out.printf("\nNumbers in reverse order\n");
            while (!S.empty())
               System.out.printf("%d ", S.pop());
            System.out.printf("\n");
         } //end main
      } //end StackTest

      class Node {
         int data;
         Node next;

         public Node(int d) {
            data = d;
            next = null;
         }
      } //end class Node

      class Stack {
         final static int RogueValue = -999999;
         Node top = null;

         public boolean empty() {
            return top == null;
         }

         public void push(int n) {
            Node p = new Node(n);
            p.next = top;
            top = p;
         } //end push

         public int pop() {
            if (this.empty()) return RogueValue; //a symbolic constant
            int hold = top.data;
            top = top.next;
            return hold;
         } //end pop

      } //end class Stack
```

The following shows a sample run of Program P4.2. As expected, it works in an identical manner to Program P4.1.

```
Enter some integers ending with 0
1 2 3 4 5 6 7 8 9 0

Numbers in reverse order
9 8 7 6 5 4 3 2 1
```

4.3 A General Stack Type

To simplify our presentation, we have worked with a stack of integers. We remind you of those places that are tied to the decision to use integers.

- In the declaration of Node, we declare an int called num.

- In push, we pass an int argument.

- In pop, we return an int result.

This means that if we need a stack of characters, say, we will have to change int to char in all of these places. Similar changes will have to be made for stacks of other types.

It would be nice if we could minimize the changes needed when a different type of stack is required. We now show how this could be done.

First, we define Node as follows:

```
class Node {
    NodeData data;
    Node next;

    public Node(NodeData d) {
        data = d;
        next = null;
    }
} //end class Node
```

The data at a node consists of the general type, NodeData. When the user defines the NodeData class, he will decide what kind of items will be stored on the stack.

The Stack class starts off the same as before:

```
public class Stack {
    Node top = null;

    public boolean empty() {
        return top == null;
    }
    ...
```

But now, push will require a NodeData argument and can be written as follows:

```
public void push(NodeData nd) {
    Node p = new Node(nd);
    p.next = top;
    top = p;
} //end push
```

Similarly, we write pop as follows. Since only NodeData should know the type of data being defined, we will let it tell us what is the rogue value.

```
public NodeData pop() {
    if (this.empty())return NodeData.getRogueValue();
    NodeData hold = top.data;
    top = top.next;
    return hold;
} //end pop
```

The observant reader will notice that all we have done so far is change int to NodeData in Node, push, and pop.

If we want to implement a stack of integers, we can define the NodeData class as follows. It is the same as before with the addition of the accessor getData().

```
public class NodeData {
    int num;

    public NodeData(int n) {
        num = n;
    }

    public int getData() {return num;}

    public static NodeData getRogueValue() {return new NodeData(-999999);}

    public int compareTo(NodeData nd) {
        if (this.num == nd.num) return 0;
        if (this.num < nd.num) return -1;
        return 1;
    }

    public String toString() {
        return num + " ";
        //" " needed to convert num to a string; may also use "" (empty string)
    }

} //end class NodeData
```

Despite all these changes to Node, Stack, and NodeData, the class StackTest of Programs P4.1 and P4.2 will work like before if we just change S.push(n) to S.push(new NodeData(n)) and S.pop() to S.pop().getData(), as shown in Program P4.3. Note that, for this program, we won't need compareTo and toString from the NodeData class, so they are omitted. As usual, we omit public from the class headers (except StackTest) so that the entire program can be kept in one file.

Program P4.3

```
import java.util.*;
public class StackTest {
    public static void main(String[] args) {
        Scanner in = new Scanner(System.in);
        Stack S = new Stack();
        System.out.printf("Enter some integers ending with 0\n");
```

```
        int n = in.nextInt();
        while (n != 0) {
            S.push(new NodeData(n));
            n = in.nextInt();
        }
        System.out.printf("\nNumbers in reverse order\n");
        while (!S.empty())
            System.out.printf("%d ", S.pop().getData());
        System.out.printf("\n");
    } //end main
} //end StackTest

class NodeData {
    int num;

    public NodeData(int n) {
        num = n;
    }

    public int getData() {return num;}

    public static NodeData getRogueValue() {return new NodeData(-999999);}

} //end class NodeData

class Node {
    NodeData data;
    Node next;

    public Node(NodeData d) {
        data = d;
        next = null;
    }
} //end class Node

class Stack {
    Node top = null;

    public boolean empty() {
        return top == null;
    }

    public void push(NodeData nd) {
        Node p = new Node(nd);
        p.next = top;
        top = p;
    } //end push

    public NodeData pop() {
        if (this.empty())return NodeData.getRogueValue();
        NodeData hold = top.data;
```

```
            top = top.next;
            return hold;
        } //end pop

    } //end class Stack
```

If we need to work with a stack of characters, we just need to change the NodeData class to the following:

```java
public class NodeData {
    char ch;

    public NodeData(char c) {
        ch = c;
    }

    public char getData() {return ch;}

    public static NodeData getRogueValue() {return new NodeData('$');}

    public int compareTo(NodeData nd) {
        if (this.ch == nd.ch) return 0;
        if (this.ch < nd.ch) return -1;
        return 1;
    }

    public String toString() {
        return ch + "";
    }
} //end class NodeData
```

4.3.1 Example: Convert from Decimal to Binary

Consider the problem of converting a positive integer from decimal to binary. We can use an integer stack, S, to do this using repeated division by 2 and saving the remainders. Here is the algorithm:

```
initialize S to empty
read the number, n
while (n > 0) {
    push n % 2 onto S
    n = n / 2
}
while (S is not empty) print pop(S)
```

This algorithm is implemented in Program P4.4. Only the class DecimalToBinary is shown. The classes NodeData, Node, and Stack are the same as in Program P4.3.

Program P4.4

```java
import java.util.*;
public class DecimalToBinary {
```

```
    public static void main(String[] args) {
        Scanner in = new Scanner(System.in);
        Stack S = new Stack();
        System.out.printf("Enter a positive integer: ");
        int n = in.nextInt();
        while (n > 0) {
            S.push(new NodeData(n % 2));
            n = n / 2;
        }
        System.out.printf("\nIts binary equivalent is ");
        while (!S.empty())
            System.out.printf("%d", S.pop().getData());
        System.out.printf("\n");
    } //end main
} //end class DecimalToBinary
```

The following is a sample run of Program P4.4:

```
Enter a positive integer: 99

Its binary equivalent is 1100011
```

4.4 How to Convert from Infix to Postfix

One of the classical uses of a stack is in the evaluation of arithmetic expressions. One of the problems with the way we normally write an arithmetic expression (*infix* form) is that it is not convenient for evaluation by a computer. For such evaluation, one method is to first convert the expression to *postfix* form. We first show how to do this conversion, followed by an explanation of how the expression is evaluated.

Consider the expression 7 + 3 * 4. What is its value? Without any knowledge about which operation should be performed first, we might work out the value from left to right as (7 + 3 = 10) * 4 = 40. However, normal rules of arithmetic state that multiplication *has higher precedence* than addition. This means that, in an expression like 7 + 3 * 4, multiplication (*) is performed before addition (+). Knowing this, the value is 7 + 12 = 19.

We can, of course, force the addition to be performed first by using brackets, as in (7 + 3) * 4. Here, the brackets mean that + is done first.

These are examples of infix expressions; the operator (+, *) is placed between its operands. One disadvantage of infix expressions is the need to use brackets to override the normal *precedence rules*.

Another way of representing expressions is to use *postfix* notation. Here, the operator comes *after* its operands and there is no need to use brackets to specify which operations to perform first. For example, the postfix form of

        7 + 3 * 4 is 7 3 4 * +

and the postfix form of

        (7 + 3) * 4 is 7 3 + 4 *

One useful observation is that the operands appear in the same order in both the infix and postfix forms but they differ in the order and placement of the operators.

Why is postfix notation useful? As mentioned, we do not need brackets to specify precedence of operators. More importantly, though, it is a convenient form for evaluating the expression.

Given the postfix form of an expression, it can be evaluated as follows:

```
initialize a stack, S, to empty
while we have not reached the end of the expression
   get the next item, x, from the expression
   if x is an operand, push it onto S
   if x is an operator, pop its operands from S, apply the operator and
            push the result onto S
endwhile
pop S; // this is the value of the expression
```

Consider the expression (7 + 3) * 4 whose postfix form is 7 3 + 4 *. It is evaluated by traversing from left to right.

1. The next item is 7; push 7 onto S; S contains 7.

2. The next item is 3; push 3 onto S; S contains 7 3 (the top is on the right).

3. The next item is +; pop 3 and 7 from S; apply + to 7 and 3, giving 10; push 10 onto S; S contains 10.

4. The next item is 4; push 4 onto S; S contains 10 4.

5. The next item is *; pop 4 and 10 from S; apply * to 10 and 4, giving 40; push 40 onto S; S contains 40.

6. We have reached the end of the expression; we pop S, getting 40—the result of the expression.

Note that when operands are popped from the stack, the first one popped is the second operand, and the second one popped is the first operand. This does not matter for addition and multiplication but would be important for subtraction and division. As an exercise, convert the following to postfix form and step through its evaluation using the algorithm above: (7 - 3) * (9 - 8 / 4).

The big question, of course, is how do we get the computer to convert an infix expression to postfix? Before presenting the algorithm, we observe that it will use an *operator stack*. We will also need a *precedence table* that gives the relative precedence of the operators. Given any two operators, the table will tell us whether they have the same precedence (like + and -) and, if not, which has greater precedence.

As the algorithm proceeds, it will output the postfix form of the given expression.

Here is the algorithm:

1. Initialize a stack of operators, S, to empty.

2. Get the next item, x, from the infix expression; if none, go to step 8 (x is either an operand, a left bracket, a right bracket, or an operator).

3. If x is an operand, output x.

4. If x is a left bracket, push it onto S.

5. If x is a right bracket, pop items off S and output popped items until a left bracket appears on top of S; pop the left bracket and discard.

6. If x is an operator, then do the following:

```
while (S is not empty) and (a left bracket is not on top of S) and
        (an operator of equal or higher precedence than x is on top of S)
   pop S and output popped item
push x onto S
```

7. Repeat from step 2.

8. Pop S and output the popped item until S is empty.

You are advised to step through the algorithm for the following expressions:

```
3 + 5
7 - 3 + 8
7 + 3 * 4
(7 + 3) * 4
(7 + 3) / (8 - 2 * 3)
(7 - 8 / 2 / 2) * ((7 - 2) * 3 - 6)
```

Let's write a program to read a simplified infix expression and output its postfix form. We assume that an operand is a single-digit integer. An operator can be one of +, -, *, or /. Brackets are allowed. The usual precedence of operators apply: + and - have the same precedence, which is lower than that of * and /, which have the same precedence. The left bracket is treated as an operator with very low precedence, less than that of + and -.

We will implement this as a function precedence that, given an operator, returns an integer representing its precedence. The actual value returned is not important as long as the relative precedence of the operators is maintained. We will use the following:

```java
public static int precedence(char c) {
    if (c == '(') return 0;
    if (c == '+' || c == '-') return 3;
    if (c == '*' || c == '/') return 5;
    return -99; //error
}
```

We could also write precedence using a switch statement as follows:

```java
public static int precedence(char c) {
    switch (c) {
        case '(': return 0;
        case '+':
        case '-': return 3;
        case '*':
        case '/': return 5;
    }//end switch
} //end precedence
```

The actual values 0, 3, and 5 are not important. Any values can be used as long as they represent the relative precedence of the operators.

We will need a function to read the input and return the next nonblank character. The function will skip over zero or more blanks, if necessary. The end-of-line character will indicate the end of the expression. Here is the function (we call it getToken):

```java
public static char getToken() throws IOException {
    int n;
    while ((n = System.in.read()) == ' ') ; //read over blanks
    if (n == '\r' || n == '\n') return '\0';
        //'\r' on Windows, MacOS and DOS; '\n' on Unix
    return (char) n;
} //end getToken
```

The operator stack is simply a stack of characters that we will implement using the NodeData class defined at the end of Section 4.3. This is shown in Program P4.5.

Step 6 of the algorithm requires us to compare the precedence of the operator on top of the stack with the current operator. This would be easy if we could "peek" at the element on top of the stack without taking it off. To do this, we write the following instance method, peek, and add it to the Stack class:

```java
public NodeData peek() {
      if (!this.empty()) return top.data;
      return null;
} //end peek
```

Putting all these together, we write Program P4.5, which implements the algorithm for converting an infix expression to postfix. The class Node is the same as that in Program P4.3. The class Stack is the same as that in Program P4.3 with the addition of peek().

Program P4.5

```java
import java.io.*;
public class InfixToPostfix {

    public static void main(String[] args) throws IOException {
        char[] post = new char[255];
        int n = readConvert(post);
        printPostfix(post, n);
    } //end main

    public static int readConvert(char[] post) throws IOException {
    //Read the expression and convert to postfix. Return the size of postfix.
        Stack S = new Stack();
        int h = 0;
        char c;
        System.out.printf("Type an infix expression and press Enter\n");
        char token = getToken();
        while (token != '\0') {
           if (Character.isDigit(token)) post[h++] = token;
           else if (token == '(') S.push(new NodeData('('));
           else if (token == ')')
              while ((c = S.pop().getData()) != '(') post[h++] = c;
           else {
              while (!S.empty() &&
                       precedence(S.peek().getData()) >= precedence(token))
                 post[h++] = S.pop().getData();
              S.push(new NodeData(token));
           }
           token = getToken();
        }
        while (!S.empty()) post[h++] = S.pop().getData();
        return h;
    } //end readConvert
```

```java
    public static void printPostfix(char[] post, int n) {
        System.out.printf("\nThe postfix form is \n");
        for (int h = 0; h < n; h++) System.out.printf("%c ", post[h]);
        System.out.printf("\n");
    } //end printPostfix

    public static char getToken() throws IOException {
        int n;
        while ((n = System.in.read()) == ' ') ; //read over blanks
        if (n == '\r') return '\0';
        return (char) n;
    } //end getToken

    public static int precedence(char c) {
    //Returns the precedence of the given operator
        if (c == '(') return 0;
        if (c == '+' || c == '-') return 3;
        if (c == '*' || c == '/') return 5;
        return -99; //error
    } //end precedence

} //end class InfixToPostfix

class NodeData {
    char ch;

    public NodeData(char c) {
        ch = c;
    }

    public char getData() {return ch;}

    public static NodeData getRogueValue() {return new NodeData('$');}

} //end class NodeData
```

The job of reading the expression and converting to postfix is delegated to the function readConvert. This outputs the postfix form to a character array, post. So as not to clutter the code with error checking, we assume that post is big enough to hold the converted expression. The function returns the number of elements in the postfix expression.

The function printPostfix simply prints the postfix expression.

The following is a sample run of Program P4.5:

```
Type an infix expression and press Enter
 (7 - 8 / 2 / 2) * ((7 - 2) * 3 - 6)

The postfix form is
7 8 2 / 2 / - 7 2 - 3 * 6 - *
```

Note that the expression can be entered with or without spaces separating the operators and operands. For instance, if the expression in the sample run were entered as follows, the correct postfix form would be produced:

```
(7 - 8/2/ 2)*((7-2) *3 - 6)
```

Program P4.5 assumes that the given expression is a valid one. However, it can be easily modified to recognize some kinds of invalid expressions. For instance, if a right bracket is missing, when we reach the end of the expression, there would be a left bracket on the stack. (If the brackets match, there would be none.) Similarly, if a left bracket is missing, when a right one is encountered and we are scanning the stack for the (missing) left one, we would not find it.

You are urged to modify Program P4.5 to catch expressions with mismatched brackets. You should also modify it to handle any integer operands, not just single-digit ones. Yet another modification is to handle other operations such as %, sqrt (square root), sin (sine), cos (cosine), tan (tangent), log (logarithm), exp (exponential), and so on.

4.4.1 Evaluating an Arithmetic Expression

Program P4.5 stores the postfix form of the expression in a character array, post. We now write a function that, given post, evaluates the expression and returns its value. The function uses the algorithm at the beginning of Section 4.4.

We will need an *integer* stack to hold the operands and intermediate results. Recall that we needed a *character* stack to hold the operators. We can neatly work with both kinds of stacks if we define NodeData as follows:

```java
public class NodeData {
    char ch;
    int num;

    public NodeData(char c) {
        ch = c;
    }

    public NodeData(int n) {
        num = n;
    }
    public NodeData(char c, int n) {
        ch = c;
        num = n;
    }

    public char getCharData() {return ch;}

    public int getIntData() {return num;}

    public static NodeData getRogueValue() {
        return new NodeData('$', -999999); //the user will choose which one is needed
    }

} //end class NodeData
```

We use the char field for the operator stack and the int field for the operand stack. Note the three constructors and the three accessors for setting and retrieving ch and num.

Using this definition of NodeData, Program P4.5 will work fine if we simply replace all occurrences of getData with getCharData.

The function eval, which evaluates an expression given its postfix form, is shown as part of Program P4.6. We test eval by placing the following as the last statement in main:

```
System.out.printf("\nIts value is %d\n", eval(post, n));
```

The classes Node and Stack are not shown in Program P4.6. The class Node is the same as that in Program P4.3. The class Stack is the same as that in Program P4.3 with the addition of peek().

Program P4.6

```java
import java.io.*;
public class EvalExpression {
   public static void main(String[] args) throws IOException {
      char[] post = new char[255];
      int n = readConvert(post);
      printPostfix(post, n);
      System.out.printf("\nIts value is %d\n", eval(post, n));
   } //end main

   public static int readConvert(char[] post) throws IOException {
   //Read the expression and convert to postfix. Return the size of postfix.
      Stack S = new Stack();
      int h = 0;
      char c;
      System.out.printf("Type an infix expression and press Enter\n");
      char token = getToken();
      while (token != '\0') {
         if (Character.isDigit(token)) post[h++] = token;
         else if (token == '(') S.push(new NodeData('('));
         else if (token == ')')
            while ((c = S.pop().getCharData()) != '(') post[h++] = c;
         else {
            while (!S.empty() &&
                    precedence(S.peek().getCharData()) >= precedence(token))
               post[h++] = S.pop().getCharData();
            S.push(new NodeData(token));
         }
         token = getToken();
      }
      while (!S.empty()) post[h++] = S.pop().getCharData();
      return h;
   } //end readConvert

   public static void printPostfix(char[] post, int n) {
      System.out.printf("\nThe postfix form is \n");
      for (int h = 0; h < n; h++) System.out.printf("%c ", post[h]);
      System.out.printf("\n");
   } //end printPostfix
```

```java
    public static char getToken() throws IOException {
        int n;
        while ((n = System.in.read()) == ' ') ; //read over blanks
        if (n == '\r') return '\0';
        return (char) n;
    } //end getToken

    public static int precedence(char c) {
    //Returns the precedence of the given operator
        if (c == '(') return 0;
        if (c == '+' || c == '-') return 3;
        if (c == '*' || c == '/') return 5;
        return -99; //error
    } //end precedence

    public static int eval(char[] post, int n) {
    //Given the postfix form of an expression, returns its value
        int a, b, c;
        Stack S = new Stack();
        for (int h = 0; h < n; h++) {
            if (Character.isDigit(post[h]))
                S.push(new NodeData(post[h] - '0'));
            else {
                b = S.pop().getIntData();
                a = S.pop().getIntData();
                if (post[h] == '+') c = a + b;
                else if (post[h] == '-') c = a - b;
                else if (post[h] == '*') c = a * b;
                else c = a / b;
                S.push(new NodeData(c));
            } //end if
        } //end for
        return S.pop().getIntData();
    } //end eval

} //end class EvalExpression

class NodeData {
    char ch;
    int num;

    public NodeData(char c) {
        ch = c;
    }

    public NodeData(int n) {
        num = n;
    }
```

```
        public NodeData(char c, int n) {
            ch = c;
            num = n;
        }

        public char getCharData() {return ch;}

        public int getIntData() {return num;}

        public static NodeData getRogueValue() {
            return new NodeData('$', -999999);
        }

    } //end class NodeData
```

The following is a sample run of Program P4.6:

```
Type an infix expression and press Enter
(7 - 8 / 2 / 2) * ((7 - 2) * 3 - 6)

The postfix form is
7 8 2 / 2 / - 7 2 - 3 * 6 - *

Its value is 45
```

4.5 Queues

A *queue* is a linear list in which items are added at one end and deleted from the other end. Familiar examples are queues at a bank, a supermarket, a concert, or a sporting event. People are supposed to join the queue at the rear and exit from the front. We would expect that a queue data structure would be useful for simulating these real-life queues.

Queues are also found inside the computer. There may be several jobs waiting to be executed, and they are held in a queue. For example, several people may each request something to be printed on a network printer. Since the printer can handle only one job at a time, the others have to be queued.

These are the basic operations we want to perform on a queue:

- Add an item to the queue (we say *enqueue*)
- Take an item off the queue (we say *dequeue*)
- Check whether the queue is empty
- Inspect the item at the head of the queue

Like with stacks, we can easily implement the queue data structure using arrays or linked lists. We will use a queue of integers for illustration purposes.

4.5.1 Implementing a Queue Using an Array

In the array implementation of a queue (of integers), we use an integer array (QA, say) for storing the numbers and two integer variables (head and tail) that indicate the item at the head of the queue and the item at the tail of the queue, respectively.

Since we are using an array, we will need to know its size in order to declare it. We will need to have some information about the problem to determine a reasonable size for the array. We will use the symbolic constant MaxQ. In our implementation, the queue will be declared full if there are MaxQ-1 elements in it and we attempt to add another.

We begin to define the class Queue as follows:

```
public class Queue {
    final static int MaxQ = 100;
    int head = 0, tail = 0;
    int[] QA = new int[MaxQ];
    ...
```

Valid values for head and tail will range from 0 to MaxQ-1. When we initialize a queue, we will set head and tail to 0; later, we will see why this is a good value.

As usual, we can create an empty queue, Q, with this:

```
Queue Q = new Queue();
```

When this statement is executed, the situation in memory can be represented as shown in Figure 4-5.

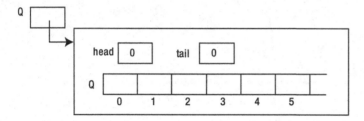

Figure 4-5. *Array representation of a queue*

This represents the empty queue. In working with queues, we will need a function that tells us whether a queue is empty. We can use the following:

```
public boolean empty() {
    return head == tail;
}
```

Shortly, we will see that given the way we will implement the *enqueue* and *dequeue* operations, the queue will be empty whenever head and tail have the same value. This value will not necessarily be 0. In fact, it may be any of the values from 0 to MaxQ-1, the valid subscripts of QA.

Consider how we might add an item to the queue. In a real queue, a person joins at the tail. We will do the same here by incrementing tail and storing the item at the location indicated by tail.

For example, to add 36, say, to the queue, we increment tail to 1 and store 36 in QA[1]; head remains at 0.

If we then add 15 to the queue, it will be stored in QA[2] and tail will be 2.

If we now add 52 to the queue, it will be stored in QA[3] and tail will be 3.

Our picture in memory will look like Figure 4-6.

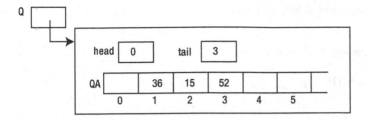

Figure 4-6. *State of the queue after adding 36, 15, and 52*

Note that head points "just in front of" the item, which is actually at the head of the queue, and tail points at the last item in the queue.

Now consider taking something off the queue. The item to be taken off is the one at the head. To remove it, we must *first* increment head and then return the value pointed to by head.

For example, if we remove 36, head will become 1, and it points "just in front of" 15, the item now at the head. Note that 36 still remains in the array, but, to all intents and purposes, it is not in the queue.

Suppose we now add 23 to the queue. It will be placed in location 4 with tail being 4 and head being 1.

The picture now looks like Figure 4-7.

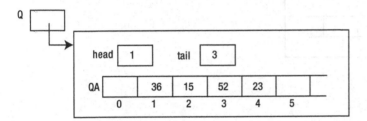

Figure 4-7. *State of the queue after removing 36 and adding 23*

There are three items in the queue; 15 is at the head, and 23 is at the tail.

Consider what happens if we continuously add items to the queue without taking off any. The value of tail will keep increasing until it reaches MaxQ-1, the last valid subscript of QA. What do we do if another item needs to be added?

We *could* say that the queue is full and stop the program. However, there are two free locations, 0 and 1. It would be better to try to use one of these. This leads us to the idea of a *circular queue*. Here, we think of the locations in the array as arranged in a circle: location MaxQ-1 is followed by location 0.

So, if tail has the value MaxQ-1, incrementing it will set it to 0.

Suppose we had not taken off any item from the queue. The value of head will still be 0. Now, what if, in attempting to add an item, tail is incremented from MaxQ-1 to 0? It now has the same value as head. In this situation, we declare that the queue is full.

We do this even though nothing is stored in location 0, which is, therefore, available to hold another item. The reason for taking this approach is that it simplifies our code for detecting when the queue is empty and when it is full. This is also the reason why we set both head and tail to 0 initially. It enables us to easily detect when the queue is full if items are inserted continuously.

To emphasize, *when the queue is declared full, it contains* MaxQ-1 *items*.

We can now write enqueue, an instance method to add an item to the queue.

```
public void enqueue(int n) {
    tail = (tail + 1) % MaxQ; //increment tail circularly
    if (tail == head) {
        System.out.printf("\nQueue is full\n");
        System.exit(1);
    }
    QA[tail] = n;
} //end enqueue
```

We first increment tail. If, by doing so, it has the same value as head, we declare that the queue is full. If not, we store the new item in position tail.

Consider Figure 4-7. If we delete 15 and 52, it changes to Figure 4-8.

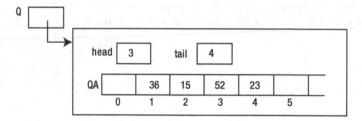

Figure 4-8. *Queue after removing 15, 52*

Now, head has the value 3, tail has the value 4, and there is one item, 23, in the queue at location 4. If we delete this last item, head and tail would both have the value 4 and the queue would be empty. This suggests that we have an *empty* queue when head has the same value as tail.

But wait! Didn't we just say that the queue is *full* when head and tail have the same value? True, but there's a difference. At any time, if head == tail, the queue is *empty*. However, if *after* incrementing tail to add an item it becomes the same as head, then the queue is full.

We can now write dequeue, a method that removes an item from the queue.

```
public int dequeue() {
    if (this.empty()) {
        System.out.printf("\nAttempt to remove from an empty queue\n");
        System.exit(2);
    }
    head = (head + 1) % MaxQ; //increment head circularly
    return QA[head];
} //end dequeue
```

If the queue is empty, an error is reported, and the program is halted. If not, we increment head and return the value in location head. Note, again, that if head has the value MaxQ -1, incrementing it sets it to 0.

To test our queue operations, we write Program P4.7, which reads an integer and prints its digits in reverse order. For example, if 12345 is read, the program prints 54321. The digits are extracted, from the right, and stored in a queue. The items in the queue are taken off, one at a time, and printed.

Program P4.7

```java
import java.util.*;
public class QueueTest {
    public static void main(String[] args) {
        Scanner in = new Scanner(System.in);
        Queue Q = new Queue();
        System.out.printf("Enter a positive integer: ");
        int n = in.nextInt();
        while (n > 0) {
            Q.enqueue(n % 10);
            n = n / 10;
        }
        System.out.printf("\nDigits in reverse order: ");
        while (!Q.empty())
            System.out.printf("%d", Q.dequeue());
        System.out.printf("\n");
    } //end main

} //end QueueTest

class Queue {
    final static int MaxQ = 100;
    int head = 0, tail = 0;
    int[] QA = new int[MaxQ];

    public boolean empty() {
        return head == tail;
    }

    public void enqueue(int n) {
        tail = (tail + 1) % MaxQ; //increment tail circularly
        if (tail == head) {
            System.out.printf("\nQueue is full\n");
            System.exit(1);
        }
        QA[tail] = n;
    } //end enqueue

    public int dequeue() {
        if (this.empty()) {
            System.out.printf("\nAttempt to remove from an empty queue\n");
            System.exit(2);
        }
        head = (head + 1) % MaxQ; //increment head circularly
        return QA[head];
    } //end dequeue

} //end class Queue
```

The following is a sample run of Program P4.7:

```
Enter a positive integer: 192837465

Digits in reverse order: 564738291
```

4.5.2 Implementing a Queue Using a Linked List

As with stacks, we can implement a queue using linked lists. This has the advantage of us not having to decide beforehand how many items to cater for. We will use two pointers, head and tail, to point to the first and last items in the queue, respectively. Figure 4-9 shows the data structure when four items (36, 15, 52, and 23) are added to the queue.

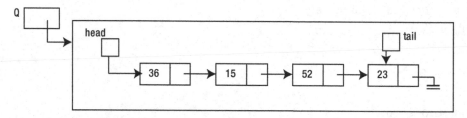

Figure 4-9. *Linked list representation of a queue*

We will implement the queue so that it works with a general data type that we will call NodeData. Each node in the queue will be created from a Node class, which we define as follows:

```
class Node {
    NodeData data;
    Node next;

    public Node(NodeData d) {
        data = d;
        next = null;
    }
} //end class Node
```

When the user defines the NodeData class, he will decide what kind of items will be stored in the queue.
The Queue class starts as follows:

```
public class Queue {
    Node head = null, tail = null;

    public boolean empty() {
        return head == null;
    }
    ...
```

We can create an empty queue with the following statement:

```
Queue Q = new Queue();
```

This will create the structure shown in Figure 4-10.

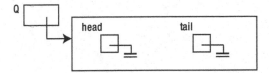

Figure 4-10. *An empty queue (linked list representation)*

To add an item to the queue, we must add it at the tail of the list. Here is enqueue:

```
public void enqueue(NodeData nd) {
    Node p = new Node(nd);
    if (this.empty()) {
        head = p;
        tail = p;
    }
    else {
        tail.next = p;
        tail = p;
    }
} //end enqueue
```

If the queue is empty, the new item becomes the only one in the queue; head and tail are set to point to it. If the queue is not empty, the item at the tail is set to point to the new one, and tail is updated to point to the new one.

To take an item off the queue, we first check whether the queue is empty. If it is, we print a message and end the program. If not, the item at the head of the queue is returned, and the node containing the item is deleted.

If, by removing an item, head becomes null, it means that the queue is empty. In this case, tail is also set to null. Here is dequeue:

```
public NodeData dequeue() {
    if (this.empty()) {
        System.out.printf("\nAttempt to remove from an empty queue\n");
        System.exit(1);
    }
    NodeData hold = head.data;
    head = head.next;
    if (head == null) tail = null;
    return hold;
} //end dequeue
```

To use the Queue class, a user needs to declare only what he wants NodeData to be. To illustrate, suppose he wants a queue of integers. He can define NodeData as follows:

```
public class NodeData {
    int num;

    public NodeData(int n) {
        num = n;
    }

    public int getIntData() {return num;}

} //end class NodeData
```

Previously, we wrote Program P4.7 which reads an integer and prints its digits in reverse order. We now rewrite it as Program P4.8 using our new Node, Queue, and NodeData classes.

Program P4.8

```
import java.util.*;
public class QueueTest {
    public static void main(String[] args) {
        Scanner in = new Scanner(System.in);
        Queue Q = new Queue();
        System.out.printf("Enter a positive integer: ");
        int n = in.nextInt();
        while (n > 0) {
            Q.enqueue(new NodeData(n % 10));
            n = n / 10;
        }
        System.out.printf("\nDigits in reverse order: ");
        while (!Q.empty())
            System.out.printf("%d", Q.dequeue().getIntData());
        System.out.printf("\n");
    } //end main
} //end QueueTest

class NodeData {
    int num;

    public NodeData(int n) {
        num = n;
    }

    public int getIntData() {return num;}

} //end class NodeData

class Node {
    NodeData data;
    Node next;
```

```
        public Node(NodeData d) {
            data = d;
            next = null;
        }
    } //end class Node

    class Queue {
        Node head = null, tail = null;

        public boolean empty() {
            return head == null;
        }

        public void enqueue(NodeData nd) {
            Node p = new Node(nd);
            if (this.empty()) {
                head = p;
                tail = p;
            }
            else {
                tail.next = p;
                tail = p;
            }
        } //end enqueue

        public NodeData dequeue() {
            if (this.empty()) {
                System.out.printf("\nAttempt to remove from an empty queue\n");
                System.exit(1);
            }
            NodeData hold = head.data;
            head = head.next;
            if (head == null) tail = null;
            return hold;
        } //end dequeue

    } //end class Queue
```

The following is a sample run of Program P4.8:

```
Enter a positive integer: 192837465

Digits in reverse order: 564738291
```

Stacks and queues are important to systems programmers and compiler writers. We have seen how stacks are used in the evaluation of arithmetic expressions. They are also used to implement the "calling" and "return" mechanism for functions. Consider the situation where function A calls function C, which calls function B, which calls function D. When a function returns, how does the computer figure out where to return to? We show how a stack can be used to do this.

139

Assume we have the following situation, where a number, like 100, represents the *return address*, which is the address of the next instruction to be executed when the function returns:

```
function A    function B    function C    function D
    .             .             .             .
    C;            D;            B;            .
100:          200:          300:
    .             .             .             .
```

When A calls C, the address 100 is pushed onto a stack, S. When C calls B, 300 is pushed onto S. When B calls D, 200 is pushed onto S. At this stage, the stack looks like the following, and control is in D:

```
(bottom of stack) 100  300  200 (top of stack)
```

When D finishes and is ready to return, the address at the top of the stack (200) is popped, and execution continues at this address. Note that this is the address immediately following the call to D.

Next, when B finishes and is ready to return, the address at the top of the stack (300) is popped, and execution continues at this address. Note that this is the address immediately following the call to B.

Finally, when C finishes and is ready to return, the address at the top of the stack (100) is popped, and execution continues at this address. Note that this is the address immediately following the call to C.

Naturally, queue data structures are used in simulating real-life queues. They are also used to implement queues in the computer. In a multiprogramming environment, several jobs may have to be queued while waiting on a particular resource such as processor time or a printer.

Stacks and queues are also used extensively in working with more advanced data structures such as trees and graphs. We will discuss trees in Chapter 8.

EXERCISES 4

1. What is an *abstract data type*?

2. What is a *stack*? What are the basic operations that can be performed on a stack?

3. What is a *queue*? What are the basic operations that can be performed on a queue?

4. Modify Program P4.5 to recognize infix expressions with mismatched brackets.

5. Program P4.5 works with single-digit operands. Modify it to handle any integer operands.

6. Modify Program P4.5 to handle expressions with operations such as %, square root, sine, cosine, tangent, logarithm, and exponential.

7. Write declarations/functions to implement a stack of `double` values.

8. Write declarations/functions to implement a queue of `double` values.

9. An integer array post is used to hold the postfix form of an arithmetic expression such that the following items are true:

   A positive number represents an operand

   -1 represents +

   -2 represents -

   -3 represents *

   -4 represents /

   0 indicates the end of the expression

   Show the contents of post for the expression (2 + 3) * (8 / 4) - 6.

   Write a function eval that, given post, returns the value of the expression.

10. An input line contains a word consisting of lowercase letters only. Explain how a stack can be used to determine whether the word is a palindrome.

11. Show how to implement a queue using two stacks.

12. Show how to implement a stack using two queues.

13. A priority queue is one in which items are added to the queue based on a priority number. Jobs with higher-priority numbers are closer to the head of the queue than those with lower-priority numbers. A job is added to the queue in front of all jobs of lower priority but after all jobs of greater or equal priority.

    Write classes to implement a priority queue. Each item in the queue has a job number (integer) and a priority number. Implement, at least, the following: (i) add a job in its appropriate place in the queue, (ii) delete the job at the head of the queue, and (iii) given a job number, remove that job from the queue.

    Ensure your methods work regardless of the state of the queue.

14. A stack, S1, contains some numbers in arbitrary order. Using another stack, S2, for temporary storage, show how to sort the numbers in S1 such that the smallest is at the top of S1 and the largest is at the bottom.

CHAPTER 5

■ ■ ■

Recursion

In this chapter, we will explain the following:

- What a recursive definition is
- How to write recursive functions in Java
- How to convert from decimal to binary
- How to print a linked list in reverse order
- How to solve Towers of Hanoi
- How to write an efficient power function
- How to sort using merge sort
- How to use recursion to keep track of pending subproblems
- How to implement backtracking using recursion by finding a path through a maze

5.1 Recursive Definition

A *recursive definition* is one that is defined in terms of itself. Perhaps the most common example is the *factorial* function. The factorial of a non-negative integer, n (written as $n!$), is defined as follows:

```
0! = 1
n! = n(n - 1)!, n > 0
```

Here, $n!$ is defined in terms of $(n - 1)!$, but what is $(n - 1)!$ exactly? To find out, we must apply the definition of factorial! In this case, we have this:

```
(n - 1)! = 1, if (n - 1) = 0
(n - 1)! = (n - 1)(n - 2)! if (n - 1) > 0
```

What is 3! now?

- Since 3 > 0, it is 3×2!.
- Since 2 > 0, 2! is 2×1!, and 3! becomes 3×2×1!.
- Since 1 > 0, 1! is 1×0!, and 3! becomes 3×2×1×0!.Since 0! is 1, we have 3! = 3×2×1×1 = 6.

Loosely, we say that $n!$ is the product of all integers from 1 to n.

Let's rewrite the definition using programming notation; we call it fact.

```
fact(0) = 1
fact(n) = n * fact(n - 1), n > 0
```

The recursive definition of a function consists of two parts.

- The base case, which gives the value of the function for a specific argument. This is also called the *anchor*, *end case*, or *terminating case*, and it allows the recursion to terminate eventually.

- The recursive (or general) case where the function is defined in terms of itself.

Shortly, we will write fact as a Java function. Before we do, we give a nonmathematical example of a recursive definition. Consider how you might define *ancestor*. Loosely, we can say that an ancestor is one's parent, grandparent, great-grandparent, and so on. But we can state this more precisely as follows:

```
a is an ancestor of b if
    (1) a is a parent of b, or
    (2) a is an ancestor of c and c is a parent of b
```

(1) is the base case and (2) is the general, recursive case where *ancestor* is defined in terms of itself.

A less serious example is the meaning of the acronym LAME. It stands for LAME, Another MP3 Encoder. Expanding LAME, we get LAME, Another MP3 Encoder, Another MP3 Encoder, and so on. We can say that LAME is a recursive acronym. It's not a true recursive definition, though, since it has no base case.

5.2 Writing Recursive Functions in Java

We have seen many examples of functions that call other functions. What we have not seen is a function that calls itself—a *recursive function*. We start off with fact.

```
public static int fact(int n) {
    if (n < 0) return 0;
    if (n == 0) return 1;
    return n * fact(n - 1);
}
```

In the last statement of the function, we have a call to the function fact, the function we are writing. The function calls itself.

Consider the following:

```
int n = fact(3);
```

It is executed as follows:

1. 3 is copied to a temporary location and this location is passed to fact where it becomes the value of n.

2. Execution reaches the last statement and fact attempts to return 3 * fact(2). However, fact(2) must be calculated before the return value is known. Think of this as just a call to a function fact with argument 2.

3. As usual, 2 is copied to a temporary location, and this location is passed to fact where it becomes the value of n. If fact were a different function, there would be no problem. But since it's the *same* function, what happens to the first value of n? It has to be saved somewhere and reinstated when *this* call to fact finishes.

4. The value is saved on something called the *run-time stack*. Each time a function calls itself, its arguments (and local variables, if any) are stored on the stack before the new arguments take effect. Also, for each call, new local variables are created. Thus, each call has its own copy of arguments and local variables.

5. When n is 2, execution reaches the last statement and fact attempts to return 2 * fact(1). However, fact(1) must be calculated before the return value is known. Think of this as just a call to a function fact with argument 1.

6. This call reaches the last statement and fact attempts to return 1 * fact(0). However, fact(0) must be calculated before the return value is known. Think of this as just a call to a function fact with argument 0.

7. At this time, the run-time stack contains the arguments 3, 2, and 1, with 1 at the top. The call fact(0) reaches the second statement and returns a value of 1.

8. The calculation 1 * fact(0) can now be completed, returning 1 as the value of fact(1).

9. The calculation 2 * fact(1) can now be completed, returning 2 as the value of fact(2).

10. The calculation 3 * fact(2) can now be completed, returning 6 as the value of fact(3).

We should emphasize that this recursive version of fact is merely for illustrative purposes. It is not an efficient way to calculate a factorial—think of all the function calls and the stacking and unstacking of arguments just to multiply the numbers from 1 to n. A more efficient function is the following:

```
public static int fact(int n) {
    int f = 1;
    while (n > 0) {
        f = f * n;
        --n;
    }
    return f;
}
```

Another example of a function that can be defined recursively is the Highest Common Factor (HCF) of two positive integers, m and n.

```
hcf(m, n) is
    (1)   m, if n is 0
    (2)   hcf(n, m % n), if n > 0
```

If m = 70 and n = 42, we have this:

```
hcf(70, 42) = hcf(42, 70 % 42) = hcf(42, 28) = hcf(28, 42 % 28)
            = hcf(28, 14) = hcf(14, 28 % 14) = hcf(14, 0) = 14
```

We can write hcf as a recursive Java function like this:

```
public static int hcf(int m, int n) {
    if (n == 0) return m;
    return hcf(n, m % n);
}
```

As a matter of interest, we can also write hcf as an iterative (as opposed to recursive) function, using Euclid's algorithm. Here it is:

```
public static int hcf(int m, int n) {
    int r;
    while (n > 0) {
        r = m % n;
        m = n;
        n = r;
    }
    return m;
}
```

Effectively, this function does explicitly what the recursive function does implicitly.

Yet another example of a recursively defined function is that of the Fibonacci numbers. We define the first two Fibonacci numbers as 1 and 1. Each new number is obtained by adding the previous two. So, the Fibonacci sequence is as follows:

```
1, 1, 2, 3, 5, 8, 13, 21, and so on.
```

Recursively, we define the nth Fibonacci number, F(n), as follows:

```
F(0) = F(1) = 1
F(n) = F(n - 1) + F(n - 2), n > 1
```

This is a Java function to return the nth Fibonacci number:

```
public static int fib(int n) {
    if (n == 0 || n == 1) return 1;
    return fib(n - 1) + fib(n - 2);
}
```

Again, we emphasize that while this function is neat, concise, and easy to understand, it is not efficient. For example, consider the calculation of F(5):

```
F(5) = F(4) + F(3) = F(3) + F(2) + F(3) = F(2) + F(1) + F(2) + F(3)
= F(1) + F(0) + F(1) + F(2) + F(3) = 1 + 1 + 1 + F(1) + F(0) + F(3)
= 1 + 1 + 1 + 1 + 1 + F(2) + F(1) =  1 + 1 + 1 + 1 + 1 + F(1) + F(0) + F(1)
= 1 + 1 + 1 + 1 + 1 + 1 + 1 + 1
= 8
```

Notice the number of function calls and additions that have to be made, whereas we can calculate F(5) straightforwardly using only four additions. You are urged to write an efficient, iterative function to return the nth Fibonacci number.

5.3 Converting a Decimal Number to Binary Using Recursion

In Section 4.3.1, we used a stack to convert an integer from decimal to binary. We will now show how to write a recursive function to perform the same task.

To see what needs to be done, suppose n is 13, which is 1101 in binary. Recall that n % 2 gives us the *last* bit of the binary equivalent of n. If, somehow, we have a way to print all but the last bit, then we can print all but the last bit followed by n % 2. But "printing all but the last bit" is the same as printing the binary equivalent of n/2.

For example, 1101 is 110 followed by 1; 110 is the binary equivalent of 6, which is 13/2, and 1 is 13 % 2. So, we can print the binary equivalent of n as follows:

```
print binary of n / 2
print n % 2
```

We use the same method to print the binary equivalent of 6. This is the binary equivalent of 6/2 = 3, which is 11, followed by 6 % 2, which is 0; this gives 110.

We use the same method to print the binary equivalent of 3. This is the binary equivalent of 3/2 = 1, which is 1, followed by 3 % 2, which is 1; this gives 11.

We use the same method to print the binary equivalent of 1. This is the binary equivalent of 1/2 = 0 followed by 1 % 2, which is 1; if we "do nothing" for 0, this will give us 1.

We stop when we get to the stage where we need to find the binary equivalent of 0. This leads us to the following function:

```java
public static void decToBin(int n) {
    if (n > 0) {
        decToBin(n / 2);
        System.out.printf("%d", n % 2);
    }
}
```

The call decToBin(13) will print 1101.

Note how much more compact this is than Program P4.4. However, it is not more efficient. The stacking/unstacking that is done explicitly in Program P4.4 is done here by the recursive mechanism provided by the language when a function calls itself. To illustrate, let's trace the call decToBin(13).

1. On the first call, n assumes the value 13.

2. While the call decToBin(13) is executing, the call decToBin(6) is made; 13 is pushed onto the runtime stack, and n assumes the value 6.

3. While the call decToBin(6) is executing, the call decToBin(3) is made; 6 is pushed onto the stack, and n assumes the value 3.

4. While the call decToBin(3) is executing, the call decToBin(1) is made; 3 is pushed onto the stack, and n assumes the value 1.

5. While the call decToBin(1) is executing, the call decToBin(0) is made; 1 is pushed onto the stack, and n assumes the value 0.

6. At this stage, the stack contains 13, 6, 3, 1.

7. Since n is 0, this call of the function returns immediately; so far, nothing has been printed.

8. When the call decToBin(0) returns, the argument on top of the stack, 1, is reinstated as the value of n.

9. Control goes to the printf statement, which prints 1 % 2, that is, 1.

10. The call decToBin(1) can now return, and the argument on top of the stack, 3, is reinstated as the value of n.

11. Control goes to the printf statement, which prints 3 % 2, that is, 1.

12. The call decToBin(3) can now return, and the argument on top of the stack, 6, is reinstated as the value of n.

13. Control goes to the printf statement, which prints 6 % 2, that is, 0.

14. The call decToBin(6) can now return, and the argument on top of the stack, 13, is reinstated as the value of n.

15. Control goes to the printf statement, which prints 13 % 2, that is, 1.

16. The call decToBin(13) can now return, and 1101 has been printed.

We can summarize the above description as follows:

```
decToBin(13)    →    decToBin(6)
                     print(13 % 2)
                →    decToBin(3)
                     print(6 % 2)
                     print(13 % 2)
                →    decToBin(1)
                     print(3 % 2)
                     print(6 % 2)
                     print(13 % 2)
                →    decToBin(0) = do nothing
                     print(1 % 2) = 1
                     print(3 % 2) = 1
                     print(6 % 2) = 0
                     print(13 % 2) = 1
```

One of the most important properties of recursive functions is that when a function calls itself, the current arguments (and local variables, if any) are pushed onto a stack. Execution of the function takes place with the new arguments and new local variables. When execution is completed, arguments (and local variables, if any) are popped from the stack, and execution resumes (with *these* popped values) with the statement following the recursive call.

Consider the following function fragment and the call test(4, 9):

```
public static void test(int m, int n) {
   char ch;
      .
   test(m + 1, n - 1);
   System.out.printf("%d %d", m, n);
      .
}
```

The function executes with m = 4, n = 9, and the local variable ch. When the recursive call is made, the following happens:

1.   The values of m, n, and ch are pushed onto a stack.

2.   test begins execution, again, with m = 5, n = 8, and a new copy of ch.

3.   Whenever this call to test finishes (perhaps even after calling itself one or more times and producing output of its own), the stack is popped, and the program resumes execution with printf (the statement after the recursive call) and the popped values of m, n, and ch. In this example, 4 9 would be printed.

5.4 Printing a Linked List in Reverse Order

Consider the problem of printing a linked list in reverse order.

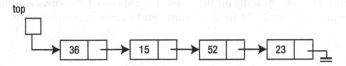

One way of doing this is to traverse the list, pushing items onto an integer stack as we meet them. When we reach the end of the list, the last number would be at the top of the stack, and the first would be at the bottom. We then pop items off the stack and print each one as it is popped.

As we may expect by now, we can use recursion to perform the stacking/unstacking. We use the following idea:

```
to print a list in reverse order
    print the list, except the first item, in reverse order
    print the first item
```

Using the list above, this says print (15 52 23) in reverse order followed by 36.

- To print (15 52 23) in reverse order, we must print (52 23) in reverse order followed by 15.

- To print (52 23) in reverse order, we must print (23) in reverse order followed by 52.

- To print (23) in reverse order, we must print nothing (the rest of the list when 23 is removed) in reverse order followed by 23.

At the end, we would have printed this: 23 52 15 36.
Another way to look at this is as follows:

```
reverse(36 15 52 23)  →   reverse(15 52 23) 36
                      →   reverse(52 23) 15 36
                      →   reverse(23) 52 15 36
                      →   reverse() 23 52 15 36
                      →   23 52 15 36
```

Here is the function, assuming that the pointer to the head of the list is of type Node and the node fields are num and next:

```java
public static void reverse(Node top) {
    if (top != null) {
        reverse(top.next);
        System.out.printf("%d ", top.num);
    }
}
```

The key to working out a recursive solution to a problem is to be able to express the solution in terms of itself but on a "smaller" problem. If the problem keeps getting smaller and smaller, eventually it will be small enough that we can solve it directly.

We see this principle in both the "decimal to binary" and "print a linked list in reverse order" problems. In the first problem, the conversion of n is expressed in terms of n/2; this will, in turn, be expressed in terms of n/4, and so on, until there is nothing to convert. In the second problem, printing the list reversed is expressed in terms of printing a shorter list (the original list minus the first element) reversed. The list gets shorter and shorter until there is nothing to reverse.

5.5 Towers of Hanoi

The Towers of Hanoi puzzle is a classic problem that can be solved using recursion. Legend has it that when the world was created, some high priests in the Temple of Brahma were given three golden pins. On one of the pins were placed 64 golden disks. The disks were all different sizes with the largest at the bottom, the smallest on the top, and no disk placed on top of a smaller one.

They were required to move the 64 disks from the given pin to another one according to the following rules:

- Move one disk at a time; only a disk at the top of a pin can be moved, and it must be moved to the top of another pin.

- No disk must be placed on top of a smaller one.

When all 64 disks have been transferred, the world will come to an end.

This is an example of a problem that can be solved easily by recursion but for which a nonrecursive solution is quite difficult. Let's denote the pins by A, B, and C with the disks originally placed on A and the destination pin being B. Pin C is used for the temporary placement of disks.

Suppose there is one disk. It can be moved directly from A to B. Next, suppose there are five disks on A, as shown in Figure 5-1.

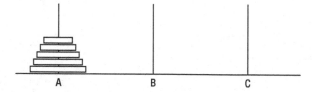

Figure 5-1. *Towers of Hanoi with five disks*

Assume we know how to transfer the top four from A to C using B. When this is done, we have Figure 5-2.

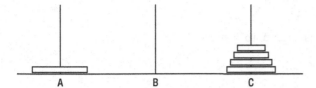

Figure 5-2. *After four disks have been moved from A to C*

We can now move the fifth disk from *A* to *B*, as shown in Figure 5-3.

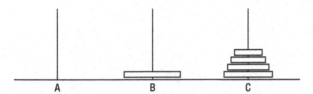

Figure 5-3. *The fifth disk is placed on B*

It remains only to transfer the four disks from *C* to *B* using *A*, which we assume we know how to do. The job is completed as shown in Figure 5-4.

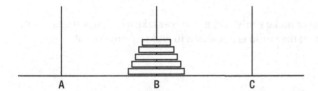

Figure 5-4. *After the four disks have been moved from C to B*

We have thus reduced the problem of transferring five disks to a problem of transferring four disks from one pin to another. This, in turn, can be reduced to a problem of moving three disks from one pin to another, and this can be reduced to two and then to one, which we know how to do. The recursive solution for *n* disks is as follows:

1. Transfer *n* - 1 disks from A to C using B.

2. Move *n*th disk from A to B.

3. Transfer *n* - 1 disks from C to B using A.

Of course, we can use this same solution for transferring *n* - 1 disks.
The following function transfers n disks from startPin to endPin using workPin:

```
public static void hanoi(int n, char startPin, char endPin, char workPin) {
    if (n > 0) {
        hanoi(n - 1, startPin, workPin, endPin);
        System.out.printf("Move disk from %c to %c\n", startPin, endPin);
        hanoi(n - 1, workPin, endPin, startPin);
    }
}
```

When called with the statement

```
hanoi(3, 'A', 'B', 'C');  //transfer 3 disks from A to B using C
```

the function prints this:

```
Move disk from A to B
Move disk from A to C
Move disk from B to C
Move disk from A to B
Move disk from C to A
Move disk from C to B
Move disk from A to B
```

How many moves are required to transfer n disks?

- If n is 1, one move is required: $(1 = 2^1 - 1)$.

- If n is 2, three moves are required: $(3 = 2^2 - 1)$.

- If n is 3, seven moves (see as shown earlier) are required: $(7 = 2^3 - 1)$.

It appears that, for n disks, the number of moves is $2^n - 1$. It can be proved that this is indeed the case. When n is 64, the number of moves is

```
2⁶⁴ - 1 = 18,446,744,073,709,551,615
```

Assuming the priests can move one disc per second, never make a mistake, and never take a rest, it will take them almost 600 billion years to complete the task. Rest assured that the world is not about to end any time soon!

5.6 Writing Power Functions

Given a number, x, and an integer, $n \geq 0$, how do we calculate x raised to the power n, that is, x^n? We can use the definition that x^n is x multiplied by itself `n-1` times. Thus, 3^4 is $3 \times 3 \times 3 \times 3$. Here is a function that uses this method:

```java
public static double power(double x, int n) {
    double pow = 1.0;
    for (int h = 1; h <= n; h++) pow = pow * x;
    return pow;
}
```

Note that if n is 0, power returns 1, the correct answer.

As written, this function performs n multiplications. However, we can write a faster function if we adopt a different approach. Suppose we want to calculate x^{16}. We can do it as follows:

- If we know x8 = x^8, we can multiply x8 by x8 to get x16, using just one more multiplication.

- If we know x4 = x^4, we can multiply x4 by x4 to get x8, using just one more multiplication.

- If we know x2 = x^2, we can multiply x2 by x2 to get x4, using just one more multiplication.

We know x; therefore, we can find x2 using one multiplication. Knowing x2, we can find x4 using one more multiplication. Knowing x4, we can find x8 using one more multiplication. Knowing x8, we can find x^{16} using one more multiplication. In all, we can find x^{16} using just four multiplications.

What if n were 15? First, we would work out $x^{15/2}$, that is, x^7 (call this x7). We would then multiply x7 by x7 to give x^{14}. Recognizing that n is odd, we would then multiply this value by x to give the required answer. To summarize:

```
xn  =  xⁿ/².xⁿ/², if n is even and
       x.xⁿ/².xⁿ/², if n is odd
```

We use this as the basis for a recursive power function that calculates x^n more efficiently than the previous function.

```
public static double power(double x, int n) {
    double y;
    if (n == 0) return 1.0;
    y = power(x, n/2);
    y = y * y;
    if (n % 2 == 0) return y;
    return x * y;
}
```

As an exercise, trace the execution of the function with n = 5 and n = 6.

5.7 Merge Sort

Consider, again, the problem of sorting a list of *n* items in ascending order. We will illustrate our ideas with a list of integers. In Section 1.9, we saw how to merge two sorted lists by traversing each list once. We now show how to use recursion and merging to sort a list. Consider the following algorithm:

```
sort list
    sort first half of list
    sort second half of list
    merge sorted halves into one sorted list
end sort
```

If we can sort the two halves and then merge them, we will have sorted the list. But how do we sort the halves? We use the same method! For instance, to "sort first half of list," we do the following:

```
sort (first half of list)
    sort first half of (first half of list)  //one quarter of the original list
    sort second half of (first half of list) //one quarter of the original list
    merge sorted halves into one sorted list
end sort
```

And so on. For each piece we have to sort, we break it into halves, sort the halves, and merge them. When do we stop using this process on a piece? When the piece consists of one element only; there is nothing to do to sort one element. We can modify our algorithm as follows:

```
sort a list
    if the list contains more than one element then
        sort first half of list
        sort second half of list
        merge sorted halves into one sorted list
    end if
end sort
```

We assume the list is stored in an array, A, from A[lo] to A[hi]. We can code the algorithm as a Java method as follows:

```java
public static void mergeSort(int[] A, int lo, int hi) {
    if (lo < hi) {                    //list contains at least 2 elements
        int mid = (lo + hi) / 2;      //get the mid-point subscript
        mergeSort(A, lo, mid);        //sort first half
        mergeSort(A, mid + 1, hi);    //sort second half
        merge(A, lo, mid, hi);        //merge sorted halves
    }
} //end mergeSort
```

This assumes that merge is available and the statement

```java
merge(A, lo, mid, hi);
```

will merge the sorted pieces in A[lo..mid] and A[mid+1..hi] so that A[lo..hi] is sorted. We will show how to write merge shortly.

But first, we show how mergeSort sorts the following list stored in an array, num:

num

57	48	79	65	33	52	15
0	1	2	3	4	5	6

The method will be called with this:

```java
mergeSort(num, 0, 6);
```

In the method, num will be known as A, lo will be 0, and hi will be 6. From these, mid will be calculated as 3, giving rise to the following two calls:

```java
mergeSort(A, 0, 3);
mergeSort(A, 4, 6);
```

Assuming that the first will sort A[0..3] and the second will sort A[4..6], we will have the following result:

A

15	33	48	52	57	65	79
0	1	2	3	4	5	6

merge will merge the pieces to produce the following:

A

15	33	48	52	57	65	79
0	1	2	3	4	5	6

Each of these calls will give rise to two further calls. The first will produce this:

```
mergeSort(A, 0, 1);
mergeSort(A, 2, 3);
```

The second will produce this:

```
mergeSort(A, 4, 5);
mergeSort(A, 6, 6);
```

As long as lo is less than hi, two further calls will be produced. If lo is equal to hi, the list consists of one element only, and the function simply returns. The following shows all the calls generated by the initial call mergeSort (num, 0, 6), in the order in which they are generated:

```
mergeSort(A, 0, 6)
  mergeSort(A, 0, 3)
    mergeSort(A, 0, 1);
      mergeSort(A, 0, 0);
      mergeSort(A, 1, 1);
    mergeSort(A, 2, 3);
      mergeSort(A, 2, 2);
      mergeSort(A, 3, 3);
  mergeSort(A, 4, 6);
    mergeSort(A, 4, 5);
      mergeSort(A, 4, 4);
      mergeSort(A, 5, 5);
    mergeSort(A, 6, 6);
```

To complete the job, we need to write merge. We can describe merge as follows:

```
public static void merge(int[] A, int lo, int mid, int hi) {
//A[lo..mid] and A[mid+1..hi] are sorted;
//merge the pieces so that A[lo..hi] are sorted
```

Note what must be done: we must merge two adjacent portions of A back into the *same* locations. The problem with this is that we *cannot* merge into the same locations *while the merge is being performed* since we may overwrite numbers before they are used. We will have to merge into another (temporary) array and then copy the merged elements back into the original locations in A.

We will use a temporary array called T; we just need to make sure it is big enough to hold the merged elements. The number of elements in the merge is hi-lo+1. We will declare T as follows:

```
int[] T = new int[hi - lo + 1];
```

Here is merge:

```
public static void merge(int[] A, int lo, int mid, int hi) {
//A[lo..mid] and A[mid+1..hi] are sorted;
//merge the pieces so that A[lo..hi] are sorted
    int[] T = new int[hi - lo + 1];
    int i = lo, j = mid + 1;
    int k = 0;
```

```
        while (i <= mid || j <= hi) {
            if (i > mid) T[k++] = A[j++];
            else if (j > hi) T[k++] = A[i++];
            else if (A[i] < A[j]) T[k++] = A[i++];
            else T[k++] = A[j++];
        }
        for (j = 0; j < hi-lo+1; j++) A[lo + j] = T[j];
    } //end merge
```

We use i to subscript the first part of A, j to subscript the second part, and k to subscript T. The method merges A[lo..mid] and A[mid+1..hi] into T[0..hi-lo].

The while loop expresses the following logic: as long as we haven't processed *all* the elements in *both* parts, we enter the loop. If we are finished with the first part (i > mid), copy an element from the second part to T. If we are finished with the second part (j > hi), copy an element from the first part to T. Otherwise, we copy the smaller of A[i] and A[j] to T.

At the end, we copy the elements from T into locations A[lo] to A[hi].

We test mergeSort with Program P5.1.

Program P5.1

```
    public class MergeSortTest {
        public static void main(String[] args) {
            int[] num = {4,8,6,16,1,9,14,2,3,5,18,13,17,7,12,11,15,10};
            int n = 18;
            mergeSort(num, 0, n-1);
            for (int h = 0; h < n; h++) System.out.printf("%d ", num[h]);
            System.out.printf("\n");
        } // end main

        public static void mergeSort(int[] A, int lo, int hi) {
            if (lo < hi) { //list contains at least 2 elements
                int mid = (lo + hi) / 2; //get the mid-point subscript
                mergeSort(A, lo, mid); //sort first half
                mergeSort(A, mid + 1, hi); //sort second half
                merge(A, lo, mid, hi); //merge sorted halves
            }
        } //end mergeSort

        public static void merge(int[] A, int lo, int mid, int hi) {
        //A[lo..mid] and A[mid+1..hi] are sorted;
        //merge the pieces so that A[lo..hi] are sorted
            int[] T = new int[hi - lo + 1];
            int i = lo, j = mid + 1;
            int k = 0;
            while (i <= mid || j <= hi) {
                if (i > mid) T[k++] = A[j++];
                else if (j > hi) T[k++] = A[i++];
                else if (A[i] < A[j]) T[k++] = A[i++];
                else T[k++] = A[j++];
            }
```

```
        for (j = 0; j < hi-lo+1; j++) A[lo + j] = T[j];
    } //end merge

} //end class MergeSortTest
```

When run, the program produces the following output:

```
1 2 3 4 5 6 7 8 9 10 11 12 13 14 15 16 17 18
```

In passing, we note that merge sort is a much faster sorting method than either selection sort or insertion sort.

5.8 Counting Organisms

Consider the following arrangement:

```
0  1  0  1  1  1  0
0  0  1  1  0  0  0
1  1  0  1  0  0  1
1  0  1  0  0  1  1
1  1  0  0  0  1  0
```

Assume that each 1 represents a cell of an organism; 0 means there is no cell. Two cells are *contiguous* if they are next to each other in the same row or same column. An organism is defined as follows:

- An organism contains at least one 1.
- Two contiguous 1s belong to the same organism.

There are five organisms in the arrangement shown. Count them!

Given an arrangement of cells in a grid, we want to write a program to count the number of organisms present.

A glance at the grid will reveal that, given a cell (1), the organism can extend in either of four directions. For *each* of these, it can extend in either of four directions, giving 16 possibilities. Each of these gives rise to four more possibilities, and so on. How do we keep track of all these possibilities, knowing which have been explored and which are still waiting to be explored?

The easiest way to do this is to let the recursive mechanism keep track for us.

To count the number of organisms, we need a way to determine which cells belong to an organism. To begin, we must find a 1. Next, we must find all 1s that are contiguous to this 1, then 1s that are contiguous to those, and so on.

To find contiguous 1s, we must look in four directions—north, east, south, and west (in any order). When we look, there are four possibilities:

1. We are outside the grid, and there is nothing to do.

2. We see a 0, and there is nothing to do.

3. We see a 1 that has been seen previously; there is nothing to do.

4. We see a 1 for the first time; we move into that position and look in four directions from there.

Step 3 implies that when we meet a 1 for the first time, we would need to mark it in some way so that if we come across this position later, we will know it has been met before and we will not attempt to process it again.

The simplest thing we can do is to change the value from 1 to 0; this ensures that nothing is done if this position is met again. This is fine if all we want to do is *count* the organisms. But if we also want to identify which cells make up an organism, we will have to mark it differently.

Presumably, we will need a variable that keeps count of the number of organisms. Let's call it orgCount. When a 1 is encountered for the first time, we will change it to orgCount + 1. Thus, the cells of organism 1 will be labeled 2, the cells of organism 2 will be labeled 3, and so on.

This is necessary since, if we start labeling from 1, we would not be able to distinguish between a 1 representing a not-yet-met cell and a 1 indicating a cell belonging to organism 1.

This "adding 1 to the label" is necessary *only while we are processing the grid*. When we print it, we will subtract 1 from the label so that, on output, organism 1 will be labeled 1, organism 2 will be labeled 2, and so on.

In writing the program, we assume that the grid data is stored in an array G and consists of m rows and n columns. We will use MaxRow and MaxCol to denote maximum values for m and n, respectively. Data for the program consists of values for m and n, followed by the cell data in row order. For example, data for the previous grid will be supplied as follows:

```
5 7
0  1  0  1  1  1  0
0  0  1  1  0  0  0
1  1  0  1  0  0  1
1  0  1  0  0  1  1
1  1  0  0  0  1  0
```

We assume that the data will be read from a file, orgs.in, and output will be sent to the file orgs.out. The gist of the program logic is as follows:

```
scan the grid from left to right, top to bottom
when we meet a 1, we have a new organism
add 1 to orgCount
call a function findOrg to mark all the cells of the organism
```

The function findOrg will implement the four possibilities outlined earlier. When it sees a 1 in grid position (i, j), say, it will call itself recursively for each of the grid positions to the north, east, south, and west of (i, j). All the details are shown in Program P5.2.

Program P5.2

```java
import java.io.*;
import java.util.*;
public class Organisms {
    static int orgCount = 0;
    public static void main(String[] args) throws IOException {
        Scanner in = new Scanner(new FileReader("orgs.in"));
        PrintWriter out = new PrintWriter(new FileWriter("orgs.out"));
        int m = in.nextInt(), n = in.nextInt();
        int[][] G = new int[m][n];
        for (int i = 0; i < m; i++)
            for (int j = 0; j < n; j++)
                G[i][j] = in.nextInt();
        for (int i = 0; i < m; i++)
            for (int j = 0; j < n; j++)
                if (G[i][j] == 1) {
                    orgCount++;
                    findOrg(G, i, j, m, n);
                }
```

```
            printOrg(out, G, m, n);
            in.close(); out.close();
        } // end main

        public static void findOrg(int[][] G, int i, int j, int m, int n) {
            if (i < 0 || i >= m || j < 0 || j >= n) return; //outside of grid
            if (G[i][j] == 0 || G[i][j] > 1) return; //no cell or cell already seen
            // else G[i][j] = 1;
            G[i][j]= orgCount + 1;        //so that this 1 is not considered again
            findOrg(G, i - 1, j, m, n);   //North
            findOrg(G, i, j + 1, m, n);   //East
            findOrg(G, i + 1, j, m, n);   //South
            findOrg(G, i, j - 1, m, n);   //West
        } //end findOrg

        public static void printOrg(PrintWriter out, int[][] G, int m, int n) {
            out.printf("\nNumber of organisms = %d\n", orgCount);
            out.printf("\nPosition of organisms are shown below\n\n");
            for (int i = 0; i < m; i++) {
                for (int j = 0; j < n; j++)
                    if (G[i][j] > 1) out.printf("%2d ", G[i][j] - 1);
                        //organism labels are one more than they should be
                    else out.printf("%2d ", G[i][j]);
                out.printf("\n");
            }
        } //end printOrg

    } //end class Organisms
```

If the file orgs.in contains the following:

```
5 7
0 1 0 1 1 1 0
0 0 1 1 0 0 0
1 1 0 1 0 0 1
1 0 1 0 0 1 1
1 1 0 0 0 1 0
```

then Program P5.2 produces the following output in the file orgs.out:

```
Number of organisms = 5

Position of organisms are shown below

0 1 0 2 2 2 0
0 0 2 2 0 0 0
3 3 0 2 0 0 4
3 0 5 0 0 4 4
3 3 0 0 0 4 0
```

Consider how findOrg identifies organism 1. In main, when i = 0 and j = 1, G[0][1] is 1, so the call findOrg(G, 0, 1, ...) will be made with G as follows:

```
0  1  0  1  1  1  0
0  0  1  1  0  0  0
1  1  0  1  0  0  1
1  0  1  0  0  1  1
1  1  0  0  0  1  0
```

In findOrg, since G[0][1] is 1, it will be set to 2, and the four calls to findOrg will be made as follows:

```
findOrg(G, -1, 1, ...); //immediate return since i < 0
findOrg(G, 0, 2, ...);  //immediate return since G[0][2] is 0
findOrg(G, 1, 1, ...);  //immediate return since G[1][1] is 0
findOrg(G, 0, -1, ...); //immediate return since j < 0
```

All of these calls return immediately, so only G[0][1] is marked with a 2.

Next, consider how findOrg identifies organism 3. In main, when i = 2 and j = 0, G[2][0] is 1, so the call findOrg(G, 2, 0, ...) will be made with G as follows (organism 2 would already have been labeled with 3):

```
0  2  0  3  3  3  0
0  0  3  3  0  0  0
1  1  0  3  0  0  1
1  0  1  0  0  1  1
1  1  0  0  0  1  0
```

(Remember that, during this phase, the label of an organism is 1 more than the number of the organism.) For this example, we will use the notation N, E, S and W (rather than subscripts) to indicate a grid position to the north, east, south, and west, respectively. At this stage, orgCount is 3 so that the cells will be labeled with 4.

The following are the calls generated to findOrg from the initial findOrg(2, 0, ...) (for clarity, we omit the first argument, G):

```
findOrg(2, 0, ...)  //G[2][0] is labeled with 4
   findOrg(N...)     //returns immediately since G[N] is 0
   findOrg(E...)     //G[E] is 1, relabeled with 4, gives rise to 4 calls
      findOrg(N...) //returns immediately since G[N] is 0
      findOrg(E...) //returns immediately since G[E] is 0
      findOrg(S...) //returns immediately since G[S] is 0
      findOrg(W...) //returns immediately since G[W] is 4
   findOrg(S...)     //G[S] is 1, relabeled with 4, gives rise to 4 calls
      findOrg(N...) //returns immediately since G[N] is 4
      findOrg(E...) //returns immediately since G[E] is 0
      findOrg(S...) //G[S] is 1, relabeled with 4, gives rise to 4 calls
         findOrg(N...) //returns immediately since G[N] is 4
         findOrg(E...) //G[E] is 1, relabeled with 4, gives rise to 4 calls
            findOrg(N...) //returns immediately since G[N] is 0
            findOrg(E...) //returns immediately since G[E] is 0
            findOrg(S...) //returns immediately since G[S] is outside grid
            findOrg(W...) //returns immediately since G[W] is 4
         findOrg(S...) //returns immediately since G[S] is outside grid
```

```
        findOrg(W...) //returns immediately since G[W] is outside grid
      findOrg(W...) //returns immediately since G[W] is outside grid
    findOrg(W...)     //returns immediately since G[W] is outside grid
```

When the call findOrg(2, 0, ...) finally returns, G would be changed to this:

```
0  2  0  3  3  3  0
0  0  3  3  0  0  0
4  4  0  3  0  0  1
4  0  1  0  0  1  1
4  4  0  0  0  1  0
```

The third organism (labeled 4) has been identified. Note that *each* cell in the organism gave rise to four calls to findOrg.

5.9 Finding a Path Through a Maze

Consider the following diagram that represents a maze:

```
##########
# #  #  #
# # # ## #
#   #    #
# ###### #
# # #S##
#      ## #
##########
```

Problem: Starting at S and moving along the open spaces, try to find a way out of the maze. The following shows how to do it with xs marking the path:

```
##########
# #xxx#  #
# #x#x## #
#xxx#xxxx#
#x######x#
#x# #x##xx
#xxxxx## #
##########
```

We want to write a program that, given a maze, determines whether a path exists. If one exists, mark the path with xs.

Given any position in the maze, there are four possible directions in which one can move: north (N), east (E), south (S), and west (W). You will not be able to move in a particular direction if you meet a wall. However, if there is an open space, you can move into it.

In writing the program, we will try the directions in the order N, E, S, and W. We will use the following strategy:

```
try N
if there is a wall, try E
else if there is a space, move to it and mark it with x
```

Whenever we go to an open space, we repeat this strategy. So, for instance, when we go east, if there is a space, we mark it and try the four directions *from this new position*.

Eventually, we will get out of the maze, or we will reach a dead-end position. For example, suppose we get to the position marked C:

```
##########
#C#   #  #
#B# # ## #
#A  #    #
#x###### #
#x# #x##
#xxxxx## #
##########
```

There are walls in all directions except south, from which we came. In this situation, we go back to the previous position and try the next possibility from there. In this example, we go back to the position south of C (call this B).

When we were at B, we would have got to C by trying the north direction. Since this failed, when we go back to B, we will try the "next" possibility, that is, east. This fails since there is a wall. So, we try south; this fails since we have already been there. Finally, we try west, which fails since there is a wall.

So, from B, we go back (we say *backtrack*) to the position from which we moved to B (call this A).

When we backtrack to A, the "next" possibility is east. There is a space, so we move into it, mark it with x, and try the first direction (north) from there.

When we backtrack from a failed position, we must "unmark" that position; that is, we must erase the x. This is necessary since a failed position will not be part of the solution path.

How do we backtrack? The recursive mechanism will take care of that for us, in a similar manner to the "counting organisms" problem. The following pseudocode shows how:

```
boolean findPath(P) {
//find a path from position P
    if P is outside the maze, at a wall or considered already, return false
    //if we get here, P is a space we can move into
    mark P with x
    if P is on the border of the maze, we are out of the maze; return true
    //try to extend the path to the North; if successful, return true
    if (findPath(N)) return true;
    //if North fails, try East, then South, then West
    if (findPath(E)) return true;
    if (findPath(S)) return true;
    if (findPath(W)) return true;
    //if all directions fail, we must unmark P and backtrack
    mark P with space
    return false; //we have failed to find a path from P
} //end findPath
```

5.9.1 Writing the Program

First we must determine how the maze data will be supplied. In the example just discussed, the maze consists of eight rows and ten columns. If we represent each wall by 1 and each space by 0, the maze is represented by the following:

```
1  1  1  1  1  1  1  1  1  1
1  0  1  0  0  0  0  1  0  0  1
1  0  1  0  1  0  1  1  0  1
1  0  0  0  1  0  0  0  0  1
1  0  1  1  1  1  1  1  0  1
1  0  1  0  1  0  1  1  0  0
1  0  0  0  0  0  1  1  0  1
1  1  1  1  1  1  1  1  1  1
```

The start position, S, is at row 6, column 6. The first line of data will specify the number of rows and columns of the maze and the coordinates of S. Thus, the first line of data will be this:

```
8 10 6 6
```

This will be followed by the maze data, above.

When we need to mark a position with an x, we will use the value 2.

Our program will read data from the file maze.in and send output to maze.out. The complete program is shown as Program P5.3.

Program P5.3

```java
import java.io.*;
import java.util.*;
public class Maze {
    static int[][]G;              //known to all methods
    static int m, n, sr, sc;     //known to all methods
    public static void main(String[] args) throws IOException {
        Scanner in = new Scanner(new FileReader("maze.in"));
        PrintWriter out = new PrintWriter(new FileWriter("maze.out"));
        getData(in);
        if (findPath(sr, sc)) printMaze(out);
        else out.printf("\nNo solution\n");
        in.close(); out.close();
    } // end main

    public static void getData(Scanner in) {
        m = in.nextInt();    n = in.nextInt();
        G = new int[m+1][n+1];
        sr = in.nextInt();    sc = in.nextInt();
        for (int r = 1; r <= m; r++)
            for (int c = 1; c <= n; c++)
                G[r][c] = in.nextInt();
    } //end getData

    public static boolean findPath(int r, int c) {
        if (r < 1 || r > m || c < 1 || c > n) return false;
        if (G[r][c] == 1) return false; //into a wall
        if (G[r][c] == 2) return false; //already considered
        // else G[r][c] = 0;
        G[r][c] = 2; //mark the path
        if (r == 1 || r == m || c == 1 || c == n) return true;
        //path found - space located on the border of the maze
```

163

```
            if (findPath(r-1, c)) return true;
            if (findPath(r, c+1)) return true;
            if (findPath(r+1, c)) return true;
            if (findPath(r, c-1)) return true;
            G[r][c] = 0; //no path found; unmark
            return false;
        } //end findPath

        public static void printMaze(PrintWriter out) {
            int r, c;
            for (r = 1; r <= m; r++) {
                for (c = 1; c <= n; c++)
                    if (r == sr && c == sc) out.printf("S");
                    else if (G[r][c] == 0) out.printf(" ");
                    else if (G[r][c] == 1) out.printf("#");
                    else out.printf("x");
                out.printf("\n");
            }
        } //end printMaze

} //end class Maze
```

Suppose the file maze.in contains the following:

```
8 10 6 6
1 1 1 1 1 1 1 1 1 1
1 0 1 0 0 0 1 0 0 1
1 0 1 0 1 0 1 1 0 1
1 0 0 0 1 0 0 0 0 1
1 0 1 1 1 1 1 1 0 1
1 0 1 0 1 0 1 1 0 0
1 0 0 0 0 0 1 1 0 1
1 1 1 1 1 1 1 1 1 1
```

Program P5.3 will write the following output to the file, maze.out:

```
##########
# #xxx#  #
# #x#x## #
#xxx#xxxx#
#x#######x#
#x# #S##xx
#xxxxx## #
##########
```

EXERCISES 5

1. Write an iterative function to return the *n*th Fibonacci number.

2. Print an integer with commas separating the thousands. For example, given 12058, print 12,058.

3. A is an array containing *n* integers. Write a recursive function to find the number of times a given integer x appears in A.

4. Write a recursive function to implement *selection sort*.

5. Write a recursive function to return the largest element in an integer array.

6. Write a recursive function to search for a given number in an `int` array.

7. Write a recursive function to search for a given number in a *sorted* `int` array.

8. What output is produced by the call W(0) of the following function?

```java
public static void W(int n) {
    System.out.printf("%3d", n);
    if (n < 10) W(n + 3);
    System.out.printf("%3d", n);
}
```

9. What output is produced by the call S('C') of the following function?

```java
public static void S(char ch) {
    if (ch < 'H') {
        S(++ch);
        System.out.printf("%c ", ch);
    }
}
```

10. In 9, what output would be produced if the statements within the `if` statement are interchanged?

11. In 9, what would happen if `++ch` is changed to `ch++`?

12. Write a recursive function, `length`, that, given a pointer to a linked list, returns the number of nodes in the list.

13. Write a recursive function, `sum`, that, given a pointer to a linked list of integers, returns the sum of the values at the nodes of the list.

14. Write a recursive function that, given a pointer to the head of a linked list of integers, returns `true` if the list is in ascending order and `false` if it is not.

15. Write a recursive method that takes an integer argument and prints the integer with one space after each digit. For example, given 7583, it prints 7 5 8 3.

16. What is printed by the call `fun(18, 3)` of the following recursive function?

```
public static void fun(int m, int n) {
    if (n > 0) {
        fun(m-1, n-1);
        System.out.printf("%d ", m);
        fun(m+1, n-1);
    }
}
```

17. What is returned by the call test(7, 2) of the following recursive function?

```
public static int test(int n, int r) {
    if (r == 0) return 1;
    if (r == 1) return n;
    if (r == n) return 1;
    return test(n-1, r-1) + test(n-1, r);
}
```

18. Consider points (*m*, *n*) in the usual Cartesian coordinate system where *m* and *n* are positive *integers*. In a *north-east* path from point A to point B, one can move only *up* and only *right* (no *down* or *left* movements are allowed). Write a function that, given the coordinates of any two points A and B, returns the *number* of north-east paths from A to B.

19. The 8-queens problem can be stated as follows: place 8 queens on a chess board so that no two queens attack each other. Two queens attack each other if they are in the same row, same column or same diagonal. Clearly, any solution must have the queens in different rows and different columns.

    We can solve the problem as follows. Place the first queen in the first column of the first row. Next, place the second queen so that it does not attack the first. If this is not possible, go back and place the first queen in the next column and try again.

    After the first two queens have been placed, place the third queen so that it does not attack the first two. If this is not possible, go back and place the second queen in the next column and try again. And so on.

    At each step, try to place the next queen so that it does not conflict with those already placed. If you succeed, try to place the next queen. If you fail, you must *backtrack* to the previously placed queen and try the next possible column. If all columns have been tried, you must backtrack to the queen before *this* queen and try the next column for *that* queen.

    The idea is similar to finding a path through a maze. Write a program to solve the 8-queens problem. Use recursion to implement the backtracking.

20. Write a program to read *n* (<= 10) and print every possible combination of *n* items. For example, if n = 3, you must print the following:

    ```
    1
    1 2
    1 2 3
    1 3
    2
    2 3
    3
    ```

CHAPTER 6

∎ ∎ ∎

Random Numbers, Games, and Simulation

In this chapter, we will explain the following:

- Random numbers

- The difference between random and pseudorandom numbers

- How to generate random numbers on a computer

- How to write a program to play a guessing game

- How to write a program to drill a user in arithmetic

- How to write a program to play Nim

- How to simulate the collection of bottle caps to spell a word

- How to simulate queues in real-life situations

- How to estimate numerical values using random numbers

6.1 Random Numbers

If you were to throw a six-sided die 100 times, each time writing down the number that shows, you would have written down 100 *random* integers *uniformly distributed* in the range 1 to 6.

If you tossed a coin 144 times and, for each toss, wrote down 0 (for heads) or 1 (for tails), you would have written 144 random integers uniformly distributed in the range 0 to 1.

If you were standing on the roadside and, as vehicles passed, you noted the last two digits of the registration number (for those vehicles that have at least two digits), you would have noted random integers uniformly distributed in the range 0 to 99.

Spin a roulette wheel (with 36 numbers) 500 times. The 500 numbers that appear are random integers uniformly distributed in the range 1 to 36.

The word *random* implies that any outcome is completely independent of any other outcome. For instance, if a 5 showed on one throw of the die, then this has no bearing on what would show on the next throw. Similarly, a 29 on the roulette wheel has no effect whatsoever on what number comes up next.

The term *uniformly distributed* means that all values are equally likely to appear. In the case of the die, you have the same chance of throwing a 1 or a 6 or any other number. And, in a large number of throws, each number will occur with roughly the same frequency.

In the case of a coin, if we toss it 144 times, we would expect heads to appear 72 times and tails to appear 72 times. In practice, these exact values are not normally obtained, but if the coin is a fair one, then the values would be close enough to the expected values to pass certain statistical tests. For example, a result of 75 heads and 69 tails is close enough to the expected value of 72 to pass the required tests.

Random numbers are widely used in simulating games of chance (such as games involving dice, coins, or cards), in playing educational games (such as creating problems in arithmetic), and in modeling real-life situations on a computer.

For example, if we want to play a game of *Snakes and Ladders*, throwing the die is simulated by the computer generating a random number from 1 to 6. Suppose we want to create problems in addition for a child, using only the numbers from 1 to 9. For each problem, the computer can generate two numbers (for example, 7 and 4) in the range 1 to 9 and give these to the child to add.

But suppose we want to simulate the traffic pattern at a road intersection governed by traffic lights. We want to time the lights in such a way that the waiting time in both directions is as short as possible. To do the simulation on a computer, we will need some data as to how fast vehicles arrive at and leave the intersection. This must be done by observation in order for the simulation to be as useful as possible.

Suppose it is determined that a random number of vehicles (between 5 and 15) going in direction 1 arrive at the intersection every 30 seconds. Also, between 8 and 20 vehicles arrive every 30 seconds going in direction 2. The computer can simulate this situation as follows:

1. Generate a random number, r1, in the range 5 to 15.

2. Generate a random number, r2, in the range 8 to 20.

r1 and r2 are taken as the numbers of vehicles that arrive at the intersection from each direction in the first 30 seconds. The process is repeated for successive 30-second periods.

6.2 Random and Pseudorandom Numbers

The value that appears when a die is thrown has no effect on what comes up on the next throw. We say that the throws have independent outcomes and the values thrown are random integers in the range 1 to 6. But when a computer is used to generate a sequence of random numbers in a given interval, it uses an algorithm.

Normally, the next number in the sequence is generated from the previous number in a prescribed and predetermined manner. This means the numbers in the sequence are not independent of each other, like they are when we throw a die, for instance. However, the numbers generated will pass the usual set of statistical tests for *randomness*, so, to all intents and purposes, they are random numbers. But, because they are generated in a very predictable manner, they are usually called *pseudorandom* numbers.

In modeling many types of situations, it does not usually matter whether we use random or pseudorandom numbers. In fact, in most applications, pseudorandom numbers work quite satisfactorily. However, consider an organization running a weekly lottery where the winning number is a six-digit number. Should a pseudorandom number generator be used to provide the winning number from one week to the next?

Since the generator produces these numbers in a completely predetermined way, it would be possible to predict the winning numbers for weeks to come. Clearly, this is not desirable (unless *you* are in charge of the random number generator!). In this situation, a truly random method of producing the winning numbers is needed.

6.3 Generating Random Numbers by Computer

In what follows, we make no distinction between random and pseudorandom numbers since, for most practical purposes, no distinction is necessary. Almost all programming languages provide some sort of random number generator, but there are slight differences in the way they operate.

In Java, we can work with random numbers using the predefined static function random in the Math class; random produces random fractions (≥ 0.0 and < 1.0). We use it by writing Math.random().

In practice, we hardly ever use random in the form provided. This is because, most times, we need random numbers in a specific range (like 1 to 6, say) rather than random fractions. However, we can easily write a function that uses random to provide random integers from m to n where m < n. Here it is:

```
public static int random(int m, int n) {
//returns a random integer from m to n, inclusive
    return (int) (Math.random() * (n - m + 1)) + m;
}
```

For example, the call random(1, 6) will return a random integer from 1 to 6, inclusive. If m = 1 and n = 6, then n-m+1 is 6. When 6 is multiplied by a fraction from 0.0 to 0.999..., we get a number from 0.0 to 5.999.... When cast with (int), we get a random integer from 0 to 5. Adding 1 gives a random integer from 1 to 6.

As another example, suppose m = 5 and n = 20. There are 20-5+1=16 numbers in the range 5 to 20. When 16 is multiplied by a fraction from 0.0 to 0.999..., we get a number from 0.0 to 15.999....When cast with (int), we get a random integer from 0 to 15. Adding 5 gives a random integer from 5 to 20.

Program P6.1 will generate and print 20 random numbers from 1 to 6. Each call to random produces the next number in the sequence. Note that the sequence may be different on another computer or on the same computer using a different compiler or run at a different time.

Program P6.1

```
import java.io.*;
public class RandomTest {
   public static void main(String[] args) throws IOException {
      for (int j = 1; j <= 20; j++) System.out.printf("%2d", random(1, 6));
      System.out.printf("\n");
   } //end main

   public static int random(int m, int n) {
   //returns a random integer from m to n, inclusive
      return (int) (Math.random() * (n - m + 1)) + m;
   } //end random

} //end class RandomTest
```

When run, Program P6.1 printed the following sequence of numbers:

4 1 5 1 3 3 1 3 1 3 6 2 3 6 5 1 3 1 1 1

When run a second time, it printed this sequence:

6 3 5 6 6 5 6 3 5 1 5 2 4 1 4 1 1 5 5 5

Each time it is run, a different sequence would be generated.

6.4 A Guessing Game

To illustrate a simple use of random numbers, let's write a program to play a guessing game. The program will "think" of a number from 1 to 100. You are required to guess the number using as few guesses as possible. The following is a sample run of the program. Underlined items are typed by the user:

```
I have thought of a number from 1 to 100.
Try to guess what it is.

Your guess? 50
Too low
Your guess? 75
Too high
Your guess? 62
Too high
Your guess? 56
Too low
Your guess? 59
Too high
Your guess? 57
Congratulations, you've got it!
```

As you can see, each time you guess, the program will tell you whether your guess is too high or too low and allow you to guess again.

The program will "think" of a number from 1 to 100 by calling random(1, 100). You will guess until you have guessed correctly or until you give up. You give up by entering 0 as your guess. Program P6.2 contains all the details.

Program P6.2

```java
import java.util.*;
public class GuessTheNumber {
    public static void main(String[] args) {
        Scanner in = new Scanner(System.in);
        System.out.printf("\nI have thought of a number from 1 to 100.\n");
        System.out.printf("Try to guess what it is.\n\n");
        int answer = random(1, 100);

        System.out.printf("Your guess? ");
        int guess = in.nextInt();
        while (guess != answer && guess != 0) {
            if (guess < answer) System.out.printf("Too low\n");
            else System.out.printf("Too high\n");
            System.out.printf("Your guess? ");
            guess = in.nextInt();
        }
        if (guess == 0) System.out.printf("Sorry, answer is %d\n", answer);
        else System.out.printf("Congratulations, you've got it!\n");
    } //end main
```

```
    public static int random(int m, int n) {
    //returns a random integer from m to n, inclusive
        return (int) (Math.random() * (n - m + 1)) + m;
    } //end random

} //end class GuessTheNumber
```

Programming note: It is a good idea to remind the user that he has the option of giving up and how to do so. To this end, the prompt can be as follows:

```
Your guess (0 to give up)?
```

6.5 Drills in Addition

We want to write a program to drill a user in simple arithmetic problems (Program P6.3). More specifically, we want to write a program to create addition problems for a user to solve. The problems will involve the addition of two numbers. But where do the numbers come from? We will let the computer "think" of the two numbers. By now, you should know that, in order to do this, the computer will generate two random numbers.

We also need to decide what size of numbers to use in the problems. This will determine, to some extent, how difficult the problems are going to be. We will use two-digit numbers, that is, numbers from 10 to 99. The program can be easily modified to handle numbers in a different range.

The program will begin by asking the user how many problems he wants to be given. The user will type the number required. He will then be asked how many attempts he wants to be given for each problem. He will enter this number. The program then proceeds to give him the requested number of problems.

The following is a sample run of the program. Underlined items are typed by the user; everything else is typed by the computer.

```
Welcome to Problems in Addition

How many problems would you like? 3
Maximum tries per problem? 2

Problem 1, Try 1 of 2
   80 + 75 = 155
Correct, well done!

Problem 2, Try 1 of 2
   17 + 29 = 36
Incorrect, try again

Problem 2, Try 2 of 2
   17 + 29 = 46
Correct, well done!

Problem 3, Try 1 of 2
   83 + 87 = 160
Incorrect, try again

Problem 3, Try 2 of 2
   83 + 87 = 180
Sorry, answer is 170

Thank you for playing. Bye...
```

All the details are shown in Program P6.3. In the interest of brevity, we have not validated the input provided by the user. However, it is strongly recommended that *all* user input be validated to ensure that your programs are as robust as possible.

Program P6.3

```
import java.util.*;
public class Arithmetic {
   public static void main(String[] args) {
      Scanner in = new Scanner(System.in);
      System.out.printf("\nWelcome to Problems in Addition\n\n");
      System.out.printf("How many problems would you like? ");
      int numProblems = in.nextInt();
      System.out.printf("Maximum tries per problem? ");
      int maxTries = in.nextInt();
      giveProblems(in, numProblems, maxTries);
      System.out.printf("\nThank you for playing. Bye...\n");
   } //end main

   public static void giveProblems(Scanner in, int amount, int maxTries) {
      int num1, num2, answer, response, tri; //'tri' since 'try' is a reserved word
      for (int h = 1; h <= amount; h++) {
         num1 = random(10, 99);
         num2 = random(10, 99);
         answer = num1 + num2;
         for (tri = 1; tri <= maxTries; tri ++) {
            System.out.printf("\nProblem %d, Try %d of %d\n", h, tri, maxTries);
            System.out.printf("%5d + %2d = ", num1, num2);
            response = in.nextInt();
            if (response == answer) {
               System.out.printf("Correct, well done!\n");
               break;
            }
            if (tri < maxTries) System.out.printf("Incorrect, try again\n");
            else System.out.printf("Sorry, answer is %d\n", answer);
         } //end for tri
      } //end for h
   } //end giveProblems

   public static int random(int m, int n) {
   //returns a random integer from m to n, inclusive
      return (int) (Math.random() * (n - m + 1)) + m;
   } //end random

} //end class Arithmetic
```

6.6 Nim

One version of the game called Nim is played between two people, A and B, say. Initially, there is a known number of matches (startAmount, say) on the table. Each player, in turn, is allowed to pick up any number of matches from 1 to some agreed maximum (maxPick, say). The player who picks up the last match loses the game.

For example, if startAmount is 20 and maxPick is 3, the game may proceed as follows:

A picks up 2, leaving 18 on the table.

B picks up 1, leaving 17 on the table.

A picks up 3, leaving 14 on the table.

B picks up 1, leaving 13 on the table.

A picks up 2, leaving 11 on the table.

B picks up 2, leaving 9 on the table.

A picks up 1, leaving 8 on the table.

B picks up 3, leaving 5 on the table.

A picks up 1, leaving 4 on the table.

B picks up 3, leaving 1 on the table.

A is forced to pick up the last match and, therefore, loses the game.

What is the best way to play the game? Obviously, the goal should be to leave your opponent with one match remaining on the table. Let's call this a *losing position*. The next question to answer is, how many matches must you leave so that, no matter how many he picks up (within the rules of the game), you can leave him with one?

In this example, the answer is 5. Whether he picks up 1, 2, or 3, you can *always* leave him with 1. If he picks up 1, you pick up 3; if he picks up 2, you pick up 2; if he picks up 3, you pick up 1. So, therefore, 5 is the next losing position.

The next question is, how many matches must you leave so that, no matter how many he picks up (within the rules of the game), you can leave him with 5? The answer is 9. Try it!

And so on. Reasoning this way, we discover that 1, 5, 9, 13, 17, and so on, are all losing positions. In other words, if you can leave your opponent with any of these number of matches, you can force a win.

In this example, the moment B left A with 17 matches, B was in a position from which he could not lose, unless he became careless.

In general, losing positions are obtained by adding 1 to multiples of maxPick+1. If maxPick is 3, multiples of 4 are 4, 8, 12, 16, and so on. Adding 1 gives the losing positions 5, 9, 13, 17, and so on.

We will write a program in which the computer plays the best possible game of Nim. If it can force the user into a losing position, it will. If the user has forced *it* into a losing position, it will pick up a random number of matches and hope that the user makes a mistake.

If remain is the number of matches remaining on the table, how can the computer determine what is the best move to make?

If remain is less than or equal to maxPick, the computer picks up remain-1 matches, leaving the user with 1. Otherwise, we perform this calculation:

```
r = remain % (maxPick + 1)
```

If r is 0, remain is a multiple of maxPick+1; the computer picks up maxPick matches, leaving the user in a losing position. In this example, if remain is 16 (a multiple of 4), the computer picks up 3, leaving the user with 13—a losing position.

If r is 1, the computer is in a losing position and picks up a random number of matches.

Otherwise, the computer picks up r-1 matches, leaving the user in a losing position. In this example, if remain is 18, r would be 2. The computer picks up 1, leaving the user with 17—a losing position.

This strategy is implemented in the function bestPick, part of Program P6.4, which pits the computer against a user in our version of Nim.

Program P6.4

```java
import java.util.*;
public class Nim {
    public static void main(String[] args) {
        Scanner in = new Scanner(System.in);
        System.out.printf("\nNumber of matches on the table? ");
        int remain = in.nextInt();
        System.out.printf("Maximum pickup per turn? ");
        int maxPick = in.nextInt();
        playGame(in, remain, maxPick);
    } //end main

    public static void playGame(Scanner in, int remain, int maxPick) {
        int userPick;
        System.out.printf("\nMatches remaining: %d\n", remain);
        while (true) { //do forever...well, until the game ends
            do {
                System.out.printf("Your turn: ");
                userPick = in.nextInt();
                if (userPick > remain)
                    System.out.printf("Cannot pick up more than %d\n", Math.min(remain, maxPick));
                else if (userPick < 1 || userPick > maxPick)
                    System.out.printf("Invalid: must be between 1 and %d\n", maxPick);
            } while (userPick > remain || userPick < 1 || userPick > maxPick);

            remain = remain - userPick;
            System.out.printf("Matches remaining: %d\n", remain);
            if (remain == 0) {
                System.out.printf("You lose!!\n");  return;
            }
            if (remain == 1) {
                System.out.printf("You win!!\n");  return;
            }
            int compPick = bestPick(remain, maxPick);
            System.out.printf("I pick up %d\n", compPick);
            remain = remain - compPick;
            System.out.printf("Matches remaining: %d\n", remain);
            if (remain == 0) {
                System.out.printf("You win!!\n");
                return;
            }
            if (remain == 1) {
                System.out.printf("I win!!\n");
                return;
            }
        } //end while (true)
    } //end playGame
```

```java
public static int bestPick(int remain, int maxPick) {
    if (remain <= maxPick) return remain - 1; //put user in losing position
    int r = remain % (maxPick + 1);
    if (r == 0) return maxPick;                //put user in losing position
    if (r == 1) return random(1, maxPick);     //computer in losing position
    return r - 1;                              //put user in losing position
}                                              //end bestPick

public static int random(int m, int n) {
//returns a random integer from m to n, inclusive
    return (int) (Math.random() * (n - m + 1)) + m;
} //end random

} //end class Nim
```

Note the use of the do...while statement for getting and validating the user's play. The general form is as follows:

```
do <statement> while (<expression>);
```

As usual, <statement> can be simple (one-line) or compound (enclosed in braces). The words do and while and the brackets and semicolon are required. The programmer supplies <statement> and <expression>. A do...while is executed as follows:

1. <statement> is executed.

2. <expression> is then evaluated; if it is true, repeat from step 1. If it is false, execution continues with the statement, if any, after the semicolon.

As long as <expression> is true, <statement> is executed. It is important to note that because of the nature of the construct, <statement> is *always executed at least once*. This is particularly useful in a situation where we want <statement> to be executed at least once. In this example, we need to prompt the user at least once for his play, hence the reason for do...while.

The following is a sample run of Program P6.4:

```
Number of matches on the table? 30
Maximum pickup per turn? 5

Matches remaining: 30
Your turn: 2
Matches remaining: 28
I pick up 3
Matches remaining: 25
Your turn: 3
Matches remaining: 22
I pick up 3
Matches remaining: 19
Your turn: 6
Invalid: must be between 1 and 5
Your turn: 1
Matches remaining: 18
I pick up 5
Matches remaining: 13
```

```
Your turn: 4
Matches remaining: 9
I pick up 2
Matches remaining: 7
Your turn: 9
Cannot pick up more than 5
Your turn: 2
Matches remaining: 5
I pick up 4
Matches remaining: 1
I win!!
```

We note, in passing, that it would be useful to provide instructions for the game when it is run.

6.7 Nonuniform Distributions

So far, the random numbers we have generated have been uniformly distributed in a given range. For instance, when we generated numbers from 10 to 99, each number in that range had the same chance of being generated. Similarly, the call random(1, 6) will generate each of the numbers 1 to 6 with equal probability.

Now suppose we want the computer to "throw" a six-sided die. Since the computer can't physically throw the die, it has to simulate the process of throwing. What is the purpose of throwing the die? It is simply to come up with a random number from 1 to 6. As we have seen, the computer knows how to do this.

If the die is fair, then each of the faces has the same chance of showing. To simulate the throwing of such a die, all we have to do is generate random numbers uniformly distributed in the range 1 to 6. We can do this with random(1, 6).

Similarly, when we toss a fair coin, heads and tails both have the same chance of showing. To simulate the tossing of such a coin on a computer, all we have to do is generate random numbers uniformly distributed in the range 1 to 2. We can let 1 represent heads and 2 represent tails.

In general, if all possible occurrences of an event (such as throwing a fair die) are equally likely, we can use uniformly distributed random numbers to simulate the event. However, if all occurrences are not equally likely, how can we simulate such an event?

To give an example, consider a *biased* coin, which comes up heads twice as often as tails. We say that the probability of heads is 2/3 and the probability of tails is 1/3. To simulate such a coin, we generate random numbers uniformly distributed in the range 1 to 3. If 1 or 2 occurs, we say that heads was thrown; if 3 occurs, we say that tails was thrown.

Thus, to simulate an event that has a nonuniform distribution, we convert it to one in which we can use uniformly distributed random numbers.

For another example, suppose that, for any day of a given month (June, say), we know the following, and only these conditions are possible:

```
probability of sun = 4/9
probability of rain = 3/9
probability of overcast = 2/9
```

We can simulate the weather for June as follows:

```
for each day in June
    r = random(1, 9)
    if (r <= 4) "the day is sunny"
    else if (r <= 7) "the day is rainy"
    else "the day is overcast"
endfor
```

We note, in passing, that we can assign *any* four numbers to sunny, any other three to rainy, and the remaining two to overcast.

6.7.1 Collecting Bottle Caps

The maker of a popular beverage is running a contest in which you must collect bottle caps to spell the word *MANGO*. It is known that in every 100 bottle caps, there are 40 *A*s, 25 *O*s, 15 *N*s, 15 *M*s, and 5 *G*s. We want to write a program to perform 20 simulations of the collection of bottle caps until we have enough caps to spell *MANGO*. For each simulation, we want to know how many caps were collected. We also want to know the average number of bottle caps collected per simulation.

The collection of a bottle cap is an event with nonuniform distribution. It is easier to collect an *A* than a *G*. To simulate the event, we can generate random numbers uniformly distributed in the range 1 to 100. To determine which letter was collected, we can use this:

```
c = random(1, 100)
if (c <= 40) we have an A
else if (c <= 65) we have an O
else if (c <= 80) we have an N
else if (c <=95) we have an M
else we have a G
```

In this example, if we want, we can scale everything by a factor of 5 and use the following:

```
c = random(1, 20)
if (c <= 8) we have an A
else if (c <= 13) we have an O
else if (c <= 16) we have an N
else if (c <=19) we have an M
else we have a G
```

Either version will work fine for this problem.

The gist of the algorithm for solving this problem is as follows:

```
totalCaps = 0
for sim = 1 to 20
    capsThisSim = perform one simulation
    print capsThisSim
    add capsThisSim to totalCaps
endfor
print totalCaps / 20
```

The logic for performing one simulation is as follows:

```
numCaps = 0
while (word not spelt) {
    collect a cap and determine the letter
    mark the letter collected
    add 1 to numCaps
}
return numCaps
```

We will use an array cap[5] to hold the status of each letter: cap[0] for *A*, cap[1] for *O*, cap[2] for *N*, cap[3] for *M*, and cap[4] for *G*. A value of 0 indicates that the corresponding letter has not been collected. When we collect an *N*, say, we set cap[2] to 1; we do so similarly for the other letters. We have collected each letter at least once when all the elements of cap are 1.

All these details are incorporated in Program P6.5.

Program P6.5

```java
public class BottleCaps {
    static int MaxSim = 20;
    static int MaxLetters = 5;
    public static void main(String[] args) {
        int sim, capsThisSim, totalCaps = 0;
        System.out.printf("\nSimulation  Caps collected\n\n");
        for (sim = 1; sim <= MaxSim; sim++) {
            capsThisSim = doOneSimulation();
            System.out.printf("%6d %13d\n", sim, capsThisSim);
            totalCaps += capsThisSim;
        }
        System.out.printf("\nAverage caps per simulation: %d\n", totalCaps/MaxSim);
    } //end main

    public static int doOneSimulation() {
        boolean[] cap = new boolean[MaxLetters];
        for (int j = 0; j < MaxLetters; j++) cap[j] = false;
        int numCaps = 0;
        while (!mango(cap)) {
            int c = random(1, 20);
            if (c <= 8) cap[0] = true;
            else if (c <= 13) cap[1] = true;
            else if (c <= 16) cap[2] = true;
            else if (c <= 19) cap[3] = true;
            else cap[4] = true;
            numCaps++;
        } //end while
        return numCaps;
    } //end doOneSimulation

    public static boolean mango(boolean[] cap) {
        for (int j = 0; j < MaxLetters; j++)
            if (cap[j] == false) return false;
        return true;
    } //end mango

    public static int random(int m, int n) {
    //returns a random integer from m to n, inclusive
        return (int) (Math.random() * (n - m + 1)) + m;
    } //end random

} //end class BottleCaps
```

When run, this program produced the following output:

Simulation	Caps collected
1	10
2	10
3	22
4	12
5	36
6	9
7	15
8	7
9	11
10	70
11	17
12	12
13	27
14	10
15	6
16	25
17	8
18	7
19	39
20	71

Average caps per simulation: 21

The results range from as few as 6 caps to as many as 71. Sometimes you get lucky, sometimes you don't. Each time the program is run, it will produce different results.

6.8 Simulation of Real-Life Problems

The computer can be used to answer certain questions about many real-life situations by using *simulation*. The process of simulation allows us to consider different solutions to a problem. This enables us to choose, with confidence, the best alternative for a given situation.

However, before the computer simulation is done, we need to collect data to enable the simulation to be as realistic as possible. For example, if we want to simulate serving customers at a bank, we would need to know (or at least estimate) the following:

- The time, $t1$, between arrivals of customers in the queue

- The time, $t2$, to serve a customer

Of course, $t1$ could vary greatly. It would depend, for instance, on the time of the day; at certain times, customers arrive more frequently than at other times. Also, different customers have different needs, so $t2$ would vary from one customer to the next. However, by observing the system in operation for a while, we can usually make assumptions like the following:

- $t1$ varies randomly between one and five minutes.

- $t2$ varies randomly between three and ten minutes.

Using these assumptions, we can do the simulation to find out how the queue length varies when there are 2, 3, 4, ..., and so on, service counters. We assume that there is one queue; the person at the head of the queue goes to whichever counter first becomes available. In practice, a bank usually assigns more counters at peak periods than at slow periods. In this case, we can do the simulation in two parts, using the assumptions that apply for each period.

These are other situations in which a similar method of simulation applies:

- *Checkout counters at supermarkets or stores*: We are normally interested in a compromise between the number of checkout counters and the average queue length. The fewer counters we have, the longer the queue will be. However, having more counters means more machines and more employees. We want to find the best compromise between the cost of operation and service to customers.

- *Gasoline stations*: How many pumps will best serve the needs of the customers?

- *Traffic lights*: What is the best timing of the lights so that the average length of the queues in all directions is kept to a minimum? In this case, we would need to gather data such as follows:

  - How often do cars arrive from direction 1 and from direction 2? The answer to this might be something like this:

    Between 5 and 15 cars arrive every minute from direction 1.

    Between 10 and 30 cars arrive every minute from direction 2.

  - How fast can cars leave in direction 1 and in direction 2? The answer might be as follows:

    20 cars can cross the intersection in direction 1 in 30 seconds.

    30 cars can cross the intersection in direction 2 in 30 seconds.

  We assume, in this simple situation, that turning is not allowed.

6.9 Simulating a Queue

Consider the situation at a bank or supermarket checkout, where customers arrive and must queue for service. Suppose there is one queue but several counters. If a counter is free, the person at the head of the queue goes to it. If all counters are busy, the customers must wait; the person at the head of the queue goes to the first available counter.

To illustrate, suppose there are two counters; we denote them by C1 and C2. To perform the simulation, we need to know the frequency with which customers arrive and the time it takes to serve a customer. Based on observation and experience, we may be able to say the following:

- The time between customer arrivals varies randomly from one to five minutes.

- The time to serve a customer varies randomly from three to ten minutes.

For the simulation to be meaningful, this data must be close to what occurs in practice. As a general rule, a simulation is only as good as the data on which it is based.

Suppose we begin at 9 a.m. We can simulate the arrival of the first ten customers by generating ten random numbers from 1 to 5, like this:

```
3 1 2 4 2 5 1 3 2 4
```

This means the first customer arrives at 9:03, the second at 9:04, the third at 9:06, the fourth at 9:10, and so on. We can simulate the service time for these customers by generating ten random numbers from 3 to 10, like this:

```
5 8 7 6 9 4 7 4 9 6
```

This means the first customer spends five minutes at the teller, the second spends eight minutes, the third spends seven minutes, and so on.

Table 6-1 shows what happens to these ten customers.

Table 6-1. *Tracking Ten Customers*

Customer	Arrives	Start Service	Counter	Service Time	Departs	Wait Time
1	9:03	9:03	C1	5	9:08	0
2	9:04	9:04	C2	8	9:12	0
3	9:06	9:08	C1	7	9:15	2
4	9:10	9:12	C2	6	9:18	2
5	9:12	9:15	C1	9	9:24	3
6	9:17	9:18	C2	4	9:22	1
7	9:18	9:22	C2	7	9:29	4
8	9:21	9:24	C1	4	9:28	3
9	9:23	9:28	C1	9	9:37	5
10	9:27	9:29	C2	6	9:35	2

- The first customer arrives at 9:03 and goes straight to C1. His service time is five minutes, so he will leave C1 at 9:08.

- The second customer arrives at 9:04 and goes straight to C2. His service time is 8 minutes, so he will leave C2 at 9:12.

- The third customer arrives at 9:06. At this time, both C1 and C2 are busy, so he must wait. C1 will be the first to become free at 9:08. This customer will begin service at 9:08. His service time is seven minutes, so he will leave C1 at 9:15. This customer had to wait in the queue for two minutes.

- The fourth customer arrives at 9:10. At this time, both C1 and C2 are busy, so he must wait. C2 will be the first to become free at 9:12. This customer will begin service at 9:12. His service time is six minutes, so he will leave C2 at 9:18. This customer had to wait in the queue for two minutes.

And so on. Work through the rest of the table to make sure you understand how those values are obtained.

Also observe that once the tellers started serving, they had no idle time. As soon as one customer left, another was waiting to be served.

6.9.1 Programming the Simulation

We now show how to write a program to produce Table 6-1. First we observe that it is no more difficult to write the program for several counters than it is for two. Hence, we will assume that there are n (n < 10) counters. For this particular example, we will set n to 2.

We will use an array depart[10] such that depart[c] will hold the time at which counter c will next become free. We will not use depart[0]. If we need to handle more than nine counters, we just need to increase the size of depart.

Suppose the customer at the head of the queue arrives at arriveTime. He will go to the first free counter. Counter c is free if the customer arrives after the last one has left counter c, that is, if arriveTime is greater than or equal to depart[c]. If no counter is free, he must wait. He will go to the counter that will become free first, that is, the one with the lowest value in the array depart; suppose this is depart[m]. He will begin service at a time that is the later of arriveTime and depart[m].

The program begins by asking for the number of counters and the number of customers to be simulated. The simulation starts from time 0, and all times are relative to this. The details are shown in Program P6.6.

Program P6.6

```java
import java.util.*;
public class SimulateQueue {
   public static void main(String[] args) {
      Scanner in = new Scanner(System.in);
      System.out.printf("\nHow many counters? ");
      int numCounters = in.nextInt();
      System.out.printf("\nHow many customers? ");
      int numCustomers = in.nextInt();

      doSimulation(numCounters, numCustomers);
   } //end main

   public static void doSimulation(int counters, int customers) {
      int m, arriveTime, startServe, serveTime, waitTime;
      int[] depart = new int[counters + 1];
      for (int h = 1; h <= counters; h++) depart[h] = 0;
      System.out.printf("\n                       Start        Service        Wait\n");
      System.out.printf("Customer Arrives Service Counter  Time   Departs Time\n\n");
      arriveTime = 0;
      for (int h = 1; h <= customers; h++) {
         arriveTime += random(1, 5);
         m = smallest(depart, 1, counters);
         startServe = Math.max(arriveTime, depart[m]);
         serveTime = random(3, 10);
         depart[m] = startServe + serveTime;
         waitTime = startServe - arriveTime;
         System.out.printf("%5d %8d %7d %6d %7d %8d %5d\n",
            h, arriveTime, startServe, m, serveTime, depart[m], waitTime);
      } //end for h
   } //end doSimulation

   public static int smallest(int list[], int lo, int hi) {
   //returns the subscript of the smallest value from list[lo..hi]
      int h, k = lo;
      for (h = lo + 1; h <= hi; h++)
         if (list[h] < list[k]) k = h;
      return k;
   }
```

```
public static int random(int m, int n) {
//returns a random integer from m to n, inclusive
    return (int) (Math.random() * (n - m + 1)) + m;
} //end random

} //end class SimulateQueue
```

A sample run of Program P6.6 is shown here:

```
How many counters? 2

How many customers? 10
```

		Start		Service		Wait
Customer	Arrives	Service	Counter	Time	Departs	Time
1	3	3	1	8	11	0
2	7	7	2	9	16	0
3	10	11	1	9	20	1
4	11	16	2	4	20	5
5	14	20	1	5	25	6
6	19	20	2	9	29	1
7	23	25	1	7	32	2
8	26	29	2	8	37	3
9	29	32	1	7	39	3
10	33	37	2	6	43	4

As you can see, the waiting time is reasonably short. However, if you run the simulation with 25 customers, you will see that the waiting time increases appreciably. What if we added another counter? With simulation, it's easy to test the effect of this without actually having to buy another machine or hire another employee.

In this case, all we have to do is enter 3 and 25 for the number of counters and customers, respectively. When we do, we will find that there is very little waiting time. We urge you to experiment with different data—counters, customers, arrival times, and service times—to see what happens.

6.10 Estimating Numerical Values Using Random Numbers

We have seen how random numbers can be used to play games and simulate real-life situations. A less obvious use is to estimate numerical values that may be difficult or cumbersome to calculate. We will show how to use random numbers to estimate the square root of a number and π (pi).

6.10.1 Estimating $\sqrt{5}$

We use random numbers to estimate the square root of 5 based on the following:

- It is between 2 and 3.

- x is less than $\sqrt{5}$ if x^2 is less than 5.

- Random numbers, with fractions, between 2 and 3 are generated. A count is kept of those numbers that are less than $\sqrt{5}$.

- Let maxCount be the total number of random numbers generated between 2 and 3. The user will supply maxCount.

- Let amountLess be the count of those numbers less than $\sqrt{5}$.

- An approximation to $\sqrt{5}$ is given by $2 + \dfrac{\text{amountLess}}{\text{maxCount}}$.

To understand the idea behind the method, consider the line segment between 2 and 3 and let the point r represent the square root of 5.

If we imagine the line between 2 and 3 completely covered with dots, we would expect that the number of dots between 2 and r would be proportional to the length of that segment. In general, the number of dots falling on any line segment would be proportional to the length of that segment—the longer the segment, the more dots will fall on it.

Now, each random number between 2 and 3 represents a dot on that line. We would expect that the more numbers we use, the more accurate would be our statement that the length of the line between 2 and r is proportional to the number of numbers falling on it and, hence, the more accurate our estimate.

Program P6.7 calculates an estimate for $\sqrt{5}$ based on this method. Remember that Math.random generates a random fraction.

When run with 1,000 numbers, this program gave 2.234 as the square root of 5. The value of $\sqrt{5}$ is 2.236 to three decimal places.

Program P6.7

```java
import java.util.*;
public class Root5 {
    public static void main(String[] args) {
        Scanner in = new Scanner(System.in);
        System.out.printf("\nHow many numbers to use? ");
        int maxCount = in.nextInt();

        int amountLess = 0;
        for (int j = 1; j <= maxCount; j++) {
            double r = 2 + Math.random();
            if (r * r < 5) ++amountLess;
        }
        System.out.printf("\nThe square root of 5 is about %5.3f\n",
                    2 + (double) amountLess / maxCount);
    } //end main

} //end class Root5
```

6.10.2 Estimating π

Consider Figure 6-1, which shows a circle within a square.

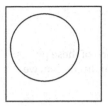

Figure 6-1. *Circle within a square*

If you close your eyes and keep stabbing at the diagram repeatedly with a pencil, you may end up with something like Figure 6-2 (considering only the dots that fall within the diagram).

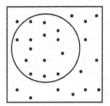

Figure 6-2. *Circle within a square after stabbing with pencil*

Note that some dots fall inside the circle and some fall outside the circle. If the dots were made "at random," it seems reasonable to expect that the number of dots inside the circle is proportional to the area of the circle—the larger the circle, the more dots will fall inside it.

Based on this, we have the following approximation:

$$\frac{area\ of\ circle}{area\ of\ square} = \frac{number\ of\ dots\ inside\ circle}{number\ of\ dots\ inside\ square}$$

Note that the number of dots inside the square also includes those inside the circle. If we imagine the entire square filled with dots, then the previous approximation will be quite accurate. We now show how to use this idea to estimate π.

Consider Figure 6-3.

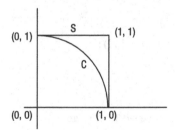

Figure 6-3. *Quarter circle and a square*

- C is a quarter circle of radius 1; S is a square of side 1.
- Area of C = $\frac{\pi}{4}$ Area of S = 1.
- A point (x, y) within C satisfies $x^2 + y^2 \le 1$, $x \ge 0$, $y \ge 0$.
- A point (x, y) within S satisfies $0 \le x \le 1$, $0 \le y \le 1$.

Suppose we generate two random fractions, that is, two values between 0 and 1; call these values x and y. Since $0 \leq x \leq 1$ and $0 \leq y \leq 1$, it follows that the point (x, y) lies within S.

This point will also lie within C if $x^2 + y^2 \leq 1$.

If we generate n pairs of random fractions, we have, in fact, generated n points within S. For each of these points, we can determine whether the point lies with C. Suppose m of these n points fall within C. From our discussion, we can assume that the following approximation holds:

$$\frac{area\ of\ C}{area\ of\ S} = \frac{m}{n}$$

The area of C is $\dfrac{\pi}{4}$ and the area of S is 1. So, the following holds:

$$\frac{\pi}{4} = \frac{m}{n}$$

Hence:

$$\pi = \frac{4\,m}{n}.$$

Based on this, we write Program P6.8 to estimate π.

Program P6.8

```
import java.util.*;
public class Pi {
    public static void main(String[] args) {
        Scanner in = new Scanner(System.in);
        int inC = 0;

        System.out.printf("\nHow many numbers to use? ");
        int inS = in.nextInt();

        for (int j = 1; j <= inS; j++) {
            double x = Math.random();
            double y = Math.random();
            if (x * x + y * y <= 1) inC++;
        }
        System.out.printf("\nAn approximation to pi is %5.3f\n", 4.0 * inC/inS);
    } //end main

} //end class Pi
```

The value of π to 3 decimal places is 3.142. When run with 1000 numbers, this program gave 3.132 as an approximation to π. When run with 2000 numbers, it gave 3.140 as the approximation.

EXERCISES 6

1. Write a program to request two numbers, *m* and *n*, and print 25 random numbers from *m* to *n*.

2. Explain the difference between random and pseudorandom numbers.

3. Modify Program P6.3 to give a user problems in subtraction.

4. Modify Program P6.3 to give a user problems in multiplication.

5. Modify Program P6.3 to incorporate a scoring system. For example, for two attempts at a problem, you can give 2 points for a correct answer on the first attempt and 1 point for a correct answer on the second attempt.

6. Rewrite Program P6.3 so that it presents the user with a menu that allows him to choose what kinds of problems he gets (addition, subtraction, or multiplication).

7. Write a program to simulate 1,000 throws of a die and determine the number of 1s, 2s, 3s, 4s, 5s, and 6s that show. Write the program (a) without using an array and (b) using an array.

8. Write a program to simulate the weather for 60 days using the probabilities in Section 6.7.

9. In the manufacture of electric bulbs, the probability that a bulb is defective is 0.01. Simulate the manufacture of 5,000 bulbs, indicating how many are defective.

10. A die is weighted such that 1s and 5s come up twice as often as any other number. Simulate 1,000 throws of this die, indicating the frequency with which each number occurs.

11. Modify Program P6.6 to calculate the average waiting time for customers and the total idle time for each counter.

12. One-Zero is a game that can be played among several players using a six-sided die. On his turn, a player can throw the die as many times as he wants. His score for that turn is the sum of the numbers he throws *provided he does not throw* a 1. If he throws a 1, his score is 0. Suppose a player decides to adopt the strategy of ending his turn after seven throws. (Of course, if he throws a 1 before the 7th throw, he must end his turn.) Write a program to play 10 turns using this strategy. For each turn, print the score obtained. Also, print the average score for the 10 turns.

    Generalize the program to request values for numTurns and maxThrowsPerTurn and print the results as described.

13. Write a program to simulate the game of *Snakes and Ladders*. The board consists of 100 squares. Snakes and ladders are input as ordered pairs of numbers, *m* and *n*. For example, the pair 17 64 means that there is a ladder from 17 to 64, and the pair 99 28 means that there is a snake from 99 to 28.

    Simulate the playing of 20 games, each game lasting a maximum of 100 moves. Print the number of games that were completed in the 100 moves and the average number of moves per game for completed games.

14. Write a program to play a modified game of Nim (Section 6.6) in which there are two heaps of matches and a player, on his turn, may choose from either one. However, in this case, a player *wins* if he picks up the last match.

15. Using the traffic lights data in Section 6.8, write a program to simulate the situation at the lights for a 30-minute period. Print the number of cars in each queue each time the light changes.

16. Write a program to estimate the square root of 59.

17. Write a program to read a positive integer n and estimate the square root of n.

18. Write a program to read a positive integer n and estimate the cube root of n.

19. Write a program to simulate the collection of bottle caps to spell *APPLE*. In every 100 caps, A and E occur 40 times each, P occurs 10 times and L occurs 10 times. Do 50 simulations and print the average number of caps per simulation.

20. The lottery requires people to pick seven numbers from the numbers 1 to 40. Write a program to randomly generate and print five sets of seven numbers each (one set per line). No number is to be repeated in any of the sets; that is, exactly 35 of the 40 numbers must be used. If a number (p, say) is generated that has been used already, the first unused number after p is used. (Assume that 1 follows 40.) For example, if 15 is generated but has been used already, 16 is tried, but if this has been used, 17 is tried, and so on, until an unused number is found.

21. A function $f(x)$ is defined for $0 \le x \le 1$, such that $0 \le f(x) < 1$ for all $0 \le x < 1$. Write a program to estimate the integral of $f(x)$ from 0 to 1. Hint: estimate the area under the curve by generating points (x, y), $0 \le x < 1, 0 \le y < 1$.

22. A gambler pays $5 to play the following game. He throws two six-sided dice. If the sum of the two numbers thrown is even, he loses his bet. If the sum is odd, he draws a card from a standard pack of 52 playing cards. If he draws an ace, 3, 5, 7 or 9, he is paid the value of the card plus $5 (ace counts as 1). If he draws any other card, he loses. Write a program to simulate the playing of 20 games and print the average amount won by the gambler per game.

CHAPTER 7

■ ■ ■

Working with Files

In this chapter, we will explain the following:

- The difference between text files and binary files

- The difference between internal and external file names

- How to write a program to compare two text files

- The try . . . catch construct

- How to perform input/output with binary files

- How to work with a binary file of records

- What are random access files

- How to create and retrieve records from random access files

- What are indexed files

- How to update a random access file using an index

7.1 Input/Output in Java

Java has a comprehensive range of classes for performing input/output. We have used System.in and System.out for reading from the standard input and writing to the standard output, respectively.

We have used, for instance, the following to read data from a file, input.txt:

```
Scanner in = new Scanner(new FileReader("input.txt"));
```

In addition, we have used the following to send output to the file, output.txt:

```
PrintWriter out = new PrintWriter(new FileWriter("output.txt"));
```

The files we have worked with have all been *text* files (files of characters). In this chapter, we will see how to work with *binary* files.

7.2 Text and Binary Files

A *text* file is a sequence of characters organized into lines. Conceptually, we think of each line as being terminated by a newline character. However, depending on the host environment, certain character translations may occur. For example, if we wrote the newline character \n to a file, it could be translated into two characters—a carriage return and a line-feed character.

Thus, there is not necessarily a one-to-one correspondence between characters written and those stored on an external device. Similarly, there may not be a one-to-one correspondence between the number of characters stored in a file and the number read.

A *binary* file is simply a sequence of bytes, with *no* character translations occurring on input or output. Thus, there *is* a one-to-one correspondence between what is read or written and what is stored in the file.

Apart from possible character translations, there are other differences between text and binary files. To illustrate, a short integer is stored using 2 bytes (16 bits); the number 3371 is stored as 00001101 00101011.

If we were to write this number to a text file, it would be written as the character 3, followed by the character 3, followed by 7, followed by 1, occupying 4 bytes in all. On the other hand, we could simply write the two bytes as is to a binary file.

Even though we could still think of them as a sequence of two "characters," the values they contain may not represent any valid characters. In fact, in this case, the decimal values of the two bytes are 13 and 43, which, interpreted as two ASCII characters, are the carriage return character (CR) and +.

Another way to look at it is that, in general, each byte in a text file contains a human-readable character, whereas, in general, each byte in a binary file contains an arbitrary bit pattern. Binary files are important for writing data directly from its internal representation to an external device, usually a disk file.

The standard input and output are considered text files. A disk file may be created as a text file or as a binary file. We will see how to do so shortly.

7.3 Internal vs. External File Name

The usual way of using a computer is via its operating system. We normally create and edit files using a word processor or a text file editor. When we create a file, we give it a name that we use whenever we need to do anything with the file. This is the name by which the file is known to the operating system.

We will refer to such a name as an *external* file name. (The term *external* is used here to mean "external to a Java program.") When we are writing a program, we may want to specify, say, the reading of data from a file. The program will need to use a file name, but, for several reasons, this name should not be an external file name. The following are the major reasons:

- The file to be read may not have been created as yet.

- If the external name is tied to the program, the program will be able to read a file with that name only. If the data is in a file with a different name, either the program will have to be changed or the file renamed.

- The program will be less portable since different operating systems have different file-naming conventions. A valid external file name on one system may be invalid on another one.

- For these reasons, a Java program uses an internal file name—we have generally used in for input and out for output. For instance, when we write the following, we associate the internal name, in, with the external file, input.txt:

```
Scanner in = new Scanner(new FileReader("input.txt"));
```

This is the only statement that mentions the external file name. The rest of the program is written in terms of in. Of course, we can be even more flexible and write this:

```
Scanner in = new Scanner(new FileReader(fileName));
```

When the program is run, we supply the name of the file in fileName, with something like this:

```
System.out.printf("Enter file name: ");
String fileName = kb.nextLine();  //Scanner kb = new Scanner(System.in);
```

This example also illustrates how to read data from the keyboard (standard input) *and* a file in the same program. For example, kb.nextInt() will read an integer typed at the keyboard, and in.nextInt() will read an integer from the file input.txt.

7.4 Example: Comparing Two Files

Consider the problem of comparing two files. The comparison is done line by line until a mismatch is found or one of the files comes to an end. Program P7.1 shows how we can solve this problem.

Program P7.1

```
import java.io.*;
import java.util.*;
public class CompareFiles {
    public static void main(String[] args) throws IOException {
        Scanner kb = new Scanner(System.in);

        System.out.printf("First file? ");
        String file1 = kb.nextLine();
        System.out.printf("Second file? ");
        String file2 = kb.nextLine();

        Scanner f1 = new Scanner(new FileReader(file1));
        Scanner f2 = new Scanner(new FileReader(file2));

        String line1 = "", line2 = "";
        int numMatch = 0;

        while (f1.hasNextLine() && f2.hasNextLine()) {
            line1 = f1.nextLine();
            line2 = f2.nextLine();
            if (!line1.equals(line2)) break;
            ++numMatch;
        }
        if (!f1.hasNextLine() && !f2.hasNextLine())
            System.out.printf("\nThe files are identical\n");
        else if (!f1.hasNextLine())   //first file ends, but not the second
            System.out.printf("\n%s, with %d lines, is a subset of %s\n",
                        file1, numMatch, file2);
```

```
        else if (!f2.hasNextLine())    //second file ends, but not the first
            System.out.printf("\n%s, with %d lines, is a subset of %s\n",
                        file2, numMatch, file1);
        else { //mismatch found
            System.out.printf("\nThe files differ at line %d\n", ++numMatch);
            System.out.printf("The lines are \n%s\n and \n%s\n", line1, line2);
        }
        f1.close();
        f2.close();
    } //end main

} //end class CompareFiles
```

The program does the following:

- It prompts for the names of the files to be compared; if any of the files does not exist, a FileNotFoundException will be thrown.

- It creates two Scanners, f1 and f2, one for each file.

- It uses hasNextLine to check whether a file has more lines to read; if true, there is at least another line to read, and if false, the end of the file has been reached.

- The variable numMatch counts the number of matching lines. One line from each file is read. If they match, 1 is added to numMatch, and another pair of lines is read. The while loop exits naturally if one (or both) of the files comes to an end; we break out of the loop if a mismatch occurs.

If the first file contains this:

```
one and one are two
two and two are four
three and three are six
four and four are eight
five and five are ten
six and six are twelve
```

and the second file contains this:

```
one and one are two
two and two are four
three and three are six
four and four are eight
this is the fifth line
six and six are twelve
```

the program will print the following:

```
The files differ at line 5
The lines are
five and five are ten
 and
this is the fifth line
```

7.5 The `try . . . catch` Construct

When a program is trying to read data, errors can arise. There may be a problem with the device, we may be trying to read beyond the end of the file, or the file we are asking to read from may not even exist. Similarly, when we attempt to write data to a file, the device may be locked or unavailable, or we may not have write permission. In such cases, Java throws an IO (input/output) Exception".

Whenever there is the possibility that a method may trigger an I/O error, either by performing some I/O operation itself or by calling a method that does, Java requires that the method declare this. One way to do so is to use `throws IOException` in the method header, as in the following:

```
public static void main(String[] args) throws IOException {
```

Another way to handle input/output errors is to use the `try . . . catch` construct. Suppose a program contains this statement:

```
Scanner in = new Scanner(new FileReader("input.txt"));
```

When run, if the program cannot find a file called `input.txt`, it will halt with a "file not found exception" error message. We can avoid this as follows:

```
try {
    Scanner in = new Scanner(new FileReader("input.txt"));
}
catch (IOException e) {
    System.out.printf("%s\n", e);
    System.out.printf("Correct the problem and try again\n");
    System.exit(1);
}
```

The `try` block consists of the word `try` followed by a block (zero or more statements enclosed in braces). Java attempts to execute the statements in the block.

The `catch` part consists of the word `catch` followed by an "exception type" in brackets, followed by a block. In this example, we expect that an I/O exception might be thrown, so we use `IOException e` after `catch`. If an exception is indeed thrown, the statements in the `catch` block are executed.

In this example, suppose the file `input.txt` exists. The `Scanner in...` statement will succeed, and the program will continue with the statement *after* the `catch` block. But if the file does *not* exist or is not available, the exception will be thrown and caught with the `catch` part.

When this happens, the statements, if any, in the catch block are executed. Java lets us put any statements in a catch block. In this case, we print the contents of the exception object, e, and a message, and the program exits. When run, with no file input.txt, this code prints the following:

```
java.io.FileNotFoundException: input.txt
Correct the problem and try again
```

The program does not *have* to exit. If the exit statement were omitted, the program would simply continue with the statement, if any, after the catch block. If we want, we could also call another method to continue execution.

To continue the example, consider the following:

```
try {
    Scanner in = new Scanner(new FileReader("input.txt"));
    n = in.nextInt();
}
```

We attempt to read the next integer from the file. Now, many things can go wrong: the file may not exist, the next item in the file may not be a valid integer, or there may be no "next" item in the file. These will throw "file not found," "input mismatch," and "no such element" exceptions, respectively. Since these are all subclasses of the class Exception, we can catch them all with the following:

```
catch (Exception e) {
    System.out.printf("%s\n", e);
    System.out.printf("Correct the problem and try again\n");
    System.exit(1);
}
```

When the file is empty, this code prints this:

```
java.util.NoSuchElementException
Correct the problem and try again
```

When the file contains the number 5.7 (not an integer), it prints this:

```
java.util.InputMismatchException
Correct the problem and try again
```

If necessary, Java allows us to catch each exception separately. We can have as many catch constructs as needed. In this example, we could write the following:

```
try {
    Scanner in = new Scanner(new FileReader("input.txt"));
    n = in.nextInt();
}
catch (FileNotFoundException e) {
    //code for file not found
}
catch (InputMismatchException e) {
    //code for "invalid integer" found
}
catch (NoSuchElementException e) {
    //code for "end of file" being reached
}
```

Sometimes, the order of the `catch` clauses matters. Suppose we want to catch "file not found" separately from all other exceptions. We may be tempted to write this:

```
try {
    Scanner in = new Scanner(new FileReader("input.txt"));
    n = in.nextInt();
}
catch (Exception e) {
    //code for all exceptions (except "file not found", presumably)
}
catch (FileNotFoundException e) {
    //code for file not found
}
```

This code would not even compile! When Java reaches the last `catch`, it will complain that `FileNotFoundException` has already been caught. This is because `FileNotFoundException` is a subclass of `Exception`. To fix the problem, we must put `catch (FileNotFoundException e)` *before* `catch (Exception e)`.

In general, subclass exceptions must come before the containing class.

7.6 Input/Output for Binary File

As mentioned earlier, a binary file contains data in a form that corresponds exactly with the internal representation of the data. For example, if a `float` variable occupies 4 bytes of memory, writing it to a binary file simply involves making an exact copy of the 4 bytes. On the other hand, writing it to a text file causes it to be converted to character form, and the characters obtained are stored in the file.

Normally, a binary file can be created only from within a program, and its contents can be read only by a program. Listing a binary file, for example, produces only "garbage" and, sometimes, generates an error. Compare a text file that can be created by typing into it and whose contents can be listed and read by a human. However, a binary file has the following advantages:

- Data can be transferred to and from a binary file much faster than for a text file since no data conversions are necessary; the data is read and written as is.

- The values of data types such as arrays and structures can be written to a binary file. For a text file, individual elements must be written.

- Data stored in a binary file usually occupies less space than the same data stored in a text file. For example, the integer –25367 (six characters) occupies 6 bytes in a text file but only 2 bytes in a binary file.

7.6.1 DataOutputStream and DataInputStream

Consider the problem of reading integers from a text file, num.txt, and writing them, in their internal form, to a (binary) file, num.bin. We assume that the numbers in num.txt are terminated by 0 and 0 is not to be written to the binary file. This can be done with Program P7.2.

Program P7.2

```
import java.io.*;
import java.util.*;
public class CreateBinaryFile {

    public static void main(String[] args) throws IOException {
        Scanner in = new Scanner(new FileReader("num.txt"));
        DataOutputStream out = new DataOutputStream(new FileOutputStream("num.bin"));
        int n = in.nextInt();
        while (n != 0) {
            out.writeInt(n);
            n = in.nextInt();
        }
        out.close();
        in.close();
    } //end main
} //end class CreateBinaryFile
```

Suppose num.txt contains the following:

```
25 18 47 96 73 89 82 13 39 0
```

When Program P7.2 is run, the numbers (except 0) will be stored in their internal form in the file, num.bin. The new statement in Program P7.2 is this:

```
DataOutputStream out = new DataOutputStream(new FileOutputStream("num.bin"));
```

A data output stream lets a program write primitive Java data types to an output stream. A file output stream is an output stream for writing data to a file. The following constructor creates an output stream connected to the file num.bin:

```
new FileOutputStream("num.bin")
```

The following are some of the methods in the DataOutputStream class. All methods write to the underlying output stream, and all values are written with the high byte first (that is, from most significant to least significant byte).

```
void writeInt(int v)        //write an int
void writeDouble(double v)  //write a double value
void writeChar(int v)       //write a char as a 2-byte value
void writeChars(String s)   //write a string as a sequence of chars
void writeFloat(float v)    //write a float value
void writeLong(long v)      //write a long value
void write(int b)           //write the low 8-bits of b
```

In Program P7.2, out.writeInt(n) writes the integer n to the file num.bin. If you try to view the contents of num.bin, all you would see is nonsense. Only a program can read and make sense of what is in the file.

Consider Program P7.3, which reads the numbers from the file num.bin and prints them.

Program P7.3

```java
import java.io.*;
public class ReadBinaryFile {
    public static void main(String[] args) throws IOException {
        DataInputStream in = new DataInputStream(new FileInputStream("num.bin"));
        int amt = 0;
        try {
            while (true) {
                int n = in.readInt();
                System.out.printf("%d ", n);
                ++amt;
            }
        }
        catch (IOException e) { }
        System.out.printf("\n\n%d numbers were read\n", amt);
    } //end main
} //end class ReadBinaryFile
```

If num.bin contains the output from Program P7.2, then Program P7.3 produces the following output:

```
25 18 47 96 73 89 82 13 39

9 numbers were read
```

The new statement in Program P7.3 is this:

```java
DataInputStream in = new DataInputStream(new FileInputStream("num.bin"));
```

A data input stream lets a program read primitive Java data types from an input stream that was created as a data output stream. A file input stream is an input stream for reading data from a file. The following constructor creates an input stream connected to the file num.bin:

```java
new FileInputStream("num.bin")
```

The following are some of the methods in the DataInputStream class:

```java
int readInt()          //read 4 input bytes and return an int value
double readDouble() //read 8 input bytes and return a double value
char readChar()        //read a char as a 2-byte value
void readFully(byte[] b) //read bytes and store in b until b is full
float readFloat()           //read 4 input bytes and return a float value
long readLong()             //read 8 input bytes and return a long value
int skipBytes(int n)       //attempts to skip n bytes of data;
                           //returns the number actually skipped
```

Generally speaking, these methods are used to read data that was written using the corresponding "write" methods from DataOutputStream.

Note the use of try . . . catch to read numbers until end-of-file is reached. Recall that there is no "end-of-data" value in the file, so we can't test for this. The while statement will read from the file continuously. When the end-of-file is reached, an EOFException is thrown. This is a subclass of IOException and so is caught.

The catch block is empty, so nothing happens there. Control goes to the following statement, which prints the amount of numbers read.

7.6.2 Binary File of Records

In the previous section, we created, and read from, a binary file of integers. We now discuss how to work with a binary file of records, where a record can consist of two or more fields.

Suppose we want to store information on car parts. For now, we assume that each part record has two fields—an int part number and a double price. Suppose we have a text file parts.txt that contains the parts data in the following format:

```
4250    12.95
3000    17.50
6699    49.99
2270    19.25
0
```

We read this data and create a binary file, parts.bin, with Program P7.4.

Program P7.4

```java
import java.io.*;
import java.util.*;
public class CreateBinaryFile1 {
    public static void main(String[] args) throws IOException {
        Scanner in = new Scanner(new FileReader("parts.txt"));
        DataOutputStream out = new DataOutputStream(new FileOutputStream("parts.bin"));
        int n = in.nextInt();
        while (n != 0) {
            out.writeInt(n);
            out.writeDouble(in.nextDouble());
            n = in.nextInt();
        }
        in.close(); out.close();
    } //end main
} //end class CreateBinaryFile1
```

Each record in parts.bin is exactly 12 bytes (4 for int + 8 for double). In the example, there are 4 records so the file will be exactly 48 bytes long. We know that the first record starts at byte 0, the second at byte 12, the third at byte 24, and the fourth at byte 36. The next record will start at byte 48.

In this scenario, we can easily calculate where record n will start; it will start at byte number $(n-1) * 12$.

To set the stage for what will come later, we will rewrite Program P7.4 using the following Part class:

```java
class Part {
    int partNum;
    double price;

    public Part(int pn, double pr) {
        partNum = pn;
        price = pr;
    }
```

```
        public void printPart() {
            System.out.printf("\nPart number: %s\n", partNum);
            System.out.printf("Price: $%3.2f\n", price);
        }
    } //end class Part
```

Program P7.5 reads the data from the text file parts.txt and creates the binary file parts.bin.

Program P7.5

```
    import java.io.*;
    import java.util.*;
    public class CreateBinaryFile2 {
        static final int EndOfData = 0;

        public static void main(String[] args) throws IOException {
            Scanner in = new Scanner(new FileReader("parts.txt"));
            DataOutputStream fp = new DataOutputStream(new FileOutputStream("parts.bin"));

            Part part = getPartData(in);
            while (part != null) {
                writePartToFile(part, fp);
                part = getPartData(in);
            }

            in.close();
            fp.close();
        } //end main

        public static Part getPartData(Scanner in) {
            int pnum = in.nextInt();
            if (pnum == EndOfData) return null;
            return new Part(pnum, in.nextDouble());
        }

        public static void writePartToFile(Part part, DataOutputStream f) throws IOException {
            f.writeInt(part.partNum);
            f.writeDouble(part.price);
            part.printPart(); //print data on standard input
        } //end writePartToFile

    } //end class CreateBinaryFile2

    //class Part goes here
```

When run, Program P7.5 produces the following output:

```
Part number: 4250
Price: $12.95

Part number: 3000
Price: $17.50

Part number: 6699
Price: $49.99

Part number: 2270
Price: $19.25
```

After the file has been created, we can read the next Part record with this:

```
public static Part readPartFromFile(DataInputStream in) throws IOException {
    return new Part(in.readInt(), in.readDouble());
} //end readPartFromFile
```

This assumes the following declaration:

```
DataInputStream in = new DataInputStream(new FileInputStream("parts.bin"));
```

7.7 Random Access Files

In the normal mode of operation, data items are read from a file in the order in which they are stored. When a file is opened, one can think of an imaginary pointer positioned at the beginning of the file. As items are read from the file, this pointer moves along by the number of bytes read. At any time, this pointer indicates where the next read (or write) operation would occur.

Normally, this pointer is moved implicitly by a read or write operation. However, Java provides facilities for moving the pointer explicitly to any position in the file. This is useful if we want to be able to read the data in random order, as opposed to sequential order.

For example, consider the parts binary file created earlier. Each record is 12 bytes long. If the first record starts at byte 0, then the nth record would start at byte $12(n-1)$. Suppose we want to read the 10th record without having to read the first nine. We work out that the 10th record starts at byte 108. If we can position the file pointer at byte 108, we can then read the 10th record.

In Java, the RandomAccessFile class provides methods for working with random access files. The following statement declares that parts.bin will be treated as a random access file; rw is the file mode, and it means "read/write"—we will be allowed to read from the file *and* write to it.

```
RandomAccessFile fp = new RandomAccessFile("parts.bin", "rw");
```

If we want to open the file in read-only mode, we use r instead of rw.

Initially, the file pointer is 0, meaning it is positioned at byte 0.

As we read data from or write data to the file, the pointer value changes. In the parts example, after we read (or write) the first record, the pointer value would be 12. After we read (or write) the 5th record, the value would be 60. Note, though, that the 5th record starts at byte 48.

At any time, `fp.getFilePointer()` returns the current value of the pointer. We can position the pointer at any byte in the file with seek. The following statement positions the pointer at byte n:

```
fp.seek(n); //n is an integer; can be as big as a long integer
```

For example, we can read the 10th record into a Part variable with this:

```
fp.seek(108);  //the 10th record starts at byte 108
Part part = new Part(fp.readInt(), fp.readDouble());
```

In general, we can read the *n*th record with this:

```
fp.seek((n - 1) * 12);  //the nth record starts at byte (n - 1) * 12
Part part = new Part(fp.readInt(), fp.readDouble());
```

We note that 12 should normally be replaced by a symbolic constant such as `PartRecordSize`.

We now expand the parts example by using a more realistic part record. Suppose that each part now has four fields: a six-character part number, a name, an amount in stock, and a price. The following is some sample data:

```
PKL070 Park-Lens 8 6.50
BLJ375 Ball-Joint 12 11.95
FLT015 Oil-Filter 23 7.95
DKP080 Disc-Pads 16 9.99
GSF555 Gas-Filter 9 4.50
END
```

The part name is written as one word so it can be read with the Scanner method next. Note that the part names do not all have the same length. And remember that in order to use a random access file, all *records* must have the same length—this way we can work out a record's position in the file. How, then, can we create a random access file of part records if the part names have different lengths?

The trick is to store each name using the same fixed amount of storage. For example, we can store each name using 20 characters. If a name is shorter than 20, we pad it with blanks to make up 20. If it is longer, we truncate it to 20. However, it is better to use a length that will accommodate the longest name.

If we use 20 characters for storing a name, what will be the size of a part record? In Java, each character is stored in 2 bytes. Hence, the part number (6 characters) will occupy 12 bytes, a name will occupy 40 bytes, the amount in stock (integer) will take up 4 bytes, and the price (double) will require 8 bytes. This gives a total of 64 bytes for each record.

We write the Part class as follows:

```
class Part {
    String partNum, name;
    int amtInStock;
    double price;

    public Part(String pn, String n, int a, double p) {
        partNum = pn;
        name = n;
        amtInStock = a;
        price = p;
    }
```

```java
    public void printPart() {
        System.out.printf("Part number: %s\n", partNum);
        System.out.printf("Part name: %s\n", name);
        System.out.printf("Amount in stock: %d\n", amtInStock);
        System.out.printf("Price: $%3.2f\n", price);
    }

} //end class Part
```

If EndOfData has the value END, we can read the data from the parts file, assuming it's in the format of the previous sample data, with this:

```java
public static Part getPartData(Scanner in) {
    String pnum = in.next();
    if (pnum.equals(EndOfData)) return null;
    return new Part(pnum, in.next(), in.nextInt(), in.nextDouble());
}
```

If there is no more data, the method returns null. Otherwise, it returns a Part object containing the next part's data.

If StringFixedLength denotes the number of characters for storing a part name, we can write a name to the file, f, with this:

```java
int n = Math.min(part.name.length(), StringFixedLength);
for (int h = 0; h < n; h++) f.writeChar(part.name.charAt(h));
for (int h = n; h < StringFixedLength; h++) f.writeChar(' ');
```

If n denotes the smaller of the actual length of the name and StringFixedLength, we first write n characters to the file. The second for statement writes blanks to the file to make up the required amount. Note that if StringFixedLength is shorter than the name, no extra blanks will be written by the last for.

To read a name from the file, we will use the following:

```java
char[] name = new char[StringFixedLength];
for (int h = 0; h < StringFixedLength; h++) name[h] = f.readChar();
String hold = new String(name, 0, StringFixedLength);
```

This reads exactly StringFixedLength characters from the file into an array. This is then converted into a String and stored in hold; hold.trim() will remove the trailing blanks, if any. We will use hold.trim() in creating the Part object read.

Program P7.6 reads the data from the text file parts.txt and creates the random access file parts.bin.

Program P7.6

```java
import java.io.*;
import java.util.*;
public class CreateRandomAccess {
    static final int StringFixedLength = 20;
    static final int PartNumSize = 6;
    static final int PartRecordSize = 64;
    static final String EndOfData = "END";
```

```
    public static void main(String[] args) throws IOException {
        Scanner in = new Scanner(new FileReader("parts.txt"));
        RandomAccessFile fp = new RandomAccessFile("parts.bin", "rw");
        Part part = getPartData(in);
        while (part != null) {
            writePartToFile(part, fp);
            part = getPartData(in);
        }
    } //end main

    public static Part getPartData(Scanner in) {
        String pnum = in.next();
        if (pnum.equals(EndOfData)) return null;
        return new Part(pnum, in.next(), in.nextInt(), in.nextDouble());
    } //end getPartData

    public static void writePartToFile(Part part, RandomAccessFile f) throws IOException {
        System.out.printf("%s %-11s %2d %5.2f %3d\n", part.partNum, part.name,
                            part.amtInStock, part.price, f.getFilePointer());
        for (int h = 0; h < PartNumSize; h++) f.writeChar(part.partNum.charAt(h));
        int n = Math.min(part.name.length(), StringFixedLength);
        for (int h = 0; h < n; h++) f.writeChar(part.name.charAt(h));
        for (int h = n; h < StringFixedLength; h++) f.writeChar(' ');
        f.writeInt(part.amtInStock);
        f.writeDouble(part.price);
    } //end writePartToFile
} //end class CreateRandomAccess

//class Part goes here
```

When run with `parts.txt` containing the previous sample data, Program P7.6 prints the following:

```
PKL070 Park-Lens    8  6.50   0
BLJ375 Ball-Joint  12 11.95  64
FLT015 Oil-Filter  23  7.95 128
DKP080 Disc-Pads   16  9.99 192
GSF555 Gas-Filter   9  4.50 256
```

The last value on each line is the file pointer; this is the byte position where the record is stored. The part name is printed left-justified in a field width of 11 using the format specification %-11s (- denotes left-justification).

We now write Program P7.7 to test whether the file has been stored correctly. It prompts the user to enter a record number, and it prints the corresponding part record.

Program P7.7

```
import java.io.*;
import java.util.*;
public class ReadRandomAccess {
    static final int StringFixedLength = 20;
    static final int PartNumSize = 6;
    static final int PartRecordSize = 64;
```

```java
    public static void main(String[] args) throws IOException {
        RandomAccessFile fp = new RandomAccessFile("parts.bin", "rw");
        Scanner kb = new Scanner(System.in);
        System.out.printf("\nEnter a record number: ");
        int n = kb.nextInt();
        while (n != 0) {
            fp.seek(PartRecordSize * (n - 1));
            readPartFromFile(fp).printPart();
            System.out.printf("\nEnter a record number: ");
            n = kb.nextInt();
        }
    } //end main

    public static Part readPartFromFile(RandomAccessFile f) throws IOException {
        String pname = "";
        for (int h = 0; h < PartNumSize; h++) pname += f.readChar();
        char[] name = new char[StringFixedLength];
        for (int h = 0; h < StringFixedLength; h++) name[h] = f.readChar();
        String hold = new String(name, 0, StringFixedLength);
        return new Part(pname, hold.trim(), f.readInt(), f.readDouble());
    } //end readPartFromFile
} //end class ReadRandomAccess

// class Part goes here
```

The following is a sample run of Program P7.7:

```
Enter a record number: 3
Part number: FLT015
Part name: Oil-Filter
Amount in stock: 23
Price: $7.95

Enter a record number: 1
Part number: PKL070
Part name: Park-Lens
Amount in stock: 8
Price: $6.50

Enter a record number: 4
Part number: DKP080
Part name: Disc-Pads
Amount in stock: 16
Price: $9.99
Enter a record number: 0
```

7.8 Indexed Files

The previous section showed how to retrieve a part record given the record number. But this is not the most natural way to retrieve records. More likely than not, we would want to retrieve records based on some *key*, in this case, the part number. It is more natural to ask, "How many of BLJ375 do we have?" rather than "How many of record 2 do we have?" The problem then is how to retrieve a record given the part number.

One approach is to use an *index*. Just as a book index lets us quickly locate information in a book, a file index enables us to quickly find records in a file. The index is created as the file is loaded. Later, it must be updated as records are added to, or deleted from, the file. In our example, an index entry will consist of a part number and a record number.

We will use the following class for creating an index:

```
class Index {
    String partNum;
    int recNum;

    public Index(String p, int r) {
        partNum = p;
        recNum = r;
    }
} //end class Index
```

We will use MaxRecords to denote the maximum number of records we will cater for. We declare an array, index, as follows:

```
Index[] index = new Index[MaxRecords + 1];
```

We will use index[0].recNum to hold numRecords, the number of records stored in the file. The index entries will be stored in index[1] to index[numRecords].

The index will be kept in order by part number. We want to create an index for the following records:

```
PKL070 Park-Lens     8   6.50
BLJ375 Ball-Joint   12  11.95
FLT015 Oil-Filter   23   7.95
DKP080 Disc-Pads    16   9.99
GSF555 Gas-Filter    9   4.50
```

We assume that the records are stored in the file in the given order. When the first record is read and stored, the index will contain this:

```
PKL070    1
```

This means that the record for PKL070 is record number 1 in the parts file. After the second record (BLJ375) is read and stored, the index will be this:

```
BLJ375    2
PKL070    1
```

Remember, we are keeping the index in order by part number. After the third record (FLT015) is read and stored, the index will be this:

```
BLJ375    2
FLT015    3
PKL070    1
```

After the fourth record (DKP080) is read and stored, the index will be this:

```
BLJ375    2
DKP080    4
FLT015    3
PKL070    1
```

Finally, after the fifth record (GSF555) is read and stored, the index will be this:

```
BLJ375    2
DKP080    4
FLT015    3
GSF555    5
PKL070    1
```

Program P7.8 illustrates how an index can be created as described.

Program P7.8

```java
import java.io.*;
import java.util.*;
public class CreateIndex {
   static final int StringFixedLength = 20;
   static final int PartNumSize = 6;
   static final int PartRecordSize = 64;
   static final int MaxRecords = 100;
   static final String EndOfData = "END";

   public static void main(String[] args) throws IOException {
      RandomAccessFile fp = new RandomAccessFile("parts.bin", "rw");
      Index[] index = new Index[MaxRecords + 1];

      createMasterIndex(index, fp);
      saveIndex(index);
      printIndex(index);
      fp.close();
   } //end main

   public static void createMasterIndex(Index[] index,
                             RandomAccessFile f) throws IOException {
      Scanner in = new Scanner(new FileReader("parts.txt"));
      int numRecords = 0;
      Part part = getPartData(in);
      while (part != null) {
         int searchResult = search(part.partNum, index, numRecords);
```

```
        if (searchResult > 0)
            System.out.printf("Duplicate part: %s ignored\n", part.partNum);
        else { //this is a new part number; insert in location -searchResult
            if (numRecords == MaxRecords) {
                System.out.printf("Too many records: only %d allowed\n", MaxRecords);
                System.exit(1);
            }
            //the index has room; shift entries to accommodate new part
            for (int h = numRecords; h >= -searchResult; h--)
                    index[h + 1] = index[h];
            index[-searchResult] = new Index(part.partNum, ++numRecords);
            writePartToFile(part, f);
        }
        part = getPartData(in);
    } //end while
    index[0] = new Index("NOPART", numRecords);
    in.close();
} //end createMasterIndex

public static Part getPartData(Scanner in) {
    String pnum = in.next();
    if (pnum.equals(EndOfData)) return null;
    return new Part(pnum, in.next(), in.nextInt(), in.nextDouble());
} //end getPartData

public static void writePartToFile(Part part, RandomAccessFile f) throws IOException {
    for (int h = 0; h < PartNumSize; h++) f.writeChar(part.partNum.charAt(h));
    int n = Math.min(part.name.length(), StringFixedLength);
    for (int h = 0; h < n; h++) f.writeChar(part.name.charAt(h));
    for (int h = n; h < StringFixedLength; h++) f.writeChar(' ');
    f.writeInt(part.amtInStock);
    f.writeDouble(part.price);
} //end writePartToFile

public static void saveIndex(Index[] index) throws IOException {
    RandomAccessFile f = new RandomAccessFile("index.bin", "rw");
    int numRecords = index[0].recNum;
    //fill the unused index positions with dummy entries
    for (int h = numRecords+1; h <= MaxRecords; h++)
        index[h] = new Index("NOPART", 0);
    f.writeInt(MaxRecords);
    for (int h = 0; h <= MaxRecords; h++) {
        for (int i = 0; i < PartNumSize; i++)
                f.writeChar(index[h].partNum.charAt(i));
        f.writeInt(index[h].recNum);
    }
    f.close();
} //end saveIndex
```

```java
    public static int search(String key, Index[] list, int n) {
    //searches list[1..n] for key. If found, it returns the location; otherwise
    //it returns the negative of the location in which key should be inserted.
        int lo = 1, hi = n;
        while (lo <= hi) {    // as long as more elements remain to consider
            int mid = (lo + hi) / 2;
            int cmp = key.compareToIgnoreCase(list[mid].partNum);
            if (cmp == 0) return mid;  // search succeeds
            if (cmp < 0) hi = mid - 1;   // key is 'less than' list[mid].partNum
            else lo = mid + 1;      // key is 'greater than' list[mid].partNum
        }
        return -lo;          // key not found; insert in location lo
    } // end search

    public static void printIndex(Index[] index) {
        System.out.printf("\nThe index is as follows: \n\n");
        int numRecords = index[0].recNum;
        for (int h = 1; h <= numRecords; h++)
            System.out.printf("%s %2d\n", index[h].partNum, index[h].recNum);
    } //end printIndex

} //end class CreateIndex

class Part {
    String partNum, name;
    int amtInStock;
    double price;

    public Part(String pn, String n, int a, double p) {
        partNum = pn;
        name = n;
        amtInStock = a;
        price = p;
    }

    public void printPart() {
        System.out.printf("Part number: %s\n", partNum);
        System.out.printf("Part name: %s\n", name);
        System.out.printf("Amount in stock: %d\n", amtInStock);
        System.out.printf("Price: $%3.2f\n", price);
    }
} //end class Part

class Index {
    String partNum;
    int recNum;

    public Index(String p, int r) {
        partNum = p;
        recNum = r;
    }
} //end class Index
```

When a part number is read, we look for it in the index. Since the index is kept in order by part number, we search it using a binary search. If the part number is present, it means the part has been stored already, so this record is ignored. If it is not present, this is a new part, so its record is stored in the parts file parts.bin, provided we have not already stored MaxRecords records.

A count is kept (in numRecords) of the number of records read. The part number and the record number are then inserted in the proper place in the index array.

When all the records have been stored, the index is saved in another file, index.bin. Before saving it, the unused portion of index (the entries after index[numRecords]) is filled with dummy records. The value of MaxRecords is the first value sent to the file. This is followed by index[0] to index[MaxRecords]. Remember that index[0].recNum contains the value of numRecords.

Suppose that parts.txt contains the following:

```
PKL070 Park-Lens 8 6.50
BLJ375 Ball-Joint 12 11.95
PKL070 Park-Lens 8 6.50
FLT015 Oil-Filter 23 7.95
DKP080 Disc-Pads 16 9.99
GSF555 Gas-Filter 9 4.50
FLT015 Oil-Filter 23 7.95
END
```

When Program P7.8 is run, it prints the following:

```
Duplicate part: PKL070 ignored
Duplicate part: FLT015 ignored

The index is as follows:

BLJ375  2
DKP080  4
FLT015  3
GSF555  5
PKL070  1
```

Next, we write a program that tests our index by first reading it from the file. The user is then asked to enter part numbers, one at a time. For each, it searches the index for the part number. If it finds it, the index entry will indicate the record number in the parts file. Using the record number, the part record is retrieved. If the part number is not found in the index, then there is no record for that part. The program is shown as Program P7.9.

Program P7.9

```java
import java.io.*;
import java.util.*;
public class UseIndex {
    static final int StringFixedLength = 20;
    static final int PartNumSize = 6;
    static final int PartRecordSize = 64;
    static int MaxRecords;

    public static void main(String[] args) throws IOException {
        RandomAccessFile fp = new RandomAccessFile("parts.bin", "rw");
```

```
        Index[] index = retrieveIndex();
        int numRecords = index[0].recNum;
        Scanner kb = new Scanner(System.in);
        System.out.printf("\nEnter a part number (E to end): ");
        String pnum = kb.next();
        while (!pnum.equalsIgnoreCase("E")) {
            int n = search(pnum, index, numRecords);
            if (n > 0) {
                fp.seek(PartRecordSize * (index[n].recNum - 1));
                readPartFromFile(fp).printPart();
            }
            else System.out.printf("Part not found\n");
            System.out.printf("\nEnter a part number (E to end): ");
            pnum = kb.next();
        } //end while
        fp.close();
    } //end main

    public static Index[] retrieveIndex() throws IOException {
        RandomAccessFile f = new RandomAccessFile("index.bin", "rw");
        int MaxRecords = f.readInt();
        Index[] index = new Index[MaxRecords + 1];
        for (int j = 0; j <= MaxRecords; j++) {
            String pnum = "";
            for (int i = 0; i < PartNumSize; i++) pnum += f.readChar();
            index[j] = new Index(pnum, f.readInt());
        }
        f.close();
        return index;
    } //end retrieveIndex

    public static Part readPartFromFile(RandomAccessFile f) throws IOException {
        String pname = "";
        for (int h = 0; h < PartNumSize; h++) pname += f.readChar();
        char[] name = new char[StringFixedLength];
        for (int h = 0; h < StringFixedLength; h++) name[h] = f.readChar();
        String hold = new String(name, 0, StringFixedLength);
        return new Part(pname, hold.trim(), f.readInt(), f.readDouble());
    } //end readPartFromFile

    public static int search(String key, Index[] list, int n) {
    //searches list[1..n] for key. If found, it returns the location; otherwise
    //it returns the negative of the location in which key should be inserted.
        int lo = 1, hi = n;
        while (lo <= hi) {    // as long as more elements remain to consider
            int mid = (lo + hi) / 2;
            int cmp = key.compareToIgnoreCase(list[mid].partNum);
            if (cmp == 0) return mid;  // search succeeds
            if (cmp < 0) hi = mid - 1;   // key is 'less than' list[mid].partNum
            else lo = mid + 1;      // key is 'greater than' list[mid].partNum
        }
```

```
        return -lo;              // key not found; insert in location lo
    } // end search

  } //end class UseIndex

  // Part and Index classes go here
```

The following is a sample run of Program P7.9:

```
Enter a part number (E to end): dkp080
Part number: DKP080
Part name: Disc-Pads
Amount in stock: 16
Price: $9.99

Enter a part number (E to end): GsF555
Part number: GSF555
Part name: Gas-Filter
Amount in stock: 9
Price: $4.50

Enter a part number (E to end): PKL060
Part not found

Enter a part number (E to end): pkl070
Part number: PKL070
Part name: Park-Lens
Amount in stock: 8
Price: $6.50

Enter a part number (E to end): e
```

Observe that the part numbers could be entered using any combination of uppercase and lowercase.

If required, we could use the index to print the records in order by part number. We simply print the records in the order in which they appear in the index. For example, using our sample data, we have the index as follows:

```
BLJ375    2
DKP080    4
FLT015    3
GSF555    5
PKL070    1
```

If we print record 2, followed by record 4, followed by record 3, followed by record 5, followed by record 1, we would have printed them in ascending order by part number. This can be done with the following function:

```
public static void printFileInOrder(Index[] index, RandomAccessFile f) throws IOException {
    System.out.printf("\nFile sorted by part number: \n\n");
    int numRecords = index[0].recNum;
    for (int h = 1; h <= numRecords; h++) {
        f.seek(PartRecordSize * (index[h].recNum - 1));
```

```
      readPartFromFile(f).printPart();
      System.out.printf("\n");
    } //end for
  } //end printFileInOrder
```

Suppose this function is added to Program P7.9 and called with the following statement after the index has been retrieved:

```
      printFileInOrder(index, fp);
```

The following will be printed:

```
File sorted by part number:

Part number: BLJ375
Part name: Ball-Joint
Amount in stock: 12
Price: $11.95

Part number: DKP080
Part name: Disc-Pads
Amount in stock: 16
Price: $9.99

Part number: FLT015
Part name: Oil-Filter
Amount in stock: 23
Price: $7.95

Part number: GSF555
Part name: Gas-Filter
Amount in stock: 9
Price: $4.50

Part number: PKL070
Part name: Park-Lens
Amount in stock: 8
Price: $6.50
```

7.9 Updating a Random Access File

The information in a file is not usually static. It must be updated from time to time. For our parts file, we may want to update it to reflect the new quantity in stock as items are sold or to reflect a change in price. We may decide to stock new parts, so we must add records to the file, and we may discontinue selling certain items, so their records must be deleted from the file.

Adding new records is done in a similar manner to loading the file in the first place. We can delete a record logically by marking it as deleted in the index or by simply removing it from the index. Later, when the file is reorganized, the record could be deleted physically (that is, not present in the new file). But how can we *change* the information in an existing record? To do this, we must do the following:

1. Locate the record in the file.

2. Read it into memory.

3. Change the desired fields.

4. Write the updated record to the *same position* in the file from which it came.

This requires that our file be opened for both reading and writing. Assuming that the file already exists, it must be opened with mode rw. We explain how to update a record whose part number is stored in key.

First we search the index for key. If it is not found, no record exists for this part. Suppose it is found in location k. Then index[k].recNum gives its record number (n, say) in the parts file. We then proceed as follows (omitting error checking in the interest of clarity):

```
fp.seek(PartRecordSize * (n - 1));
Part part = readPartFromFile(fp);
```

The record is now in memory in the variable part. Suppose we need to subtract amtSold from the amount in stock. This could be done with this:

```
if (amtSold > part.amtInStock)
    System.out.printf("Cannot sell more than you have: ignored\n");
else part.amtInStock -= amtSold;
```

Other fields (except the part number, since this is used to identify the record) could be updated similarly. When all changes have been made, the updated record is in memory in part. It must now be written back to the file in the same position from which it came. This could be done with this:

```
fp.seek(PartRecordSize * (n - 1));
writePartToFile(part, fp);
```

Note that we must call seek again since, after having read the record the first time, the file is positioned at the beginning of the *next* record. We must re-position it at the beginning of the record just read before writing the updated record. The net effect is that the updated record overwrites the old one.

Program P7.10 updates the amtInStock field of records in the parts file. The user is asked to enter a part number and the amount sold. The program searches the index for the part number using a binary search. If found, the record is retrieved from the file, updated in memory, and written back to the file. This is repeated until the user enters E.

Program P7.10

```
import java.io.*;
import java.util.*;
public class UpdateFile {
    static final int StringFixedLength = 20;
    static final int PartNumSize = 6;
    static final int PartRecordSize = 64;
    static int MaxRecords;

    public static void main(String[] args) throws IOException {
        Scanner in = new Scanner(System.in);
        Index[] index = retrieveIndex();
        int numRecords = index[0].recNum;
```

```
            System.out.printf("\nEnter part number (E to end): ");
            String pnum = in.next();
            while (!pnum.equalsIgnoreCase("E")) {
                updateRecord(pnum, index, numRecords);
                System.out.printf("\nEnter part number (E to end): ");
                pnum = in.next();
            } //end while
        } //end main

        public static void updateRecord(String pnum, Index[] index, int max) throws IOException {
            Scanner in = new Scanner(System.in);
            RandomAccessFile fp = new RandomAccessFile("parts.bin", "rw");

            int n = search(pnum, index, max);
            if (n < 0) System.out.printf("Part not found\n");
            else {
                fp.seek(PartRecordSize * (index[n].recNum - 1));
                Part part = readPartFromFile(fp);
                System.out.printf("Enter amount sold: ");
                int amtSold = in.nextInt();
                if (amtSold > part.amtInStock)
                    System.out.printf("You have %d: cannot sell more, ignored\n",
                                part.amtInStock);
                else {
                    part.amtInStock -= amtSold;
                    System.out.printf("Amount remaining: %d\n", part.amtInStock);
                    fp.seek(PartRecordSize * (index[n].recNum - 1));
                    writePartToFile(part, fp);
                    System.out.printf("%s %-11s %2d %5.2f\n", part.partNum, part.name,
                                                  part.amtInStock, part.price);
                } //end if
            } //end if
            fp.close();
        } //end updateRecord

        public static Index[] retrieveIndex() throws IOException {
            RandomAccessFile f = new RandomAccessFile("index.bin", "rw");
            int MaxRecords = f.readInt();
            Index[] index = new Index[MaxRecords + 1];
            for (int j = 0; j <= MaxRecords; j++) {
                String pnum = "";
                for (int i = 0; i < PartNumSize; i++) pnum += f.readChar();
                index[j] = new Index(pnum, f.readInt());
            }
            f.close();
            return index;
        } //end retrieveIndex
```

```
    public static Part readPartFromFile(RandomAccessFile f) throws IOException {
        String pname = "";
        for (int h = 0; h < PartNumSize; h++) pname += f.readChar();
        char[] name = new char[StringFixedLength];
        for (int h = 0; h < StringFixedLength; h++) name[h] = f.readChar();
        String hold = new String(name, 0, StringFixedLength);
        return new Part(pname, hold.trim(), f.readInt(), f.readDouble());
    } //end readPartFromFile

    public static void writePartToFile(Part part, RandomAccessFile f) throws IOException {
        for (int h = 0; h < PartNumSize; h++) f.writeChar(part.partNum.charAt(h));
        int n = Math.min(part.name.length(), StringFixedLength);
        for (int h = 0; h < n; h++) f.writeChar(part.name.charAt(h));
        for (int h = n; h < StringFixedLength; h++) f.writeChar(' ');
        f.writeInt(part.amtInStock);
        f.writeDouble(part.price);
    } //end writePartToFile

    public static int search(String key, Index[] list, int n) {
    //searches list[1..n] for key. If found, it returns the location; otherwise
    //it returns the negative of the location in which key should be inserted.
        int lo = 1, hi = n;
        while (lo <= hi) {   // as long as more elements remain to consider
            int mid = (lo + hi) / 2;
            int cmp = key.compareToIgnoreCase(list[mid].partNum);
            if (cmp == 0) return mid;      // search succeeds
            if (cmp < 0) hi = mid - 1;     // key is 'less than' list[mid].partNum
            else lo = mid + 1;             // key is 'greater than' list[mid].partNum
        }
        return -lo;                        // key not found; insert in location lo
    } // end search

} //end class UpdateFile

// Part and Index classes go here
```

The following is a sample run of Program P7.10:

```
Enter part number (E to end): blj375
Enter amount sold: 2
Amount remaining: 10
BLJ375 Ball-Joint   10 11.95

Enter part number (E to end): blj375
Enter amount sold: 11
You have 10: cannot sell more, ignored

Enter part number (E to end): dkp080
Enter amount sold: 4
Amount remaining: 12
DKP080 Disc-Pads   12   9.99
```

```
Enter part number (E to end): gsf55
Part not found

Enter part number (E to end): gsf555
Enter amount sold: 1
Amount remaining: 8
GSF555 Gas-Filter   8   4.50

Enter part number (E to end): e
```

EXERCISES 7

1. What is the difference between a file opened with "`r`" and one opened with "`rw`"?

2. Write a program to determine whether two binary files are identical. If they are different, print the first byte number at which they differ.

3. Write a program to read a (binary) file of integers, sort the integers and write them back to the same file. Assume that all the numbers can be stored in an array.

4. Repeat (3) but assume that only 20 numbers can be stored in memory (in an array) at any one time. Hint: you will need to use at least 2 additional files for temporary output.

5. Write a program to read two sorted files of integers and merge the values to a third sorted file.

6. Write a program to read a text file and produce another text file in which all lines are less than some given length. Make sure to break lines in sensible places; for example, avoid breaking words or putting isolated punctuation marks at the beginning of a line.

7. What is the purpose of creating an index for a file?

    The following are some records from an employee file. The fields are employee number (the key), name, job title, telephone number, monthly salary and tax to be deducted.

    ```
    STF425, Julie Johnson, Secretary, 623-3321, 2500, 600
    COM319, Ian McLean, Programmer, 676-1319, 3200, 800
    SYS777, Jean Kendall, Systems Analyst, 671-2025, 4200, 1100
    JNR591, Lincoln Kadoo, Operator, 657-0266, 2800, 700
    MSN815, Camille Kelly, Clerical Assistant, 652-5345, 2100, 500
    STF273, Anella Bayne, Data Entry Manager, 632-5324, 3500, 850
    SYS925, Riaz Ali, Senior Programmer, 636-8679, 4800, 1300
    ```

    Assume that the records are stored in a binary file in the order given.

    a. How can a record be retrieved given the record number?

    b. How can a record be retrieved given the key of the record?

    c.   As the file is loaded, create an index in which the keys are in the order given. How is such an index searched for a given key?

    d.   As the file is loaded, create an index in which the keys are sorted. Given a key, how is the corresponding record retrieved?

    Discuss what changes must be made to the index when records are added to and deleted from the file.

8.   For the "parts file" application discussed in this chapter, write methods for (i) adding new records and (ii) deleting records.

CHAPTER 8

■ ■ ■

Introduction to Binary Trees

In this chapter, we will explain the following:

- The difference between a tree and a binary tree

- How to perform pre-order, in-order, and post-order traversals of a binary tree

- How to represent a binary tree in a computer program

- How to build a binary tree from given data

- What a binary search tree is and how to build one

- How to write a program to do a word-frequency count of words in a passage

- How to use an array as a binary tree representation

- How to write some recursive functions to obtain information about a binary tree

- How to delete a node from a binary search tree

8.1 Trees

A *tree* is a finite set of nodes such that the following are both true:

- There is one specially designated node called the *root* of the tree.

- The remaining nodes are partitioned into $m \geq 0$ disjoint sets $T_1, T_2, ..., T_m$, and each of these sets is a tree.

The trees $T_1, T_2, ..., T_m$, are called the *subtrees* of the root. We use a recursive definition since recursion is an innate characteristic of tree structures. Figure 8-1 illustrates a tree. By convention, the root is drawn at the top, and the tree grows downward.

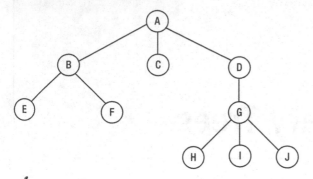

Figure 8-1. *A tree*

The root is A. There are three subtrees rooted at B, C, and D, respectively. The tree rooted at B has two subtrees, the one rooted at C has no subtrees, and the one rooted at D has one subtree. Each node of a tree is the root of a subtree.

The *degree* of a node is the number of subtrees of the node. Think of it as the number of lines leaving the node. For example, degree(A) = 3, degree(C) = 0, degree(D) = 1, and degree(G) = 3.

We use the terms *parent, child,* and *sibling* to refer to the nodes of a tree. For example, the parent A has three children, which are B, C, and D; the parent B has two children, which are E and F; and the parent D has one child, G, which has three children: H, I, and J. Note that a node may be the child of one node but the parent of another.

Sibling nodes are child nodes of the same parent. For example, B, C, and D are siblings; E and F are siblings; and H, I, and J are siblings.

In a tree, a node may have several children but, except for the root, only one parent. The root has no parent. Put another way, a nonroot node has exactly one line leading *into* it.

A *terminal* node (also called a *leaf*) is a node of degree 0. A *branch* node is a nonterminal node. In Figure 8-1, C, E, F, H, I, and J are leaves, while A, B, D, and G are branch nodes.

The *moment* of a tree is the number of nodes in the tree. The tree in Figure 8-1 has moment 10.

The *weight* of a tree is the number of leaves in the tree. The tree in Figure 8-1 has weight 6.

The *level* (or *depth*) of a node is the number of branches that must be traversed on the path to the node from the root. The root has level 0.

In the tree in Figure 8-1, B, C, and D are at level 1; E, F, and G are at level 2; and H, I, and J are at level 3. The level of a node is a measure of the depth of the node in the tree.

The *height* of a tree is the number of levels in the tree. The tree in Figure 8-1 has height 4. Note that the height of a tree is one more than its highest level.

If the relative order of the subtrees $T_1, T_2, ..., T_m$ is important, the tree is an *ordered* tree. If order is unimportant, the tree is *oriented*.

A *forest* is a set of zero or more disjoint trees, as shown in Figure 8-2.

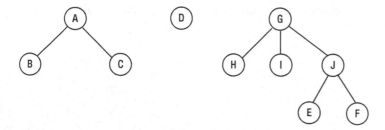

Figure 8-2. *A forest of three disjoint trees*

While general trees are of some interest, by far the most important kind of tree is a binary tree.

8.2 Binary Trees

A *binary tree* is a classic example of a nonlinear data structure—compare this to a linear list where we identify a first item, a next item, and a last item. A binary tree is a special case of the more general *tree* data structure, but it is the most useful and most widely used kind of tree. A binary tree is best defined using the following recursive definition:

A *binary tree*

a.   is empty

or

b.   consists of a root and two subtrees—a left and a right—with each subtree being
    a binary tree

A consequence of this definition is that a node always has two subtrees, any of which may be empty. Another consequence is that if a node has *one* nonempty subtree, it is important to distinguish whether it is on the left or right. Here's an example:

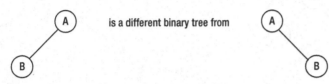

is a different binary tree from

The first has an empty right subtree, while the second has an empty left subtree. However, as *trees*, they are the same.

The following are examples of binary trees.

Here's a binary tree with one node, the root:

Here are binary trees with two nodes:

Here are binary trees with three nodes:

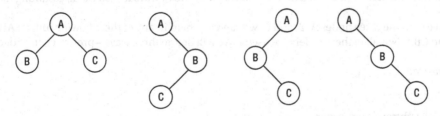

Here are binary trees with all left subtrees empty and all right subtrees empty:

Here is a binary tree where each node, except the leaves, has exactly two subtrees; this is called a *complete* binary tree:

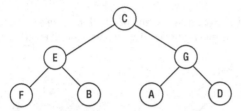

Here is a general binary tree:

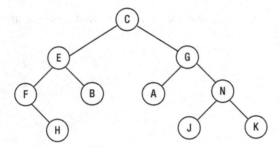

8.3 Traversing a Binary Tree

In many applications, we want to visit the nodes of a binary tree in some systematic way. For now, we'll think of "visit" as simply printing the information at the node. For a tree of n nodes, there are $n!$ ways to visit them, assuming that each node is visited once.

For example, for a tree with the three nodes A, B, and C, we can visit them in any of the following orders: ABC, ACB, BCA, BAC, CAB, and CBA. Not all of these orders are useful. We will define three ways—pre-order, in-order, and post-order—that are useful.

This is *pre-order t raversal*:

1.   Visit the root.

2.   Traverse the left subtree in pre-order.

3.   Traverse the right subtree in pre-order.

Note that the traversal is defined recursively. In steps 2 and 3, we must reapply the definition of pre-order traversal, which says "visit the root, and so on."

The *pre-order* traversal of this tree

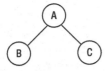

is A B C.

The *pre-order* traversal of this tree

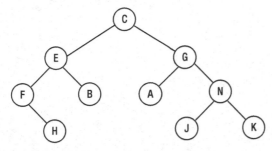

is C E F H B G A N J K.

This is *in-order traversal*:

1. Traverse the left subtree in in-order.

2. Visit the root.

3. Traverse the right subtree in in-order.

Here we traverse the left subtree first, then the root, and then the right subtree.
The *in-order* traversal of this tree

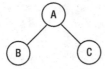

is B A C.

The *in-order* traversal of this tree

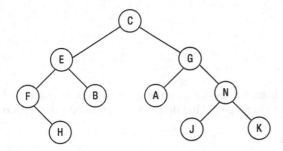

is F H E B C A G J N K

This is *post-order traversal*:

1. Traverse the left subtree in post-order.

2. Traverse the right subtree in post-order.

3. Visit the root.

Here we traverse the left and right subtrees *before* visiting the root.
The *post-order* traversal of this tree

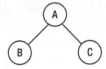

is B C A.
The *post-order* traversal of this tree

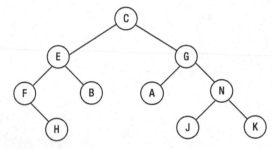

is H F B E A J K N G C.

Note that the traversals derive their names from the place where we visit the root relative to the traversal of the left and right subtrees. As another example, consider a binary tree that can represent the following arithmetic expression:

(54 + 37) / (72 - 5 * 13)

Here is the tree:

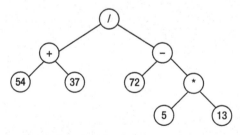

The leaves of the tree contain the operands, and the branch nodes contain the operators. Given a node containing an operator, the left subtree represents the first operand, and the right subtree represents the second operand.

The pre-order traversal is: / + 54 37 - 72 * 5 13
The in-order traversal is: 54 + 37 / 72 - 5 * 13
The post-order traversal is: 54 37 + 72 5 13 * - /

The post-order traversal can be used in conjunction with a stack to evaluate the expression. The algorithm is as follows:

```
initialize a stack, S, to empty
while we have not reached the end of the traversal
   get the next item, x
   if x is an operand, push it onto S
   if x is an operator
      pop its operands from S,
      apply the operator
      push the result onto S
   endif
endwhile
pop S; // this is the value of the expression
```

Consider the post-order traversal: 54 37 + 72 5 13 * - /. It is evaluated as follows:

1. The next item is 54; push 54 onto S; S contains 54.

2. The next item is 37; push 37 onto S; S contains 54 37 (the top is on the right).

3. The next item is +; pop 37 and 54 from S; apply + to 54 and 37, giving 91; push 91 onto S; S contains 91.

4. The next item is 72; push 72 onto S; S contains 91 72.

5. The next items are 5 and 13; these are pushed onto S; S contains 91 72 5 13.

6. The next item is *; pop 13 and 5 from S; apply * to 5 and 13, giving 65; push 65 onto S; S contains 91 72 65.

7. The next item is –; pop 65 and 72 from S; apply – to 72 and 65, giving 7; push 7 onto S; S contains 91 7.

8. The next item is /; pop 7 and 91 from S; apply / to 91and 7, giving 13; push 13 onto S; S contains 13.

9. We have reached the end of the traversal; we pop S, getting 13—the result of the expression.

Note that when operands are popped from the stack, the first one popped is the second operand, and the second one popped is the first operand. This does not matter for addition and multiplication but is important for subtraction and division.

8.4 Representing a Binary Tree

As a minimum, each node of a binary tree consists of three fields: a field containing the data at the node, a pointer to the left subtree, and a pointer to the right subtree. For example, suppose the data to be stored at each node is a word. We can begin by writing a class (TreeNode, say) with three instance variables and a constructor that creates a TreeNode object.

```
class TreeNode {
   NodeData data;
   TreeNode left, right;
```

```
        TreeNode(NodeData d) {
            data = d;
            left = right = null;
        }
}
```

To keep our options open, we have defined TreeNode in terms of a general data type that we call NodeData. Any program that wants to use TreeNode must provide its own definition of NodeData.

For example, if the data at a node is an integer, NodeData could be defined as follows:

```
class NodeData {
    int num;

    public NodeData(int n) {
        num = n;
    }
} //end class NodeData
```

A similar definition can be used if the data is a character. But we are not restricted to single-field data. Any number of fields can be used. Later, we will write a program to do a frequency count of words in a passage. Each node will contain a word and its frequency count. For that program, NodeData will contain the following, among other things:

```
class NodeData {
    String word;
    int freq;

    public NodeData(String w) {
        word = w;
        freq = 0;
    }
} //end class NodeData
```

In addition to the nodes of the tree, we will need to know the root of the tree. Keep in mind that once we know the root, we have access to all the nodes in the tree via the left and right pointers. Thus, a binary tree is defined solely by its root. We will develop a BinaryTree class to work with binary trees. The only instance variable will be root. The class will start as follows:

```
class BinaryTree {
    TreeNode root;          // the only field in this class

    BinaryTree() {
        root = null;
    }
    //methods in the class
} //end class BinaryTree
```

The constructor is not really necessary since Java will set root to null when a BinaryTree object is created. However, we include it to emphasize that, in an empty binary tree, root is null.

If you want, you can put the TreeNode class in its own file, TreeNode.java, and declare it public. However, in our programs, we will put the TreeNode class in the same file as BinaryTree since it is used only by BinaryTree. To do so, we must omit the word public and write class TreeNode.

8.5 Building a Binary Tree

Let's write a function to build a binary tree. Suppose we want to build a tree consisting of a single node, like this:

The data will be supplied as A @ @. Each @ denotes the position of a null pointer.
To build the following, we will supply the data as A B @ @ C @ @:

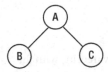

Each node is immediately followed by its left subtree and then its right subtree.
By comparison, to build the following, we will supply the data as A B @ C @ @ @.

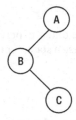

The two @s after C denote its left and right subtrees (null), and the last @ denotes the right subtree of A (null).
And to build the following, we supply the data as C E F @ H @ @ B @ @ G A @ @ N J @ @ K @ @.

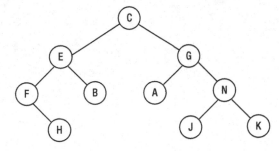

Given data in this format, the following function will build the tree and return a pointer to its root:

```
static TreeNode buildTree(Scanner in) {
    String str = in.next();
    if (str.equals("@")) return null;
    TreeNode p = new TreeNode(new NodeData(str));
    p.left = buildTree(in);
    p.right = buildTree(in);
    return p;
} //end buildTree
```

The function will read data from the input stream associated with the Scanner, in. It uses the following definition of NodeData:

```
class NodeData {
    String word;

    public NodeData(String w) {
        word = w;
    }
} //end class NodeData
```

We will call buildTree from the following constructor:

```
public BinaryTree(Scanner in) {
    root = buildTree(in);
}
```

Suppose a user class has its tree data stored in the file btree.in. It can create a binary tree, bt, with the following code:

```
Scanner in = new Scanner(new FileReader("btree.in"));
BinaryTree bt = new BinaryTree(in);
```

Having built the tree, we should want to check that it has been built properly. One way to do that is to perform traversals. Suppose we want to print the nodes of bt in pre-order. It would be nice to be able to use a statement such as this:

```
bt.preOrder();
```

To do so, we would need to write an instance method preOrder in the BinaryTree class. The method is shown in the following listing of the class. It also includes the methods inOrder and postOrder. We also retain the no-arg constructor so the user can start with an empty binary tree, if desired.

The BinaryTree class

```
import java.util.*;
public class BinaryTree {
    TreeNode root;

    public BinaryTree() {
        root = null;
    }
    public BinaryTree(Scanner in) {
        root = buildTree(in);
    }

    public static TreeNode buildTree(Scanner in) {
        String str = in.next();
        if (str.equals("@")) return null;
        TreeNode p = new TreeNode(new NodeData(str));
        p.left = buildTree(in);
        p.right = buildTree(in);
```

```
            return p;
        } //end buildTree

        public void preOrder() {
            preOrderTraversal(root);
        }

        public void preOrderTraversal(TreeNode node) {
            if (node!= null) {
                node.data.visit();
                preOrderTraversal(node.left);
                preOrderTraversal(node.right);
            }
        } //end preOrderTraversal

        public void inOrder() {
            inOrderTraversal(root);
        }

        public void inOrderTraversal(TreeNode node) {
            if (node!= null) {
                inOrderTraversal(node.left);
                node.data.visit();
                inOrderTraversal(node.right);
            }
        } //end inOrderTraversal

        public void postOrder() {
            postOrderTraversal(root);
        }

        public void postOrderTraversal(TreeNode node) {
            if (node!= null) {
                postOrderTraversal(node.left);
                postOrderTraversal(node.right);
                node.data.visit();
            }
        } //end postOrderTraversal

    } //end class BinaryTree
```

The traversals all use the statement node.data.visit();. Since node.data is a NodeData object, the NodeData class should contain the method visit. In this example, we just print the value at the node, so we write visit as follows:

```
public void visit() {
    System.out.printf("%s ", word);
}
```

We now write Program P8.1, which builds a binary tree and prints the nodes in pre-order, in-order, and post-order. As usual, we can declare the class BinaryTree as public and store it in its own file, BinaryTree.java. We can also declare the class TreeNode as public and store it in its own file, TeeeNode.java. However, if you prefer to have the entire program in one file, BinaryTreeTest.java, you can omit the word public and include the classes TreeNode and BinaryTree in the positions indicated in Program P8.1.

Program P8.1

```java
import java.io.*;
import java.util.*;
public class BinaryTreeTest {

    public static void main(String[] args) throws IOException {
        Scanner in = new Scanner(new FileReader("btree.in"));
        BinaryTree bt = new BinaryTree(in);
        System.out.printf("\nThe pre-order traversal is: ");
        bt.preOrder();
        System.out.printf("\n\nThe in-order traversal is: ");
        bt.inOrder();
        System.out.printf("\n\nThe post-order traversal is: ");
        bt.postOrder();
        System.out.printf("\n\n");
        in.close();
    } // end main
} //end class BinaryTreeTest

class NodeData {
    String word;

    public NodeData(String w) {
        word = w;
    }

    public void visit() {
        System.out.printf("%s ", word);
    }
} //end class NodeData

// class TreeNode goes here

// class BinaryTree goes here
```

If btree.in contains C E F @ H @ @ B @ @ G A @ @ N J @ @ K @ @, then Program P8.1 builds the following tree:

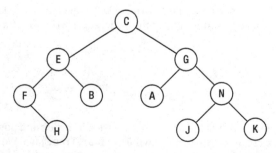

It then prints the traversals as follows:

The pre-order traversal is: C E F H B G A N J K

The in-order traversal is: F H E B C A G J N K

The post-order traversal is: H F B E A J K N G C

The `buildTree` method is not restricted to single-character data; any string (not containing whitespace since we use %s to read the data) can be used.

For example, if btree.in contains this:

hat din bun @ @ fan @ @ rum kit @ @ win @ @

then Program P8.1 builds the following tree:

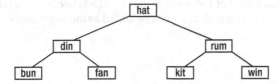

It then prints the traversals as follows:

The pre-order traversal is: hat din bun fan rum kit win

The in-order traversal is: bun din fan hat kit rum win

The post-order traversal is: bun fan din kit win rum hat

In passing, note that the in-order and pre-order traversals of a binary tree uniquely define that tree. It's the same for in-order and post-order. However, pre-order and post-order do not uniquely define the tree. In other words, it is possible to have two *different* trees A and B where the pre-order and post-order traversals of A are the same as the pre-order and post-order traversals of B, respectively. As an exercise, give an example of two such trees.

8.6 Binary Search Trees

Consider one possible binary tree built with the three-letter words shown in Figure 8-3.

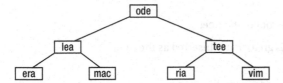

Figure 8-3. *Binary search tree with some three-letter words*

This is a special kind of binary tree. It has the property that, given *any* node, a word in the left subtree is "smaller," and a word in the right subtree is "greater" than the word at the node. (Here, *smaller* and *greater* refer to alphabetical order.)

Such a tree is called a *binary search tree* (BST). It facilitates the search for a given key using a method of searching similar to the binary search of an array.

Consider the search for ria. Starting at the root, ria is compared with ode. Since ria is greater (in alphabetical order) than ode, we can conclude that if it is in the tree, it must be in the right subtree. It must be so since all the nodes in the left subtree are smaller than ode.

Following the right subtree of ode, we next compare ria with tee. Since ria is smaller than tee, we follow the left subtree of tee. We then compare ria with ria, and the search ends successfully.

But what if we were searching for fun?

1. fun is smaller than ode, so we go left.

2. fun is smaller than lea, so we go left again.

3. fun is greater than era, so we must go right.

But since the right subtree of era is empty, we can conclude that fun is not in the tree. If it is necessary to add fun to the tree, note that we have also found the place where it must be added. It must be added as the right subtree of era, as shown in Figure 8-4.

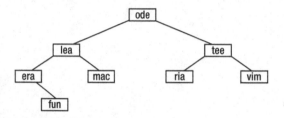

Figure 8-4. *BST after adding fun*

Thus, not only does the binary search tree facilitate searching, but if an item is not found, it can be easily inserted. It combines the speed advantage of a binary search with the easy insertion of a linked list.

The tree drawn in Figure 8-3 is the optimal binary search tree for the seven given words. This means that it is the best possible tree for these words in the sense that no shallower binary tree can be built from these words. It gives the same number of comparisons to find a key as a binary search on a linear array containing these words.

But this is not the only possible search tree for these words. Suppose the words came in one at a time, and as each word came in, it was added to the tree in such a way that the tree remained a binary search tree. The final tree built will depend on the order in which the words came in. For example, suppose the words came in this order:

        mac tee ode era ria lea vim

Initially the tree is empty. When mac comes in, it becomes the root of the tree.

-   tee comes next and is compared with mac. Since tee is greater, it is inserted as the right subtree of mac.

-   ode comes next and is greater than mac, so we go right; ode is smaller than tee, so it inserted as the left subtree of tee.

-   era is next and is smaller than mac, so it is inserted as the left subtree of mac.

The tree built so far is shown in Figure 8-5.

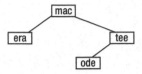

Figure 8-5. *BST after adding mac, tee, ode, era*

- ria is next and is greater than mac, so we go right; it is smaller than tee, so we go left; it is greater than ode, so it is inserted as the right subtree of ode.

Following this procedure, lea is inserted as the right subtree of era, and vim is inserted as the right subtree of tee, giving the final tree shown in Figure 8-6.

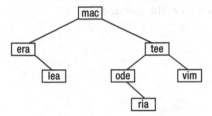

Figure 8-6. *BST after adding all seven words*

Note that the tree obtained is quite different from the optimal search tree. The number of comparisons required to find a given word has also changed. For instance, ria now requires four comparisons; it required three previously, and lea now requires three as opposed to two previously. But it's not all bad news; era now requires two as compared to three previously.

It can be proved that if the words come in random order, then the average search time for a given word is approximately 1.4 times the average for the optimal search tree, that is, $1.4\log_2 n$, for a tree of n nodes.

But what about the worst case? If the words come in alphabetical order, then the tree built will be that shown in Figure 8-7.

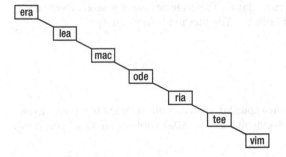

Figure 8-7. *A degenerate tree*

Searching such a tree is reduced to a sequential search of a linked list. This kind of tree is called a *degenerate* tree. Certain orders of the words will give some very unbalanced trees. As an exercise, draw the trees obtained for the following orders of the words:

- vim tee ria ode mac lea era

- era vim lea tee mac ria ode

- vim era lea tee ria mac ode

- lea mac vim tee era ria ode

8.7 Building a Binary Search Tree

We now write a function to find or insert an item in a binary search tree. Assuming the previous definitions of TreeNode and BinaryTree, we write the function findOrInsert, an instance method in the BinaryTree class. The function searches the tree for a NodeData item, d. If it is found, it returns a pointer to the node. If it is not found, the item is inserted in the tree in its appropriate place, and the function returns a pointer to the new node.

```
public TreeNode findOrInsert(NodeData d) {
    if (root == null) return root = new TreeNode(d);
    TreeNode curr = root;
    int cmp;
    while ((cmp = d.compareTo(curr.data)) != 0) {
        if (cmp < 0) { //try left
            if (curr.left == null) return  curr.left = new TreeNode(d);
            curr = curr.left;
        }
        else { //try right
            if (curr.right == null) return curr.right = new TreeNode(d);
            curr = curr.right;
        }
    }
    //d is in the tree; return pointer to the node
    return curr;
} //end findOrInsert
```

In the while condition, we use the expression d.compareTo(curr.data). This suggests that we need to write a compareTo method in the NodeData class to compare two NodeData objects. The method is shown here:

```
public int compareTo(NodeData d) {
    return this.word.compareTo(d.word);
}
```

It simply calls the compareTo method from the String class since NodeData consists only of a String object. Even if there were other fields in the class, we could, if we wanted, still decide that two NodeData objects are to be compared based on the word field or on any other field.

8.7.1 Example: Word Frequency Count

We will illustrate the ideas developed so far by writing a program to do a frequency count of the words in a passage. We will store the words in a binary search tree. The tree is searched for each incoming word. If the word is not found, it is added to the tree, and its frequency count is set to 1. If the word is found, then its frequency count is incremented by 1. At the end of the input, an in-order traversal of the tree gives the words in alphabetical order.

First, we must define the NodeData class. This will consist of two fields (a word and its frequency), a constructor, a function to add 1 to the frequency, compareTo and visit. Here is the class:

```
class NodeData {
    String word;
    int freq;

    public NodeData(String w) {
        word = w;
        freq = 0;
    }
    public void incrFreq() {
        ++freq;
    }

    public int compareTo(NodeData d) {
        return this.word.compareTo(d.word);
    }

    public void visit() {
        WordFrequencyBST.out.printf("%-15s %2d\n", word, freq);
    }
} //end class NodeData
```

Note the method to increase the frequency by 1. In visit, we print the data at a node using the object WordFrequencyBST.out. We will write the class WordFrequencyBST shortly, but, for now, note that we will let it determine where the output should go, and out specifies the output stream. If you wanted, you could send the results to the standard output stream using System.out.printf.

The gist of the algorithm for building the search tree is as follows:

```
create empty tree; set root to NULL
while (there is another word) {
    get the word
    search for word in tree; insert if necessary and set frequency to 0
    add 1 to frequency //for an old word or a newly inserted one
}
print words and frequencies
```

For our program, we will define a word to be any consecutive sequence of uppercase or lowercase letters. In other words, any nonletter will delimit a word. In particular, whitespace and punctuation marks will delimit a word. If in is a Scanner object, we can specify this information with this statement:

```
in.useDelimiter("[^a-zA-Z]+");  // ^ means "not"
```

The part inside the square brackets means "any character that is *not* a lowercase or uppercase letter," and the + means one or more of those characters.

Normally, Scanner uses whitespace to delimit the tokens read using next(). However, we can change that and specify whatever characters we want to be used as delimiters. For example, to use a colon as a delimiter, we can write this:

```
in.useDelimiter(":");
```

When we use in.next() in our program, it will return a string consisting of the characters up to, but not including, the next colon. To use a colon or a comma, say, as a delimiter, we can write this:

```
in.useDelimiter("[:,]"); //make a set using [ and ]
```

The square brackets denote a set. To use a colon, comma, period, or question mark, we write this:

```
in.useDelimiter("[:,\\.\\?]");
```

The period and question mark are so-called *meta* characters (used for a special purpose), so we must specify each using an escape sequence: \. and \?. Recall that, within a string, \ is specified by \\.

If we want to specify that a delimiter is any character that is *not* a lowercase letter, we write this:

```
in.useDelimiter("[^a-z]");  // ^ denotes negation, "not"
```

The expression a-z denotes a range—from a to z.

If we add + after the right square bracket, it denotes a sequence of "one or more" nonlowercase characters. So, since we want that a delimiter to be a sequence of "one or more" nonletters (neither uppercase nor lowercase), we write this:

```
in.useDelimiter("[^a-zA-Z]+");
```

We now write Program P8.2 to do the frequency count of words in the file wordFreq.in. It simply reflects the algorithm we outlined previously.

Program P8.2

```
import java.io.*;
import java.util.*;
public class WordFrequencyBST {
    static Scanner in;
    static PrintWriter out;

    public static void main(String[] args) throws IOException {
        in = new Scanner(new FileReader("wordFreq.in"));
        out = new PrintWriter(new FileWriter("wordFreq.out"));

        BinaryTree bst = new BinaryTree();

        in.useDelimiter("[^a-zA-Z]+");
        while (in.hasNext()) {
            String word = in.next().toLowerCase();
            TreeNode node = bst.findOrInsert(new NodeData(word));
            node.data.incrFreq();
        }
        out.printf("\nWords        Frequency\n\n");
        bst.inOrder();
        in.close(); out.close();
    } // end main

} //end class WordFrequencyBST
```

```
class NodeData {
    String word;
    int freq;

    public NodeData(String w) {
        word = w;
        freq = 0;
    }
    public void incrFreq() {
        ++freq;
    }

    public int compareTo(NodeData d) {
        return this.word.compareTo(d.word);
    }

    public void visit() {
        WordFrequencyBST.out.printf("%-15s %2d\n", word, freq);
    }
} //end class NodeData

// class TreeNode goes here

// class BinaryTree (with findOrInsert added) goes here
```

Note that in and out are declared as static class variables. This is not necessary for in, which could have been declared in main since it is used only there. However, the visit method of the NodeData class needs to know where to send the output, so it needs access to out. We give it access by declaring out as a class variable.

Since findOrInsert requires a NodeData object as its argument, we must create a NodeData object from word before calling it in this statement:

```
TreeNode node = bst.findOrInsert(new NodeData(word));
```

An in-order traversal of the search tree yields the words in alphabetical order.
Suppose the file wordFreq.in contains the following data:

```
If you can trust yourself when all men doubt you;
If you can dream - and not make dreams your master;
If you can talk with crowds and keep your virtue;
If all men count with you, but none too much;
If neither foes nor loving friends can hurt you;
```

When Program P8.2 is run, it sends its output to the file, wordFreq.out. Here is the output:

Words	Frequency
all	2
and	2
but	1
can	4
count	1
crowds	1
doubt	1
dream	1
dreams	1
foes	1
friends	1
hurt	1
if	5
keep	1
loving	1
make	1
master	1
men	2
much	1
neither	1
none	1
nor	1
not	1
talk	1
too	1
trust	1
virtue	1
when	1
with	2
you	6
your	2
yourself	1

8.8 Building a Binary Tree with Parent Pointers

We have seen how to perform pre-order, in-order, and post-order traversals using recursion (which is implemented using a stack) or an explicit stack. We now look at a third possibility. First, let's build the tree so that it contains "parent" pointers.

Each node now contains an additional field—a pointer to its parent. The parent field of the root will be null. For example, in the tree shown in Figure 8-8, H's parent field points to F, A's parent field points to G, and G's parent field points to C.

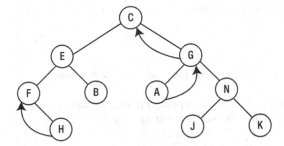

Figure 8-8. *A binary tree with some parent pointers*

To represent such a tree, we now declare TreeNode as follows:

```
class TreeNode {
    NodeData data;
    TreeNode left, right, parent;

    public TreeNode(NodeData d) {
        data = d;
        left = right = parent = null;
    }
} //end class TreeNode
```

We can now rewrite buildTree as follows:

```
public static TreeNode buildTree(Scanner in) {
    String str = in.next();
    if (str.equals("@")) return null;
    TreeNode p = new TreeNode(new NodeData(str));
    p.left = buildTree(in);
    if (p.left != null) p.left.parent = p;
    p.right = buildTree(in);
    if (p.right != null) p.right.parent = p;
    return p;
} //end buildTree
```

After we build the left subtree of a node p, we check whether it is null. If it is, there is nothing further to do. If it is not and q is its root, we set q.parent to p. Similar remarks apply to the right subtree.

With parent fields, we can do traversals without recursion and the stacking/unstacking of arguments and local variables implied by it. For example, we can perform an in-order traversal as follows:

```
get the first node in in-order; call it "node"
while (node is not null) {
    visit node
    get next node in in-order
}
```

Given the non-null root of a tree, we can find the first node in in-order with this:

```
TreeNode node = root;
while (node.left != null) node = node.left;
```

We go as far left as possible. When we can't go any further, we have reached the first node in in-order. After the code is executed, node will point to the first node in in-order.

The main problem to solve is the following: given a pointer to any node, return a pointer to its *in-order successor*, that is, the node that comes *after* it in in-order, if any. The last node in in-order will have no successor.

There are two cases to consider:

1. If the node has a nonempty right subtree, then its in-order successor is the first node in the in-order traversal of that right subtree. We can find it with the following code, which returns a pointer to the in-order successor:

```
if (node.right != null) {
    node = node.right;
    while (node.left != null) node = node.left;
    return node;
}
```

For example, consider the following tree:

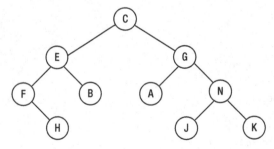

The in-order successor of G is found by going right once (to N) and then as far left as possible (to J). J is the in-order successor of G.

2. If the node has an empty right subtree, then its in-order successor is one of its ancestors. Which one? It's the lowest ancestor for which the given node is in its *left* subtree. For example, what is the in-order successor of B?

   We look at B's parent, E. Since B is in the right subtree of E, it is not E.

   We then look at E's parent, C. Since E (and hence, B) is in the left subtree of C, we conclude that C is the in-order successor of B.

   Note, however, that K, being the last node in in-order, has no successor. If we follow parent pointers from K, we never find one with K in its left subtree. In this case, our function will return null.

Using these ideas, we write inOrderTraversal as an instance method in the BinaryTree class and inOrderSuccessor as a static method called by it.

```
public void inOrderTraversal() {
    if (root == null) return;
    //find first node in in-order
    TreeNode node = root;
    while (node.left != null) node = node.left;
    while (node != null) {
        node.data.visit(); //from the NodeData class
        node = inOrderSuccessor(node);
    }
} //end inOrderTraversal

private static TreeNode inOrderSuccessor(TreeNode node) {
    if (node.right != null) {
        node = node.right;
        while (node.left != null) node = node.left;
        return node;
    }
    //node has no right subtree; search for the lowest ancestor of the
    //node for which the node is in the ancestor's left subtree
    //return null if there is no successor (node is the last in in-order)
    TreeNode parent = node.parent;
    while (parent != null && parent.right == node) {
        node = parent;
        parent = node.parent;
    }
    return parent;
} //end inOrderSuccessor
```

As an exercise, write similar functions to perform pre-order and post-order traversals. We will write a program to test inOrderTraversal in the next section.

8.8.1 Building a Binary Search Tree with Parent Pointers

We can modify the findOrInsert function from the BinaryTree class to build a search tree with parent pointers. This can be done with the following:

```
public TreeNode findOrInsert(NodeData d) {
//Searches the tree for d; if found, returns a pointer to the node.
//If not found, d is added and a pointer to the new node returned.
//The parent field of d is set to point to its parent.
    TreeNode curr, node;
    int cmp;

    if (root == null) {
        node = new TreeNode(d);
        node.parent = null;
        return root = node;
    }
    curr = root;
```

```
        while ((cmp = d.compareTo(curr.data)) != 0) {
            if (cmp < 0) { //try left
                if (curr.left == null) {
                    curr.left  = new TreeNode(d);
                    curr.left.parent = curr;
                    return curr.left;
                }
                curr = curr.left;
            }
            else { //try right
                if (curr.right == null)  {
                    curr.right = new TreeNode(d);
                    curr.right.parent = curr;
                    return curr.right;
                }
                curr = curr.right;
            } //end else
        } //end while
        return curr;  //d is in the tree; return pointer to the node
    } //end findOrInsert
```

When we need to add a node (N, say) to the tree, if curr points to the node from which the new node will hang, we simply set the parent field of N to curr.

We can test findOrInsert and inOrderTraversal with Program P8.3.

Program P8.3

```
    import java.io.*;
    import java.util.*;
    public class P8_3BinarySearchTreeTest {
        public static void main(String[] args) throws IOException {

            Scanner in = new Scanner(new FileReader("words.in"));

            BinaryTree bst = new BinaryTree();

            in.useDelimiter("[^a-zA-Z]+");
            while (in.hasNext()) {
                String word = in.next().toLowerCase();
                TreeNode node = bst.findOrInsert(new NodeData(word));
            }
            System.out.printf("\n\nThe in-order traversal is: ");
            bst.inOrderTraversal();
            System.out.printf("\n");
            in.close();
        } // end main

    } //end class P8_3BinarySearchTreeTest
```

```java
class NodeData {
   String word;

   public NodeData(String w) {
      word = w;
   }
   public int compareTo(NodeData d) {
      return this.word.compareTo(d.word);
   }

   public void visit() {
      System.out.printf("%s ", word);
   }
} //end class NodeData

class TreeNode {
   NodeData data;
   TreeNode left, right, parent;

   public TreeNode(NodeData d) {
      data = d;
      left = right = parent = null;
   }
} //end class TreeNode

//The BinaryTree class - only the methods relevant to this problem are shown
class BinaryTree {
   TreeNode root;

   public BinaryTree() {
      root = null;
   }

    public void inOrderTraversal() {
      if (root == null) return;
      //find first node in in-order
      TreeNode node = root;
      while (node.left != null) node = node.left;
      while (node != null) {
         node.data.visit(); //from the NodeData class
         node = inOrderSuccessor(node);
      }
   } //end inOrderTraversal

   private static TreeNode inOrderSuccessor(TreeNode node) {
      if (node.right != null) {
         node = node.right;
         while (node.left != null) node = node.left;
         return node;
      }
```

```
            //node has no right subtree; search for the lowest ancestor of the
            //node for which the node is in the ancestor's left subtree
            //return null if there is no successor (node is the last in in-order)
            TreeNode parent = node.parent;
            while (parent != null && parent.right == node) {
                node = parent;
                parent = node.parent;
            }
            return parent;
        } //end inOrderSuccessor

        //The method findOrInsert from this Section goes here
    } //end class BinaryTree
```

Program P8.3 reads words from the file words.in, builds the search tree, and performs an in-order traversal to print the words in alphabetical order. For example, suppose words.in contains the following:

```
mac tee ode era ria lea vim
```

Program P8.3 builds the following binary search tree with parent pointers:

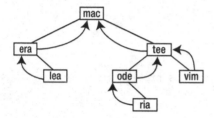

It then prints this:

```
The in-order traversal is: era lea mac ode ria tee vim
```

8.9 Level-Order Traversal

In addition to pre-order, in-order, and post-order, another useful traversal is *level-order*. Here we traverse the tree level by level, starting at the root. At each level, we traverse the nodes from left to right. For example, suppose we have the following tree:

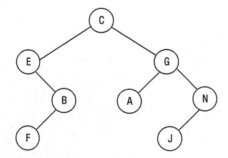

Its level-order traversal is C E G B A N F J.

To perform a level-order traversal, we will need to use a queue. The following algorithm shows how:

```
add the root to the queue, Q
while (Q is not empty) {
   remove item at the head of Q and store in p
   visit p
   if (left(p) is not null) add left(p) to Q
   if (right(p) is not null) add right(p) to Q
}
```

For the previous tree, the following occurs:

- Put C on Q.

- Q is not empty, so remove and visit C; add E and G to Q, which now has E G.

- Q is not empty, so remove and visit E; add B to Q, which now has G B.

- Q is not empty; remove and visit G; add A and N to Q, which now has B A N.

- Q is not empty; remove and visit B; add F to Q, which now has A N F.

- Q is not empty; remove and visit A; add nothing to Q, which now has N F.

- Q is not empty; remove and visit N; add J to Q, which now has F J.

- Q is not empty; remove and visit F; add nothing to Q, which now has J.

- Q is not empty; remove and visit J; add nothing to Q, which is now empty.

- Q is empty; the traversal ends having visited the nodes in the order C E G B A N F J.

We will need the following to perform the queue operations. First, we define the class `QueueData` as follows:

```
public class QueueData {
   TreeNode node;

   public QueueData(TreeNode n) {
      node = n;
   }
} //end class QueueData
```

Next, we define the class QNode:

```
public class QNode {
   QueueData data;
   QNode next;

   public QNode(QueueData d) {
      data = d;
      next = null;
   }
} //end class QNode
```

And, finally, here's the class Queue:

```java
public class Queue {
    QNode head = null, tail = null;

    public boolean empty() {
        return head == null;
    }

    public void enqueue(QueueData nd) {
        QNode p = new QNode(nd);
        if (this.empty()) {
            head = p;
            tail = p;
        }
        else {
            tail.next = p;
            tail = p;
        }
    } //end enqueue

    public QueueData dequeue() {
        if (this.empty()) {
            System.out.printf("\nAttempt to remove from an empty queue\n");
            System.exit(1);
        }
        QueueData hold = head.data;
        head = head.next;
        if (head == null) tail = null;
        return hold;
    } //end dequeue
} //end class Queue
```

Note that if you put QueueData in the same file as Queue or the program that uses Queue, you must omit the word public. Similar remarks apply to the class QNode.

Using Queue and QueueData, we can write the instance method levelOrderTraversal in BinaryTree as follows:

```java
public void levelOrderTraversal() {
    Queue Q = new Queue();
    Q.enqueue(new QueueData(root));
    while (!Q.empty()) {
        QueueData temp = Q.dequeue();
        temp.node.data.visit();
        if (temp.node.left != null) Q.enqueue(new QueueData(temp.node.left));
        if (temp.node.right != null) Q.enqueue(new QueueData(temp.node.right));
    }
} //end levelOrderTraversal
```

Putting it all together, we write Program P8.4, which builds a tree using data from the file, btree.in, and performs a level-order traversal. Note that, in order to put the entire program in one file, only the class containing main is declared public. In the other classes, only the methods relevant to this problem are shown.

Program P8.4

```java
import java.io.*;
import java.util.*;
public class LevelOrderTest {
    public static void main(String[] args) throws IOException {

        Scanner in = new Scanner(new FileReader("btree.in"));
        BinaryTree bt = new BinaryTree(in);

        System.out.printf("\n\nThe level-order traversal is: ");
        bt.levelOrderTraversal();
        System.out.printf("\n");
        in.close();
    } // end main

} //end class LevelOrderTest

class NodeData {
    String word;

    public NodeData(String w) {
        word = w;
    }
    public void visit() {
        System.out.printf("%s ", word);
    }
} //end class NodeData

class TreeNode {
    NodeData data;
    TreeNode left, right, parent;

    public TreeNode(NodeData d) {
        data = d;
        left = right = parent = null;
    }
} //end class TreeNode

//The BinaryTree class - only the methods relevant to this problem are shown
class BinaryTree {
    TreeNode root;

    public BinaryTree() {
        root = null;
    }

    public BinaryTree(Scanner in) {
        root = buildTree(in);
    }
```

```java
    public static TreeNode buildTree(Scanner in) {
     String str = in.next();
        if (str.equals("@")) return null;
        TreeNode p = new TreeNode(new NodeData(str));
        p.left = buildTree(in);
        p.right = buildTree(in);
        return p;
    } //end buildTree

    public void levelOrderTraversal() {
        Queue Q = new Queue();
        Q.enqueue(new QueueData(root));
        while (!Q.empty()) {
           QueueData temp = Q.dequeue();
           temp.node.data.visit();
           if (temp.node.left != null) Q.enqueue(new QueueData(temp.node.left));
           if (temp.node.right != null) Q.enqueue(new QueueData(temp.node.right));
        }
    } //end levelOrderTraversal

} //end class BinaryTree

class QueueData {
    TreeNode node;

    public QueueData(TreeNode n) {
        node = n;
    }
} //end class QueueData

class QNode {
    QueueData data;
    QNode next;

    public QNode(QueueData d) {
        data = d;
        next = null;
    }
} //end class QNode

class Queue {
    QNode head = null, tail = null;

    public boolean empty() {
        return head == null;
    }

    public void enqueue(QueueData nd) {
        QNode p = new QNode(nd);
        if (this.empty()) {
           head = p;
           tail = p;
        }
```

```
        else {
            tail.next = p;
            tail = p;
        }
    } //end enqueue

    public QueueData dequeue() {
        if (this.empty()) {
            System.out.printf("\nAttempt to remove from an empty queue\n");
            System.exit(1);
        }
        QueueData hold = head.data;
        head = head.next;
        if (head == null) tail = null;
        return hold;
    } //end dequeue

} //end class Queue
```

Suppose the file btree.in contains this:

```
C E @ B F @ @ @ G A @ @ N J @ @
```

Program P8.4 will build the tree shown at the start of this section and print the following:

```
The level-order traversal is: C E G B A N F J
```

8.10 Some Useful Binary Tree Functions

We now show you how to write some functions (in the class BinaryTree) that return information about a binary tree. The first counts the number of nodes in a tree:

```
    public int numNodes() {
        return countNodes(root);
    }

    private int countNodes(TreeNode root) {
        if (root == null) return 0;
        return 1 + countNodes(root.left) + countNodes(root.right);
    }
```

If bt is a binary tree, bt.numNodes() will return the number of nodes in the tree. Counting the nodes is delegated to the private function countNodes.

The next function returns the number of leaves in the tree:

```
    public int numLeaves() {
        return countLeaves(root);
    }
```

```
private int countLeaves(TreeNode root) {
    if (root == null) return 0;
    if (root.left == null && root.right == null) return 1;
    return countLeaves(root.left) + countLeaves(root.right);
}
```

And the next returns the height of the tree:

```
public int height() {
    return numLevels(root);
}

private int numLevels(TreeNode root) {
    if (root == null) return 0;
    return 1 + Math.max(numLevels(root.left), numLevels(root.right));
}
```

Math.max returns the larger of its two arguments.

You are advised to dry-run these functions on some sample trees to verify that they do return the correct values.

8.11 Binary Search Tree Deletion

Consider the problem of deleting a node from a binary search tree (BST) so that it remains a BST. There are three cases to consider:

1. The node is a leaf.

2. (a) The node has no left subtree.

   (b) The node has no right subtree.

3. The node has non-empty left and right subtrees.

We illustrate these cases using the BST shown in Figure 8-9.

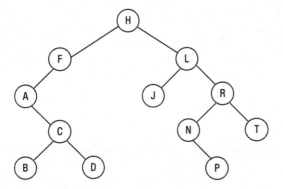

Figure 8-9. *A binary search tree*

Case 1 is easy. For example, to delete P, we simply set the right subtree of N to null. Case 2 is also easy. To delete A (no left subtree), we replace it by C, its right subtree. And to delete F (no right subtree), we replace it by A, its left subtree.

Case 3 is a bit more difficult since we have to worry about what to do with the two subtrees hanging off the node. For example, how do we delete L? One approach is to replace L by its in-order successor, N, which *must* have an empty left subtree. Why? Because, by definition, the in-order successor of a node is the first node (in order) in its right subtree. And this first node (in any tree) is found by going as far left as possible.

Since N has no left subtree, we will set its left link to the left subtree of L. We will set the left link of the parent of N (R in this case) to point to P, the right subtree of N. Finally, we will set the right link of N to point to the right subtree of L, giving the tree shown in Figure 8-10.

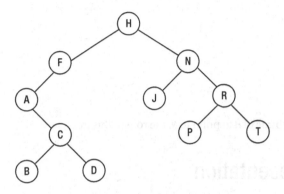

Figure 8-10. *BST after deletion of L in Figure 8-9*

Another way to look at it is to imagine the contents of node N being copied into node L. And the left link of the parent of N (which is R) is set to point to the right subtree of N (which is P).

In our algorithm, we will treat the node to be deleted as the root of a subtree. We will delete the root and return a pointer to the root of the reconstructed tree.

```
deleteNode(TreeNode T) {
    if (T == null) return null
    if (right(T) == null) return left(T)  //cases 1 and 2b
    R = right(T)
    if (left(T) == null) return R //case 2a
        if (left(R) == null) {
        left(R) == left(T)
    return R
}


while (left(R) != null) { //will be executed at least once
    P = R
    R = left(R)
}
```

```
        //R is pointing to the in-order successor of T;
        //P is its parent
        left(R) = left(T)
        left(P) = right(R)
        right(R) = right(T)
        return R
    } //end deleteNode
```

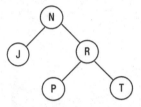

Suppose we call deleteNode with a pointer to the node L (Figure 8-9) as argument. The function will delete L and return a pointer to the following tree:

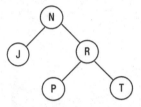

Since L was the right subtree of H, we can now set the right subtree of H to point to N, the root of this tree.

8.12 An Array as a Binary Tree Representation

A *complete* binary tree is one in which every nonleaf node has two nonempty subtrees and all leaves are at the same level. Figure 8-11 shows some complete binary trees.

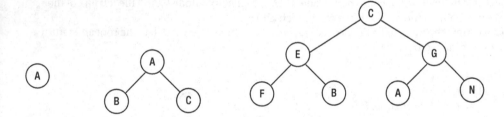

Figure 8-11. *Complete binary trees*

The first is a complete binary tree of height 1, the second is a complete binary tree of height 2, and the third is a complete binary tree of height 3. For a complete binary tree of height n, the number of nodes in the tree is $2^n - 1$.

Consider the third tree. Let's number the nodes as shown in Figure 8-12.

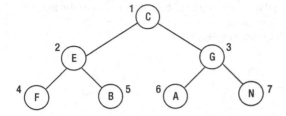

Figure 8-12. *Numbering the nodes, level by level*

Starting from 1 at the root, we number the nodes in order from top to bottom and from left to right at each level. Observe that if a node has label *n*, its left subtree has label 2*n*, and its right subtree has label 2*n* + 1. If the nodes are stored in an array T[1..7], like this:

T

C	E	G	F	B	A	N
1	2	3	4	5	6	7

then

- T[1] is the root.

- The left subtree of T[i] is T[2i] if 2i <= 7 and null otherwise.

- The right subtree of T[i] is T[2i+1] if 2i+1 <= 7 and null otherwise.

- The parent of T[i] is T[i/2] (integer division).

Based on this, the array is a representation of a complete binary tree. In other words, given the array, we can easily construct the binary tree it represents.

An array represents a complete binary tree if the number of elements in the array is $2^n - 1$, for some *n*. If the number of elements is some other value, the array represents an *almost complete* binary tree.

An *almost complete binary tree* is one in which:

- All levels, except possibly the lowest, are completely filled.

- The nodes (all leaves) at the lowest level are as far left as possible.

If the nodes are numbered as shown earlier, then all leaves will be labeled with consecutive numbers from n/2+1 to n. The last nonleaf node will have label n/2. For example, consider the tree with ten nodes drawn and labeled as in Figure 8-13.

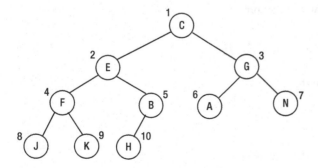

Figure 8-13. *A tree of ten nodes labeled level by level*

Note that the leaves are numbered from 6 to 10. If, for instance, H were the right subtree of B instead of the left, the tree would not be "almost complete" since the leaves on the lowest level would not be "as far left as possible."

The following array of size 10 can represent this almost complete binary tree:

T

C	E	G	F	B	A	N	J	K	H
1	2	3	4	5	6	7	8	9	10

In general, if the tree is represented by an array T[1..n], then the following holds:

- T[1] is the root.

- The left subtree of T[i] is T[2i] if 2i <= n and null otherwise.

- The right subtree of T[i] is T[2i+1] if 2i+1 <= n and null otherwise.

- The parent of T[i] is T[i/2] (integer division).

Looked at another way, there is exactly one almost complete binary tree with *n* nodes, and an array of size *n* represents this tree.

An almost complete binary tree has no "holes" in it; there is no room to add a node in between existing nodes. The only place to add a node is after the last one.

For instance, Figure 8-14 is not "almost complete" since there is a "hole" at the right subtree of B.

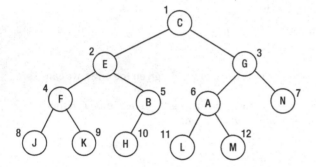

Figure 8-14. *Empty right subtree of B makes this not "almost complete"*

With the hole, the left subtree of A (in position 6) is *not* now in position 6*2 = 12, and the right subtree is not in position 6*2+1 =13. This relationship holds only when the tree is almost complete.

Given an array T[1..n] representing an almost complete binary tree with *n* nodes, we can perform an in-order traversal of the tree with the call inOrder(1, n) of the following function:

```
public static void inOrder(int h, int n) {
    if (h <= n) {
        inOrder(h * 2, n);
        visit(h); //or visit(T[h]), if you wish
        inOrder(h * 2 + 1, n);
    }
} //end inOrder
```

We can write similar functions for pre-order and post-order traversals.

By comparison to a complete binary tree, a *full binary tree* is one in which every node, except a leaf, has *exactly two* nonempty subtrees. Figure 8-15 is an example of a full binary tree.

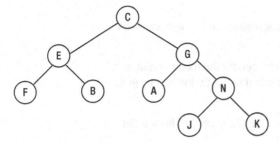

Figure 8-15. *A full binary tree*

Note that a complete binary tree is always full, but as shown in Figure 8-15, a full binary tree is not necessarily complete. An almost complete binary tree may or may not be full.

The tree in Figure 8-16 is almost complete but not full (G has *one* nonempty subtree).

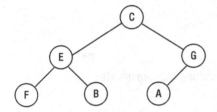

Figure 8-16. *An almost complete but not full binary tree*

However, if node A is removed, the tree will be almost complete *and* full.

In the next chapter, we will explain how to sort an array by interpreting it as an almost complete binary tree.

EXERCISES 8

1. A binary tree consists of an integer key field and pointers to the left subtree, right subtree, and parent. Write the declarations required for building a tree, and write the code to create an empty tree.

2. Each node of a binary tree has fields left, right, key, and parent.

    Write a function to return the in-order successor of any given node x. Hint: if the right subtree of node x is empty and x has a successor y, then y is the lowest ancestor of x, which contains x in its *left* subtree.

    Write a function to return the pre-order successor of any given node x.

    Write a function to return the post-order successor of any given node x.

    Using these functions, write functions to perform the in-order, pre-order, and post-order traversals of a given binary tree.

3. Do Exercise 2 assuming the tree is stored in an array.

4. Write a function that, given the root of a binary search tree, deletes the smallest node and returns a pointer to the root of the reconstructed tree.

5. Write a function that, given the root of a binary search tree, deletes the largest node and returns a pointer to the root of the reconstructed tree.

6. Write a function that, given the root of a binary search tree, deletes the root and returns a pointer to the root of the reconstructed tree. Write the function replacing the root by (i) its in-order successor and (ii) its in-order predecessor.

7. Draw a nondegenerate binary tree of five nodes such that the pre-order and level-order traversals produce identical results.

8. Write a function that, given the root of binary tree, returns the *width* of the tree, that is, the maximum number of nodes at any level.

9. A binary search tree contains integers. For each of the following sequences, state whether it could be the sequence of values examined in searching for the number 36. If it cannot, state why.

    ```
    7 25 42 40 33 34 39 36
    92 22 91 24 89 20 35 36
    95 20 90 24 92 27 30 36
    7 46 41 21 26 39 37 24 36
    ```

10. Draw the binary search tree (BST) obtained for the following keys assuming they are inserted in the following order: 56 30 61 39 47 35 75 13 21 64 26 73 18.

    There is one almost complete BST for the previous keys. Draw it.

    List the keys in an order that will produce the almost complete BST.

    Assuming that the almost complete tree is stored in a one-dimensional array num[1..13], write a recursive function for printing the integers in post-order.

11. An imaginary "external" node is attached to each null pointer of a binary tree of *n* nodes. How many external nodes are there?

    If I is the sum of the levels of the original tree nodes and *E* is the sum of the levels of the external nodes, prove that $E - I = 2n$. (I is called the *internal path length*.)

    Write a recursive function that, given the root of a binary tree, returns I.

    Write a nonrecursive function that, given the root of a binary tree, returns I.

12. Draw the binary tree whose in-order and post-order traversals of the nodes are as follows:

    In-order: G D P K E N F A T L

    Post-order: G P D K F N T A L E

13. Draw the binary tree whose pre-order and in-order traversals of the nodes are as follows:

    Pre-order: N D G K P E T F A L

    In-order: G D P K E N F A T L

14. Draw two different binary trees such that the pre-order and post-order traversals of the one tree are identical to the pre-order and post-order traversals of the other tree.

15. Write a recursive function that, given the root of a binary tree and a key, searches for the key using (i) a pre-order, (ii) an in-order, and (iii) a post-order traversal. If found, return the node containing the key; otherwise, return `null`.

16. Store the following integers in an array `bst[1..15]` such that `bst` represents a complete binary search tree:

    34 23 45 46 37 78 90 2 40 20 87 53 12 15 91

17. Each node of a *binary search tree* contains three fields—`left`, `right`, and `data`—with their usual meanings; `data` is a positive integer field. Write an *efficient* function that, given the root of the tree and `key`, returns the *smallest* number in the tree that is *greater* than `key`. If there is no such number, return -1.

18. Write a program that takes a Java program as input and outputs the program, numbering the lines, followed by an alphabetical cross-reference listing of all user identifiers; that is, a user identifier is followed by the numbers of all lines in which the identifier appears. If an identifier appears more than once in a given line, the line number must be repeated the number of times it appears.

    The cross-reference listing must *not* contain Java reserved words, words within character strings, or words within comments.

CHAPTER 9

■ ■ ■

Advanced Sorting

In this chapter, we will explain the following:

- What a heap is and how to perform heapsort using `siftDown`
- How to build a heap using `siftUp`
- How to analyze the performance of heapsort
- How a heap can be used to implement a priority queue
- How to sort a list of items using quicksort
- How to find the *k*th smallest item in a list
- How to sort a list of items using Shell (diminishing increment) sort

In Chapter 1, we discussed two simple methods (selection and insertion sort) for sorting a list of items. In this chapter, we take a detailed look at some faster methods—heapsort, quicksort, and Shell (diminishing increment) sort.

9.1 Heapsort

Heapsort is a method of sorting that *interprets* the elements in an array as an almost complete binary tree. Consider the following array, which is to be sorted in ascending order:

num

37	25	43	65	48	84	73	18	79	56	69	32
1	2	3	4	5	6	7	8	9	10	11	12

We can think of this array as an almost complete binary tree with 12 nodes, as shown in Figure 9-1.

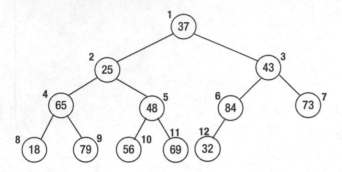

Figure 9-1. *A binary tree view of the array*

Suppose we now require that the value at each node be greater than or equal to the values in its left and right subtrees, if present. As it is, only node 6 and the leaves have this property. Shortly, we will see how to rearrange the nodes so that *all* nodes satisfy this condition. But, first, we give such a structure a name:

> A **heap** is an almost complete binary tree such that the value at the root is greater than or equal to the values at the left and right children, and the left and right subtrees are also heaps.

An immediate consequence of this definition is that the largest value is at the root. Such a heap is referred to as a *max-heap*. We define a *min-heap* with the word *greater* replaced by *smaller*. In a min-heap, the *smallest* value is at the root.

Let's now convert the binary tree in Figure 9-1 into a max-heap.

9.1.1 Converting a Binary Tree into a Max-Heap

First, we observe that all the leaves are heaps since they have no children.

Starting at the last nonleaf node (6, in the example), we convert the tree rooted there into a max-heap. If the value at the node is greater than its children, there is nothing to do. This is the case with node 6, since 84 is bigger than 32.

Next, we move on to node 5. The value here, 48, is smaller than at least one child (both, in this case, 56 and 69). We first find the larger child (69) and interchange it with node 5. Thus, 69 ends up in node 5, and 48 ends up in node 11.

Next, we go to node 4. The larger child, 79, is moved to node 4, and 65 is moved to node 9. At this stage, the tree looks like that in Figure 9-2.

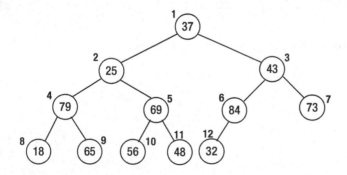

Figure 9-2. *The tree after nodes 6, 5, and 4 have been processed*

Continuing at node 3, 43 must be moved. The larger child is 84, so we interchange the values at nodes 3 and 6. The value now at node 6 (43) is bigger than its child (32), so there is nothing more to do. Note, however, that if the value at node 6 were 28, say, it would have had to be exchanged with 32.

Moving to node 2, 25 is exchanged with its larger child, 79. But 25 now in node 4 is smaller than 65, its right child in node 9. Thus, these two values must be exchanged.

Finally, at node 1, 37 is exchanged with its larger child, 84. It is further exchanged with its (new) larger child, 73, giving the tree, which is now a heap, shown in Figure 9-3.

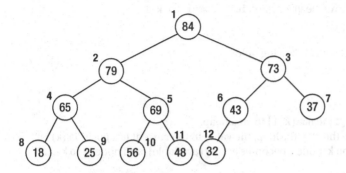

Figure 9-3. *The final tree, which is now a heap*

9.1.2 The Sorting Process

After conversion to a heap, note that the largest value, 84, is at the root of the tree. Now that the values in the array form a heap, we can sort them in ascending order as follows:

- Store the last item, 32, in a temporary location. Next, move 84 to the last position (node 12), freeing node 1. Then, imagine 32 is in node 1 and move it so that items 1 to 11 become a heap. This will be done as follows:

- 32 is exchanged with its bigger child, 79, which now moves into node 1. Then, 32 is further exchanged with its (new) bigger child, 69, which moves into node 2.

Finally, 32 is exchanged with 56, giving us Figure 9-4.

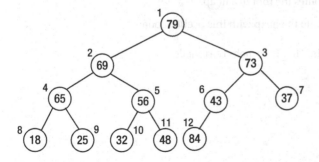

Figure 9-4. *After 84 has been placed and the heap is reorganized*

At this stage, the second largest number, 79, is in node 1. This is placed in node 11, and 48 is "sifted down" from node 1 until items 1 to 10 form a heap. Now, the third largest number, 73, will be at the root. This is placed in node 10, and so on. The process is repeated until the array is sorted.

After the initial heap is built, the sorting process can be described with the following pseudocode:

```
for k = n downto 2 do
    item = num[k]      //extract current last item
    num[k] = num[1]    //move top of heap to current last node
    siftDown(item, num, 1, k-1)  //restore heap properties from 1 to k-1
end for
```

where siftDown(item, num, 1, k-1) assumes that the following hold:

- num[1] is empty.

- num[2] to num[k-1] form a heap.

Starting at position 1, item is inserted so that num[1] to num[k-1] form a heap.

In the sorting process described above, each time through the loop, the value in the current last position (k) is stored in item. The value at node 1 is moved to position k; node 1 becomes empty (available), and nodes 2 to k-1 all satisfy the heap property.

The call siftDown(item, num, 1, k-1) will add item so that num[1] to num[k-1] contain a heap. This ensures that the next highest number is at node 1.

The nice thing about siftDown (when we write it) is that it can be used to create the initial heap from the given array. Recall the process of creating a heap described in Section 9.1.1. At each node (h, say), we "sifted the value down" so that we formed a heap rooted at h. To use siftDown in this situation, we generalize it as follows:

```
void siftDown(int key, int num[], int root, int last)
```

This assumes the following:

- num[root] is empty.

- last is the last entry in the array, num.

- num[root*2], if it exists (root*2 £ last), is the root of a heap.

- num[root*2+1], if it exists (root*2+1 £ last), is the root of a heap.

Starting at root, key is inserted so that num[root] becomes the root of a heap.

Given an array of values num[1] to num[n], we could build the heap with this pseudocode:

```
for h = n/2 downto 1 do              // n/2 is the last non-leaf node
siftDown(num[h], num, h, n)
```

We now show how to write siftDown.

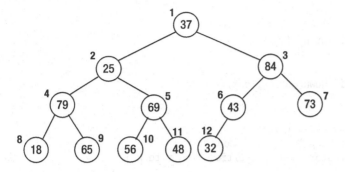

Figure 9-5. *A heap, except for nodes 1 and 2*

Consider Figure 9-5.

Except for nodes 1 and 2, all the other nodes satisfy the heap property in that they are bigger than or equal to their children. Suppose we want to make node 2 the root of a heap. As it is, the value 25 is smaller than its children (79 and 69). We want to write siftDown so that the following call will do the job:

```
siftDown(25, num, 2, 12)
```

Here, 25 is the key, num is the array, 2 is the root, and 12 is the position of the last node.

After this, each of nodes 2 to 12 will be the root of a heap, and the following call will ensure that the entire array contains a heap:

```
siftDown(37, num, 1, 12)
```

The gist of siftDown is as follows:

```
find the bigger child of num[root]; //suppose it is in node m
if (key >= num[m]) we are done; put key in num[root]
//key is smaller than the bigger child
store num[m] in num[root]  //promote bigger child
set root to m
```

The process is repeated until the value at root is bigger than its children or there are no children. Here is siftDown:

```
public static void siftDown(int key, int[] num, int root, int last) {
    int bigger = 2 * root;
    while (bigger <= last) { //while there is at least one child
        if (bigger < last) //there is a right child as well; find the bigger
            if (num[bigger+1] > num[bigger]) bigger++;
        //'bigger' holds the index of the bigger child
        if (key >= num[bigger]) break;
        //key is smaller; promote num[bigger]
        num[root] = num[bigger];
        root = bigger;
        bigger = 2 * root;
    }
    num[root] = key;
} //end siftDown
```

We can now write heapSort as follows:

```
public static void heapSort(int[] num, int n) {
    //sort num[1] to num[n]
    //convert the array to a heap
    for (int k = n / 2; k >= 1; k--) siftDown(num[k], num, k, n);

    for (int k = n; k > 1; k--) {
        int item = num[k]; //extract current last item
        num[k] = num[1];   //move top of heap to current last node
        siftDown(item, num, 1, k-1); //restore heap properties from 1 to k-1
    }
} //end heapSort
```

We can test heapSort with Program P9.1.

Program P9.1

```
import java.io.*;
public class HeapSortTest {
    public static void main(String[] args) throws IOException {
        int[] num = {0, 37, 25, 43, 65, 48, 84, 73, 18, 79, 56, 69, 32};
        int n = 12;
        heapSort(num, n);
        for (int h = 1; h <= n; h++) System.out.printf("%d ", num[h]);
        System.out.printf("\n");
    }

    public static void heapSort(int[] num, int n) {
        //sort num[1] to num[n]
        //convert the array to a heap
        for (int k = n / 2; k >= 1; k--) siftDown(num[k], num, k, n);

        for (int k = n; k > 1; k--) {
            int item = num[k]; //extract current last item
            num[k] = num[1];   //move top of heap to current last node
            siftDown(item, num, 1, k-1); //restore heap properties from 1 to k-1
        }
    } //end heapSort

    public static void siftDown(int key, int[] num, int root, int last) {
        int bigger = 2 * root;
        while (bigger <= last) { //while there is at least one child
            if (bigger < last) //there is a right child as well; find the bigger
                if (num[bigger+1] > num[bigger]) bigger++;
            //'bigger' holds the index of the bigger child
            if (key >= num[bigger]) break;
            //key is smaller; promote num[bigger]
            num[root] = num[bigger];
            root = bigger;
            bigger = 2 * root;
        }
```

```
          num[root] = key;
     } //end siftDown

  } //end class HeapSortTest
```

When run, Program P9.1 produces the following output (num[1] to num[12] sorted):

```
18 25 32 37 43 48 56 65 69 73 79 84
```

Programming note: As written, heapSort sorts an array assuming that *n* elements are stored from subscripts 1 to n. If they are stored from 0 to n-1, appropriate adjustments would have to be made. They would be based mainly on the following observations:

- The root is stored in num[0].

- The left child of node h is node 2h+1 if 2h+1 < n.

- The right child of node h is node 2h+2 if 2h+2 < n.

- The parent of node h is node (h-1)/2 (integer division).

- The last nonleaf node is (n-2)/2 (integer division).

You can verify these observations using the tree (n = 12) shown in Figure 9-6.

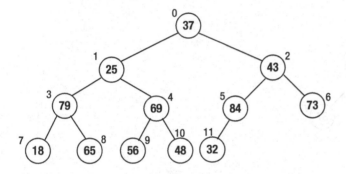

Figure 9-6. *A binary tree stored in an array starting at 0*

You are urged to rewrite heapSort so that it sorts the array num[0..n-1]. As a hint, note that the only change required in siftDown is in the calculation of bigger. Instead of 2 * root, we now use 2 * root + 1.

9.2 Building a Heap Using siftUp

Consider the problem of adding a new node to an existing heap. Specifically, suppose num[1] to num[n] contain a heap. We want to add a new number, newKey, so that num[1] to num[n+1] contain a heap that includes newKey. We assume the array has room for the new key.

For example, suppose we have the heap shown in Figure 9-7 and we want to add 40 to the heap. When the new number is added, the heap will contain 13 elements. We imagine 40 is placed in num[13] (but do not store it there, as yet) and compare it with its parent 43 in num[6]. Since 40 is smaller, the heap property is satisfied; we place 40 in num[13], and the process ends.

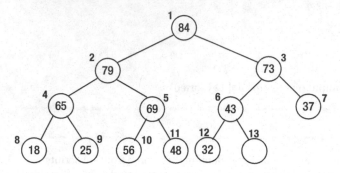

Figure 9-7. *A heap to which we will add a new item*

But suppose we want to add 80 to the heap. We imagine 80 is placed in num[13] (but do not actually store it there, as yet) and compare it with its parent 43 in num[6]. Since 80 is bigger, we move 43 to num[13] and imagine 80 being placed in num[6].

Next, we compare 80 with its parent 73 in num[3]. It is bigger, so we move 73 to num[6] and imagine 80 being placed in num[3].

We then compare 80 with its parent 84 in num[1]. It is smaller, so we place 80 in num[3], and the process ends.

Note that if we were adding 90 to the heap, 84 would be moved to num[3], and 90 would be inserted in num[1]. It is now the largest number in the heap.

Figure 9-8 shows the heap after 80 is added.

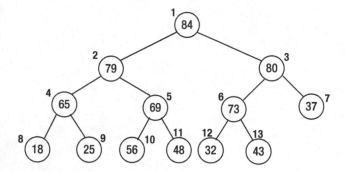

Figure 9-8. *The heap after 80 is added*

The following code adds newKey to a heap stored in num[1] to num[n]:

```
child = n + 1;
parent = child / 2;
while (parent > 0) {
    if (newKey <= num[parent]) break;
    num[child] = num[parent]; //move down parent
    child = parent;
    parent = child / 2;
}
num[child] = newKey;
n = n + 1;
```

The process described is usually referred to as *sifting up*. We can rewrite this code as a function siftUp. We assume that siftUp is given an array heap[1..n] such that heap[1..n-1] contains a heap and heap[n] is to be sifted up so that heap[1..n] contains a heap. In other words, heap[n] plays the role of newKey in the previous discussion.

We show siftUp as part of Program P9.2, which creates a heap out of numbers stored in a file, heap.in.

Program P9.2

```java
import java.io.*;
import java.util.*;
public class SiftUpTest {
    final static int MaxHeapSize = 100;
    public static void main (String[] args) throws IOException {
        Scanner in = new Scanner(new FileReader("heap.in"));
        int[] num = new int[MaxHeapSize + 1];
        int n = 0, number;

        while (in.hasNextInt()) {
            number = in.nextInt();
            if (n < MaxHeapSize) { //check if array has room
                num[++n] = number;
                siftUp(num, n);
            }
        }

        for (int h = 1; h <= n; h++) System.out.printf("%d ", num[h]);
        System.out.printf("\n");
        in.close();
    } //end main

    public static void siftUp(int[] heap, int n) {
    //heap[1] to heap[n-1] contain a heap
    //sifts up the value in heap[n] so that heap[1..n] contains a heap
        int siftItem = heap[n];
        int child = n;
        int parent = child / 2;
        while (parent > 0) {
            if (siftItem <= heap[parent]) break;
            heap[child] = heap[parent]; //move down parent
            child = parent;
            parent = child / 2;
        }
        heap[child] = siftItem;
    } //end siftUp

} //end class SiftUpTest
```

Suppose heap.in contains the following:

37 25 43 65 48 84 73 18 79 56 69 32

Program P9.2 will build the heap (described next) and print the following:

---

84 79 73 48 69 37 65 18 25 43 56 32

After 37, 25, and 43 are read, we will have Figure 9-9.

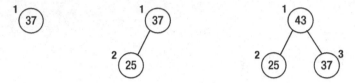

Figure 9-9. *Heap after processing 37, 25, 43*

After 65, 48, 84, and 73 are read, we will have Figure 9-10.

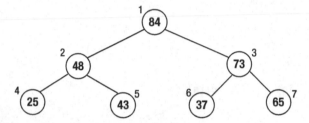

Figure 9-10. *Heap after processing 65, 48, 84, 73*

And after 18, 79, 56, 69, and 32 are read, we will have the final heap shown in Figure 9-11.

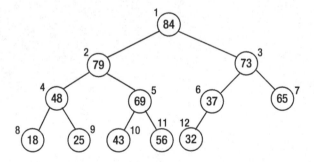

Figure 9-11. *Final heap after processing 18, 79, 56, 69, 32*

Note that the heap in Figure 9-11 is different from that of Figure 9-3 even though they are formed from the same numbers. What hasn't changed is that the largest value, 84, is at the root.

If the values are already stored in an array num[1..n], we can create a heap with the following:

```
for (int k = 2; k <= n; k++) siftUp(num, k);
```

9.3 Analysis of Heapsort

Is siftUp or siftDown better for creating a heap? Keep in mind that the most times any node will ever have to move is $\log_2 n$.

In siftDown, we process $n/2$ nodes, and at each step, we make two comparisons: one to find the bigger child and one to compare the node value with the bigger child. In a simplistic analysis, in the worst case, we will need to make $2*n/2*\log_2 n = n\log_2 n$ comparisons. However, a more careful analysis will show that we need to make, at most, only $4n$ comparisons.

In siftUp, we process $n-1$ nodes. At each step, we make one comparison: the node with its parent. In a simplistic analysis, in the worst case, we make $(n-1)\log_2 n$ comparisons. However, it is possible that all the leaves may have to travel all the way to the top of the tree. In this case, we have $n/2$ nodes having to travel a distance of $\log_2 n$, giving a total of $(n/2)\log_2 n$ comparisons. And that's only for the leaves. In the end, a more careful analysis still gives us approximately $n\log_2 n$ comparisons for siftUp.

The difference in performance is hinged on the following: in siftDown, there is no work to do for half the nodes (the leaves); siftUp has the most work to do for these nodes.

Whichever method we use for creating the initial heap, heapsort will sort an array of size n making at most $2n\log_2 n$ comparisons and $n\log_2 n$ assignments. This is very fast. In addition, heapsort is *stable* in the sense that its performance is always at worst $2n\log_2 n$, regardless of the order of the items in the given array.

To give an idea of how fast heapsort (and all sorting methods that are of order $O(n\log_2 n)$, such as quicksort and mergesort) is, let's compare it with selection sort, which makes roughly $\frac{1}{2} n^2$ comparisons to sort n items (Table 9-1).

Table 9-1. *Comparison of Heapsort with Selection Sort*

n	selection(comp)	heap(comp)	select(sec)	heap(sec)
100	5,000	1,329	0.005	0.001
1,000	500,000	19,932	0.5	0.020
10,000	50,000,000	265,754	50	0.266
100,000	5,000,000,000	3,321,928	5000	3.322
1,000,000	500,000,000,000	39,863,137	500000	39.863

The second and third columns show the number of comparisons that each method makes. The last two columns show the running time of each method (in seconds) assuming that the computer can process 1 million comparisons per second. For example, to sort 1 million items, selection sort will take 500,000 seconds (almost 6 days!), whereas heapsort will do it in less than 40 seconds.

9.4 Heaps and Priority Queues

A *priority queue* is one in which each item is assigned some "priority" and its position in the queue is based on this priority. The item with top priority is placed at the head of the queue. The following are some typical operations that may be performed on a priority queue:

- Remove (serve) the item with the highest priority
- Add an item with a given priority
- Remove (delete without serving) an item from the queue
- Change the priority of an item, adjusting its position based on its new priority

We can think of priority as an integer—the bigger the integer, the higher the priority.

Immediately, we can surmise that if we implement the queue as a max-heap, the item with the highest priority will be at the root, so it can be easily removed. Reorganizing the heap will simply involve "sifting down" the last item from the root.

Adding an item will involve placing the item in the position after the current last one and sifting it up until it finds its correct position.

To delete an arbitrary item from the queue, we will need to know its position. Deleting it will involve replacing it with the current last item and sifting it up or down to find its correct position. The heap will shrink by one item.

If we change the priority of an item, we may need to sift it either up or down to find its correct position. Of course, it may also remain in its original position, depending on the change.

In many situations (for example, a job queue on a multitasking computer), the priority of a job may increase over time so that it eventually gets served. In these situations, a job moves closer to the top of the heap with each change; thus, only sifting up is required.

In a typical situation, information about the items in a priority queue is held in another structure that can be quickly searched, for example a binary search tree. One field in the node will contain the index of the item in the array used to implement the priority queue.

Using the job queue example, suppose we want to add an item to the queue. We can search the tree by job number, say, and add the item to the tree. Its priority number is used to determine its position in the queue. This position is stored in the tree node.

If, later, the priority changes, the item's position in the queue is adjusted, and this new position is stored in the tree node. Note that adjusting this item may also involve changing the position of other items (as they move up or down the heap), and the tree will have to be updated for these items as well.

9.5 Sorting a List of Items with Quicksort

At the heart of quicksort is the notion of *partitioning* the list with respect to one of the values called a *pivot*. For example, suppose we are given the following list to be sorted:

num

53	12	98	63	18	32	80	46	72	21
1	2	3	4	5	6	7	8	9	10

We can *partition* it with respect to the first value, 53. This means placing 53 in such a position that all values to the left of it are smaller and all values to the right are greater than or equal to it. Shortly, we will describe an algorithm that will partition num as follows:

num

21	12	18	32	46	53	80	98	72	63
1	2	3	4	5	6	7	8	9	10

The value 53 is used as the *pivot*. It is placed in position 6. All values to the left of 53 are smaller than 53, and all values to the right are greater. The location in which the pivot is placed is called the *division point* (dp, say). By definition, 53 is in its final sorted position.

If we can sort num[1..dp-1] and num[dp+1..n], we would have sorted the entire list. But we can use the same process to sort these pieces, indicating that a recursive procedure is appropriate.

Assuming a function `partition` is available that partitions a given section of an array and returns the division point, we can write `quicksort` as follows:

```
public static void quicksort(int[] A, int lo, int hi) {
//sorts A[lo] to A[hi] in ascending order
   if (lo < hi) {
       int dp = partition(A, lo, hi);
       quicksort(A, lo, dp-1);
       quicksort(A, dp+1, hi);
   }
} //end quicksort
```

The call `quicksort(num, 1, n)` will sort `num[1..n]` in ascending order.

We now look at how `partition` may be written. Consider the following array:

num

53	12	98	63	18	32	80	46	72	21
1	2	3	4	5	6	7	8	9	10

We will partition it with respect to `num[1]`, 53 (the pivot) by making one pass through the array. We will look at each number in turn. If it is bigger than the pivot, we do nothing. If it is smaller, we move it to the left side of the array. Initially, we set the variable `lastSmall` to 1; as the method proceeds, `lastSmall` will be the index of the last item that is known to be smaller than the pivot. We partition `num` as follows:

1. Compare 12 with 53; it is smaller, so add 1 to `lastSmall` (making it 2) and swap `num[2]` with itself.

2. Compare 98 with 53; it is bigger, so move on.

3. Compare 63 with 53; it is bigger, so move on.

4. Compare 18 with 53; it is smaller, so add 1 to `lastSmall` (making it 3) and swap `num[3]`, 98, with 18.

At this stage, we have this:

num

53	12	18	63	98	32	80	46	72	21
1	2	3	4	5	6	7	8	9	10

5. Compare 32 with 53; it is smaller, so add 1 to `lastSmall` (making it 4) and swap `num[4]`, 63, with 32.

6. Compare 80 with 53; it is bigger, so move on.

7. Compare 46 with 53; it is smaller, so add 1 to `lastSmall` (making it 5) and swap `num[5]`, 98, with 46.

At this stage, we have the following:

num

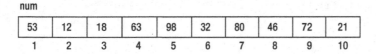

53	12	18	32	46	63	80	98	72	21
1	2	3	4	5	6	7	8	9	10

8. Compare 72 with 53; it is bigger, so move on.

9. Compare 21 with 53; it is smaller, so add 1 to lastSmall (making it 6) and swap num[6], 63, with 21.

10. We have come to the end of the array; swap num[1] and num[lastSmall]; this moves the pivot into its final position (6, in this example).

We end up with this:

num

21	12	18	32	46	53	80	98	72	63
1	2	3	4	5	6	7	8	9	10

The division point is denoted by lastSmall (6).

We can express the method just described as a function partition1. The function is shown as part of Program P9.3, which we write to test quicksort and partition1.

Program P9.3

```java
import java.io.*;
public class QuicksortTest {

    public static void main(String[] args) throws IOException {
        int[] num = {0, 37, 25, 43, 65, 48, 84, 73, 18, 79, 56, 69, 32};
        int n = 12;
        quicksort(num, 1, n);
        for (int h = 1; h <= n; h++) System.out.printf("%d ", num[h]);
        System.out.printf("\n");
    }

    public static void quicksort(int[] A, int lo, int hi) {
    //sorts A[lo] to A[hi] in ascending order
        if (lo < hi) {
            int dp = partition1(A, lo, hi);
            quicksort(A, lo, dp-1);
            quicksort(A, dp+1, hi);
        }
    } //end quicksort

    public static int partition1(int[] A, int lo, int hi) {
    //partition A[lo] to A[hi] using A[lo] as the pivot
        int pivot = A[lo];
        int lastSmall = lo;
        for (int j = lo + 1; j <= hi; j++)
            if (A[j] < pivot) {
                ++lastSmall;
                swap(A, lastSmall, j);
            }
        //end for
        swap(A, lo, lastSmall);
        return lastSmall;  //return the division point
    } //end partition1
```

```
    public static void swap(int[] list, int i, int j) {
    //swap list[i] and list[j]
        int hold = list[i];
        list[i] = list[j];
        list[j] = hold;
    }

} //end class QuicksortTest
```

When run, Program P9.3 produces the following output (num[1] to num[12] sorted):

18 25 32 37 43 48 56 65 69 73 79 84

Quicksort is one of those methods whose performance can range from very fast to very slow. Typically, it is of order O($n\log_2 n$), and for random data, the number of comparisons varies between $n\log_2 n$ and $3n\log_2 n$. However, things can get worse.

The idea behind partitioning is to break up the given portion into two fairly equal pieces. Whether this happens depends, to a large extent, on the value that is chosen as the pivot.

In the function, we choose the first element as the pivot. This will work well in most cases, especially for random data. However, if the first element happens to be the smallest, the partitioning operation becomes almost useless since the division point will simply be the first position. The "left" piece will be empty, and the "right" piece will be only one element smaller than the given sublist. Similar remarks apply if the pivot is the largest element.

While the algorithm will still work, it will be slowed considerably. For example, if the given array is sorted, quicksort will become as slow as selection sort.

One way to avoid this problem is to choose a random element as the pivot, not merely the first one. While it is still possible that this method will choose the smallest (or the largest), that choice will be merely by chance.

Yet another method is to choose the median of the first (A[lo]), last (A[hi]), and middle (A[(lo+hi)/2]) items as the pivot.

You are advised to experiment with various ways of choosing the pivot.

Our experiments showed that choosing a random element as the pivot was simple and effective, even for sorted data. In fact, in many cases, the method ran faster with sorted data than with random data, an unusual result for quicksort.

One possible disadvantage of quicksort is that, depending on the actual data being sorted, the overhead of the recursive calls may be high. We will see how to minimize this in Section 9.5.2. On the plus side, quicksort uses very little extra storage. On the other hand, mergesort (which is also recursive) needs extra storage (the same size as the array being sorted) to facilitate the merging of sorted pieces. Heapsort has neither of these disadvantages. It is *not* recursive and uses very little extra storage. And, as noted in Section 9.3, heapsort is *stable* in that its performance is always at worst $2n\log_2 n$, regardless of the order of the items in the given array.

9.5.1 Another Way to Partition

There are many ways to achieve the goal of partitioning—splitting the list into two parts such that the elements in the left part are smaller than the elements in the right part. Our first method, shown earlier, placed the pivot in its final position. For variety, we will look at another way to partition. While this method still partitions with respect to a pivot, it does *not* place the pivot in its final sorted position. As we will see, this is not a problem.

Consider, again, the array num[1..n] where n = 10.

num

53	12	98	63	18	32	80	46	72	21
1	2	3	4	5	6	7	8	9	10

We choose 53 as the pivot. The general idea is to scan from the right looking for a key that is smaller than, or equal to, the pivot. We then scan from the left for a key that is greater than, or equal to, the pivot. We swap these two values; this process effectively puts smaller values to the left and bigger values to the right.

We use two variables, lo and hi, to mark our positions on the left and right. Initially, we set lo to 0 and hi to 11 (n+1). We then loop as follows:

1. Subtract 1 from hi (making it 10).

2. Compare num[hi], 21, with 53; it is smaller, so stop scanning from the right with hi = 10.

3. Add 1 to lo (making it 1).

4. Compare num[lo], 53, with 53; it is not smaller, so stop scanning from the left with lo = 1.

5. lo (1) is less than hi (10), so swap num[lo] and num[hi].

6. Subtract 1 from hi (making it 9).

7. Compare num[hi], 72, with 53; it is bigger, so decrease hi (making it 8). Compare num[hi], 46, with 53; it is smaller, so stop scanning from the right with hi = 8.

8. Add 1 to lo (making it 2).

9. Compare num[lo], 12, with 53; it is smaller, so add 1 to lo (making it 3). Compare num[lo], 98, with 53; it is bigger, so stop scanning from the left with lo = 3.

10. lo (3) is less than hi (8), so swap num[lo] and num[hi].

At this stage, we have lo = 3, hi = 8 and num as follows:

num

21	12	46	63	18	32	80	98	72	53
1	2	3	4	5	6	7	8	9	10

11. Subtract 1 from hi (making it 7).

12. Compare num[hi], 80, with 53; it is bigger, so decrease hi (making it 6). Compare num[hi], 32, with 53; it is smaller, so stop scanning from the right with hi = 6.

13. Add 1 to lo (making it 4).

14. Compare num[lo], 63, with 53; it is bigger, so stop scanning from the left with lo = 4.

15. lo (4) is less than hi (6), so swap num[lo] and num[hi], giving this:

num

21	12	46	32	18	63	80	98	72	53
1	2	3	4	5	6	7	8	9	10

16. Subtract 1 from hi (making it 5).

17. Compare num[hi], 18, with 53; it is smaller, so stop scanning from the right with hi = 5.

18. Add 1 to lo (making it 5).

19. Compare num[lo], 18, with 53; it is smaller, so add 1 to lo (making it 6). Compare num[lo], 63, with 53; it is bigger, so stop scanning from the left with lo = 6.

20. lo (6) is *not* less than hi (5), so the algorithm ends.

The value of hi is such that the values in num[1..hi] are smaller than those in num[hi+1..n]. Here, the values in num[1..5] are smaller than those in num[6..10]. Note that 53 is not in its final sorted position. However, this is not a problem since, to sort the array, all we need to do is sort num[1..hi] and num[hi+1..n].

We can express the procedure just described as partition2:

```
public static int partition2(int[] A, int lo, int hi) {
//return dp such that A[lo..dp] <= A[dp+1..hi]
    int pivot = A[lo];
    --lo; ++hi;
    while (lo < hi) {
        do --hi; while (A[hi] > pivot);
        do ++lo; while (A[lo] < pivot);
        if (lo < hi) swap(A, lo, hi);
    }
    return hi;
} //end partition2
```

With *this* version of partition, we can write quicksort2 as follows:

```
public static void quicksort2(int[] A, int lo, int hi) {
//sorts A[lo] to A[hi] in ascending order
    if (lo < hi) {
        int dp = partition2(A, lo, hi);
        quicksort2(A, lo, dp);
        quicksort2(A, dp+1, hi);
    }
}
```

In partition2, we choose the first element as the pivot. However, as discussed, choosing a random element will give better results. We can do this with the following code:

```
swap(A, lo, random(lo, hi));
int pivot = A[lo];
```

Here, random can be written like this:

```
public static int random(int m, int n) {
//returns a random integer from m to n, inclusive
    return (int) (Math.random() * (n - m + 1)) + m;
}
```

9.5.2 Nonrecursive Quicksort

In the versions of quicksort shown earlier, after a sublist is partitioned, we call quicksort with the left part followed by the right part. For most cases, this will work fine. However, it is possible that, for large n, the number of pending recursive calls can get so large so as to generate a "recursive stack overflow" error.

In our experiments, this occurred with n = 7000 if the given data was already sorted and the first element was chosen as the pivot. However, there was no problem even for n = 100000 if a random element was chosen as the pivot.

Another approach is to write quicksort nonrecursively. This would require us to stack the pieces of the list that remain to be sorted. It can be shown that when a sublist is subdivided, if we process the *smaller* sublist first, the number of stack elements will be restricted to at most $\log_2 n$.

For example, suppose we are sorting A[1..99] and the first division point is 40. Assume we are using partition2, which does not put the pivot in its final sorted position. Thus, we must sort A[1..40] and A[41..99] to complete the sort. We will stack (41, 99) and deal with A[1..40] (the shorter sublist) first.

Suppose the division point for A[1..40] is 25. We will stack (1, 25) and process A[26..40] first. At this stage, we have two sublists—(41, 99) and (1, 25)—on the stack that remain to be sorted. Attempting to sort A[26..40] will cause another sublist to be added to the stack, and so on. In our implementation, we will also add the shorter sublist to the stack, but this will be taken off immediately and processed.

The result mentioned here assures us that there will never be more than $\log_2 99 = 7$ (rounded up) elements on the stack at any given time. Even for n = 1,000,000, we are guaranteed that the number of stack items will not exceed 20.

Of course, we will have to manipulate the stack ourselves. Each stack element will consist of two integers (left and right, say) meaning that the portion of the list from left to right remains to be sorted. We can define NodeData as follows:

```java
class NodeData {
   int left, right;

   public NodeData (int a, int b) {
      left = a;
      right = b;
   }

   public static NodeData getRogueValue() {return new NodeData(-1, -1);}

} //end class NodeData
```

We will use the stack implementation from Section 4.3. We now write quicksort3 based on the previous discussion. It is shown as part of the self-contained Program P9.4. This program reads numbers from the file quick.in, sorts the numbers using quicksort3, and prints the sorted numbers, ten per line.

Program P9.4

```java
import java.io.*;
import java.util.*;
public class Quicksort3Test {
   final static int MaxNumbers = 100;
   public static void main (String[] args) throws IOException {
      Scanner in = new Scanner(new FileReader("quick.in"));
      int[] num = new int[MaxNumbers+1];
      int n = 0, number;

      while (in.hasNextInt()) {
         number = in.nextInt();
         if (n < MaxNumbers) num[++n] = number; //store if array has room
      }

      quicksort3(num, 1, n);
      for (int h = 1; h <= n; h++) {
         System.out.printf("%d ", num[h]);
         if (h % 10 == 0) System.out.printf("\n"); //print 10 numbers per line
      }
      System.out.printf("\n");
   } //end main
```

```
    public static void quicksort3(int[] A, int lo, int hi) {
        Stack S = new Stack();
        S.push(new NodeData(lo, hi));
        int stackItems = 1, maxStackItems = 1;

        while (!S.empty()) {
            --stackItems;
            NodeData d = S.pop();
            if (d.left < d.right) { //if the sublist is > 1 element
                int dp = partition2(A, d.left, d.right);
                if (dp - d.left + 1 < d.right - dp) {  //compare lengths of sublists
                    S.push(new NodeData(dp+1, d.right));
                    S.push(new NodeData(d.left, dp));
                }
                else {
                    S.push(new NodeData(d.left, dp));
                    S.push(new NodeData(dp+1, d.right));
                }
                stackItems += 2;    //two items added to stack
            } //end if
            if (stackItems > maxStackItems) maxStackItems = stackItems;
        } //end while
        System.out.printf("Max stack items: %d\n\n", maxStackItems);
    } //end quicksort3

    public static int partition2(int[] A, int lo, int hi) {
    //return dp such that A[lo..dp] <= A[dp+1..hi]
        int pivot = A[lo];
        --lo; ++hi;
        while (lo < hi) {
            do --hi; while (A[hi] > pivot);
            do ++lo; while (A[lo] < pivot);
            if (lo < hi) swap(A, lo, hi);
        }
        return hi;
    } //end partition2

    public static void swap(int[] list, int i, int j) {
    //swap list[i] and list[j]
        int hold = list[i];
        list[i] = list[j];
        list[j] = hold;
    } //end swap

} //end class Quicksort3Test

class NodeData {
    int left, right;
```

```
        public NodeData(int a, int b) {
            left = a;
            right = b;
        }

        public static NodeData getRogueValue() {return new NodeData(-1, -1);}

    } //end class NodeData

class Node {
    NodeData data;
    Node next;

    public Node(NodeData d) {
        data = d;
        next = null;
    }

} //end class Node

class Stack {
    Node top = null;

    public boolean empty() {
        return top == null;
    }

    public void push(NodeData nd) {
        Node p = new Node(nd);
        p.next = top;
        top = p;
    } //end push

    public NodeData pop() {
        if (this.empty())return NodeData.getRogueValue();
        NodeData hold = top.data;
        top = top.next;
        return hold;
    } //end pop

} //end class Stack
```

In quicksort3, when partition2 returns, the lengths of the two sublists are compared, and the longer one is placed on the stack first followed by the shorter one. This ensures that the shorter one will be taken off first and processed before the longer one.

We also added statements to quicksort3 to keep track of the maximum number of items on the stack at any given time. When used to sort 100000 integers, the maximum number of stack items was 13. This is less than the theoretical maximum, $\log_2 100000 = 17$, rounded up.

Suppose quick.in contains the following numbers:

```
43 25 66 37 65 48 84 73 60 79 56 69 32 87 23 99 85 28 14 78 39 51 44 35
46 90 26 96 88 31 17 81 42 54 93 38 22 63 40 68 50 86 75 21 77 58 72 19
```

When Program P9.4 is run, it produces the following output:

```
Max stack items: 5

14 17 19 21 22 23 25 26 28 31
32 35 37 38 39 40 42 43 44 46
48 50 51 54 56 58 60 63 65 66
68 69 72 73 75 77 78 79 81 84
85 86 87 88 90 93 96 99
```

As written, even if a sublist consists of two items only, the method will go through the whole process of calling partition, checking the lengths of the sublists, and stacking the two sublists. This seems an awful lot of work to sort two items.

We can make quicksort more efficient by using a simple method (insertion sort, say) to sort sublists that are shorter than some predefined length (8, say). You are urged to write quicksort with this change and experiment with different values of the predefined length.

9.5.3 Finding the kth Smallest Number

Consider the problem of finding the kth smallest number in a list of n numbers. One way to do this is to sort the n numbers and pick out the kth one. If the numbers are stored in an array A[1..n], we simply retrieve A[k] after sorting.

Another, more efficient way is to use the idea of partitioning. We will use that version of partition that places the pivot in its final sorted position. Consider an array A[1..99] and suppose a call to partition returns a division point of 40. This means that the pivot has been placed in A[40] with smaller numbers to the left and bigger numbers to the right. In other words, the 40th smallest number has been placed in A[40]. So, if k is 40, we have our answer immediately.

What if k were 59? We know that the 40 smallest numbers occupy A[1..40]. So, the 59th must be in A[41..99], and we can confine our search to this part of the array. In other words, with one call to partition, we can eliminate 40 numbers from consideration. The idea is similar to *binary search*.

Suppose the next call to partition returns 65. We now know the 65th smallest number and the 59th will be in A[41..64]; we have eliminated A[66..99] from consideration. We repeat this process each time, reducing the size of the part that contains the 59th smallest number. Eventually, partition will return 59, and we will have our answer.

The following is one way to write kthSmall; it uses partition1:

```
public static int kthSmall(int[] A, int k, int lo, int hi) {
//returns the kth smallest from A[lo] to A[hi]
    int kShift = lo + k - 1; //shift k to the given portion, A[lo..hi]
    if (kShift < lo || kShift > hi) return -9999;
    int dp = partition1(A, lo, hi);
    while (dp != kShift) {
        if (kShift < dp) hi = dp - 1; //kth smallest is in the left part
        else lo = dp + 1;            //kth smallest is in the right part
        dp = partition1(A, lo, hi);
    }
    return A[dp];
} //end kthSmall
```

For instance, the call kthSmall(num, 59, 1, 99) will return the 59th smallest number from num[1..99]. Note, however, that the call kthSmall(num, 10, 30, 75) will return the 10th smallest number from num[30..75].

As an exercise, write the recursive version of kthSmall.

9.6 Shell (Diminishing Increment) Sort

Shell sort (named after Donald Shell) uses a series of *increments* to govern the sorting process. It makes several passes over the data, with the last pass being the same as insertion sort. For the other passes, elements that are a fixed distance apart (for instance, five apart) are sorted using the same technique as insertion sort.

For example, to sort the following array, we use three increments—8, 3, and 1:

num

67	90	28	84	29	58	25	32	16	64	13	71	82	10	51	57
1	2	3	4	5	6	7	8	9	10	11	12	13	14	15	16

The increments decrease in size (hence the term *diminishing increment sort*), with the last one being 1.

Using increment 8, we eight-sort the array. This means we sort the elements that are eight apart. We sort elements 1 and 9, 2 and 10, 3 and 11, 4 and 12, 5 and 13, 6 and 14, 7 and 15, and 8 and 16. This will transform num into this:

16	64	13	71	29	10	25	32	67	90	28	84	82	58	51	57
1	2	3	4	5	6	7	8	9	10	11	12	13	14	15	16

Next, we three-sort the array; that is, we sort elements that are three apart. We sort elements (1, 4, 7, 10, 13, 16), (2, 5, 8, 11, 14), and (3, 6, 9, 12, 15). This gives us the following:

16	28	10	25	29	13	57	32	51	71	58	67	82	64	84	90
1	2	3	4	5	6	7	8	9	10	11	12	13	14	15	16

Note that, at each step, the array is a little closer to being sorted. Finally, we perform a one-sort, sorting the entire list, giving the final sorted order:

10	13	16	25	28	29	32	51	57	58	64	67	71	82	84	90
1	2	3	4	5	6	7	8	9	10	11	12	13	14	15	16

You may ask, why didn't we just do a one-sort from the beginning and sort the entire list? The idea here is that when we reach the stage of doing a one-sort, the array is more or less in order, and if we use a method that works better with partially ordered data (such as insertion sort), then the sort can proceed quickly. Recall that insertion sort can take as few as n comparisons (if the data is already sorted) or as many as $\frac{1}{2}n^2$ comparisons (if the data is sorted in descending order and we want ascending) to sort a list of n items.

When the increment is large, the pieces to sort are small. In the example, when the increment is eight, each piece consists of two elements only. Presumably, we can sort a small list quickly. When the increment is small, the pieces to sort are bigger. However, by the time we get to the small increments, the data is partially sorted, and we can sort the pieces quickly if we use a method that takes advantage of order in the data.

We will use a slightly modified version of insertion sort to sort elements that are h apart rather than one apart.

In insertion sort, when we come to process num[k], we assume that num[1..k-1] are sorted and insert num[k] among the previous items so that num[1..k] are sorted.

Suppose the increment is h, and consider how we might process num[k] where k is any valid subscript. Remember, our goal is to sort items that are h apart. So, we must sort num[k] with respect to num[k-h], num[k-2h], num[k-3h], and so on, provided these elements fall within the array. When we come to process num[k], if the previous items that are h apart are sorted among themselves, we must simply insert num[k] among those items so that the sublist ending at num[k] is sorted.

To illustrate, suppose h = 3 and k = 4. There is only one element before num[4] that is three away, that is, num[1]. So, when we come to process num[4], we can assume that num[1], by itself, is sorted. We insert num[4] relative to num[1] so that num[1] and num[4] are sorted.

Similarly, there is only one element before num[5] that is three away, that is, num[2]. So, when we come to process num[5], we can assume that num[2], by itself, is sorted. We insert num[5] relative to num[2] so that num[2] and num[5] are sorted. Similar remarks apply to num[3] and num[6].

When we get to num[7], the two items before num[7] (num[1] and num[4]) are sorted. We insert num[7] such that num[1], num[4], and num[7] are sorted.

When we get to num[8], the two items before num[8] (num[2] and num[5]) are sorted. We insert num[8] such that num[2], num[5], and num[8] are sorted.

When we get to num[9], the two items before num[9] (num[3] and num[6]) are sorted. We insert num[9] such that num[3], num[6], and num[9] are sorted.

When we get to num[10], the three items before num[10] (num[1], num[4], and num[7]) are sorted. We insert num[10] such that num[1], num[4], num[7], and num[10] are sorted.

And so on. Starting at h+1, we step through the array processing each item with respect to previous items that are multiples of h away.

In the example, when h = 3, we said we must sort elements (1, 4, 7, 10, 13, 16), (2, 5, 8, 11, 14), and (3, 6, 9, 12, 15). This is true, but our algorithm will not sort items (1, 4, 7, 10, 13, 16), followed by items (2, 5, 8, 11, 14) followed by items (3, 6, 9, 12, 15).

Rather, it will sort them in parallel by sorting the pieces in the following order: (1, 4), (2, 5), (3, 6), (1, 4, 7), (2, 5, 8), (3, 6, 9), (1, 4, 7, 10), (2, 5, 8, 11), (3, 6, 9, 12), (1, 4, 7, 10, 13), (2, 5, 8, 11, 14), (3, 6, 9, 12, 15), and finally (1, 4, 7, 10, 13, 16). This may sound more difficult, but it is actually easier to code, since we merely need to step through the array starting at h+1.

The following will perform an h-sort on A[1..n]:

```java
public static void hsort(int[] A, int n, int h) {
    for (int k = h + 1; k <= n; k++) {
        int j = k - h;
        int key = A[k];
        while (j > 0 && key < A[j]) {
            A[j + h] = A[j];
            j = j - h;
        }
        A[j + h] = key;
    }
} //end hsort
```

Alert readers will realize that if we set h to 1, this becomes insertion sort.

Programming note: If we want to sort A[0..n-1], we must change the for statement to the following and use j >= 0 in the while statement:

```java
for (int k = h; k < n; k++)
```

Given a series of increments $h_t, h_{t-1}, ..., h_1 = 1$, we simply call hsort with each increment, from largest to smallest, to effect the sort.

We write Program P9.5, which reads numbers from the file shell.in, sorts them using Shell sort (with three increments—8, 3 and 1), and prints the sorted list, ten numbers per line.

Program P9.5

```java
import java.io.*;
import java.util.*;
public class ShellSortTest {
    final static int MaxNumbers = 100;
    public static void main (String[] args) throws IOException {
```

```
            Scanner in = new Scanner(new FileReader("shell.in"));
            int[] num = new int[MaxNumbers+1];
            int n = 0, number;
            while (in.hasNextInt()) {
                number = in.nextInt();
                if (n < MaxNumbers) num[++n] = number; //store if array has room
            }

            //perform Shell sort with increments 8, 3 and 1
            hsort(num, n, 8);
            hsort(num, n, 3);
            hsort(num, n, 1);

            for (int h = 1; h <= n; h++) {
                System.out.printf("%d ", num[h]);
                if (h % 10 == 0) System.out.printf("\n"); //print 10 numbers per line
            }
            System.out.printf("\n");
        } //end main

    public static void hsort(int[] A, int n, int h) {
        for (int k = h + 1; k <= n; k++) {
            int j = k - h;
            int key = A[k];
            while (j > 0 && key < A[j]) {
                A[j + h] = A[j];
                j = j - h;
            }
            A[j + h] = key;
        } //end for
    } //end hsort

} //end class ShellSortTest
```

Suppose shell.in contains the following numbers:

```
43 25 66 37 65 48 84 73 60 79 56 69 32 87 23 99 85 28 14 78 39 51 44 35
46 90 26 96 88 31 17 81 42 54 93 38 22 63 40 68 50 86 75 21 77 58 72 19
```

When Program P9.5 is run, it produces the following output:

```
14 17 19 21 22 23 25 26 28 31
32 35 37 38 39 40 42 43 44 46
48 50 51 54 56 58 60 63 65 66
68 69 72 73 75 77 78 79 81 84
85 86 87 88 90 93 96 99
```

We note, in passing, that our code would be more flexible if the increments are stored in an array (incr, say) and hsort is called with each element of the array in turn. For example, suppose incr[0] contains the number of increments (m, say), and incr[1] to incr[m] contain the increments in decreasing order with incr[m] = 1. We could call hsort with each increment as follows:

```
for (int i = 1; i <= incr[0]; i++) hsort(num, n, incr[i]);
```

One question that arises is how do we decide which increments to use for a given n? Many methods have been proposed; the following gives reasonable results:

```
let h₁ = 1
generate h_{s+1} = 3h_s + 1, for s = 1, 2, 3,...
stop when h_{t+2} ≥ n; use h₁ to h_t as the increments for the sort
```

In other words, we generate terms of the sequence until a term is greater than or equal to n. Discard the last two and use the others as the increments for the sort.

For example, if n = 100, we generate $h_1 = 1$, $h_2 = 4$, $h_3 = 13$, $h_4 = 40$, $h_5 = 121$. Since $h_5 > 100$, we use h_1, h_2, and h_3 as the increments to sort 100 items.

The performance of Shell sort lies somewhere between the simple $O(n^2)$ methods (insertion, selection) and the $O(n\log_2 n)$ methods (heapsort, quicksort, mergesort). Its order is approximately $O(n^{1.3})$ for n in a practical range tending to $O(n(\log_2 n)^2)$ as n tends to infinity.

As an exercise, write a program to sort a list using Shell sort, counting the number of comparisons and assignments made in sorting the list.

EXERCISES 9

1. Write a program to compare the performance of the sorting methods discussed in this chapter with respect to "number of comparisons" and "number of assignments". For quicksort, compare the performance of choosing the first element as the pivot with choosing a random element.

   Run the program to (i) sort 10, 100, 1000, 10000 and 100000 elements supplied in random order and (ii) sort 10, 100, 1000, 10000 and 100000 elements that are already sorted.

2. A function makeHeap is passed an integer array A. If A[o] contains n, then A[1] to A[n] contain numbers in arbitrary order. Write makeHeap such that A[1] to A[n] contain a max-heap (*largest* value at the root). Your function must create the heap by processing the elements in the order A[2], A[3],...,A[n].

3. A heap is stored in a one-dimensional integer array num[1..n] with the *largest* value in position 1. Give an efficient algorithm that deletes the root and rearranges the other elements so that the heap now occupies num[1] to num[n-1].

4. A heap is stored in a one-dimensional integer array A[o..max] with the *largest* value in position 1. A[o] specifies the number of elements in the heap at any time. Write a function to add a new value v to the heap. Your function should work if the heap is initially empty and should print a message if there is no room to store v.

5. Write code to read a set of positive integers (terminated by 0) and create a heap in an array
    H with the *smallest* value at the top of the heap. As each integer is read, it is inserted among
    the existing items such that the heap properties are maintained. At any time, if *n* numbers
    have been read then H[1..n] must contain a heap. Assume that H is large enough to hold all
    the integers.

    Given the data: 51 26 32 45 38 89 29 58 34 23 0

    show the contents of H after each number has been read and processed.

6. A function is given an integer array A and two subscripts m and n. The function must
    rearrange the elements A[m] to A[n] and return a subscript d such that all elements to
    the left of d are less than or equal to A[d] and all elements to the right of d are greater
    than A[d].

7. Write a function that, given an integer array num and an integer n, sorts the elements num[1]
    to num[n] using Shell sort. The function must return the number of key comparisons made in
    performing the sort. You may use any reasonable method for determining increments.

8. A single integer array A[1..n] contains the following: A[1..k] contains a min-heap and
    A[k+1..n] contains arbitrary values. Write efficient code to merge the two portions so that
    A[1..n] contains one min-heap. Do *not* use any other array.

9. An *integer* max-heap is stored in an array (A, say) such that the size of the heap (n, say) is
    stored in A[0] and A[1] to A[n] contain the elements of the heap with the *largest* value
    in A[1].

    (i)   Write a function deleteMax which, given an array like A, deletes the largest element and
          reorganizes the array so that it remains a heap.

    (ii) Given two arrays A and B containing heaps as described above, write programming
          code to merge the elements of A and B into another array C such that C is in ascending
          order. Your method must proceed by comparing an element of A with one in B. You may
          assume that deleteMax is available.

10. Write a recursive function for finding the kth smallest number in an array of *n* numbers,
    without sorting the array.

11. Write insertion sort using a binary search to determine the position in which A[j] will be
    inserted among the sorted sublist A[1..j-1].

12. A sorting algorithm is said to be *stable* if equal keys retain their original relative order after
    sorting. Which of the sorting methods discussed are stable?

13. You are given a list of *n* numbers. Write efficient algorithms to find (i) the smallest (ii) the
    largest (iii) the mean (iv) the median (the middle value) and (v) the mode (the value that
    appears most often).

    Write an efficient algorithm to find all five values.

14. It is known that every number in a list of *n distinct* numbers is between 100 and 9999.
    Devise an efficient method for sorting the numbers.

    Modify the method to sort the list if it may contain duplicate numbers.

15. Modify merge sort (Chapter 5) and quicksort so that if a sublist to be sorted is smaller than some pre-defined size, it is sorted using insertion sort.

16. You are given a list of *n* numbers and another number x. You must find the smallest number in the list that is greater than or equal to x. You must then delete this number from the list and replace it by a new number y, retaining the list structure. Devise ways of solving this problem using (i) unsorted array (ii) sorted array (iii) sorted linked list (iv) binary search tree (v) heap.

    Which of these is the most efficient?

17. You are given a (long) list of English words. Write a program to determine which of those words are anagrams of each other. Output consists of each group of anagrams (two or more words) followed by a blank line. Two words are anagrams if they consist of the same letters, such as (teacher, cheater), (sister, resist).

18. Each value in A[1..n] is either 1, 2 or 3. You are required to find the *minimal* number of *exchanges* to sort the array. For example, the array

2	2	1	3	3	3	2	3	1
1	2	3	4	5	6	7	8	9

can be sorted with four exchanges, in order: (1, 3) (4, 7) (2, 9) (5, 9). Another solution is (1, 3) (2, 9) (4, 7) (5, 9). The array cannot be sorted with less than four exchanges.

CHAPTER 10

■ ■ ■

Hashing

In this chapter, we will explain the following:

- The fundamental ideas on which hashing is based

- How to solve the search and insert problem using hashing

- How to delete an item from a hash table

- How to resolve collisions using linear probing

- How to resolve collisions using quadratic probing

- How to resolve collisions using chaining

- How to resolve collisions using linear probing with double hashing

- How to link items in order using arrays

10.1 Hashing Fundamentals

Searching for an item in a (large) table is a common operation in many applications. In this chapter, we discuss *hashing*, a fast method for performing this search. The main idea behind hashing is to use the key of an item (for example, the vehicle registration number of a vehicle record) to determine *where* in the table (the *hash table*) the item is stored. The key is first converted to a number (if it is not already one), and this number is mapped (we say *hashed*) to a table location. The method used to convert a key to a table location is called the *hash function*.

It is entirely possible, of course, for two or more keys to hash to the same location. When this happens, we say we have a *collision*, and we must find a way to resolve the collision. The efficiency (or otherwise) of hashing is determined to a large extent by the method used to resolve collisions. Much of the chapter is devoted to a discussion of these methods.

10.1.1 The Search and Insert Problem

The classical statement of the search and insert problem is as follows:

> *Given a list of items (the list may be empty initially), search for a given item in the list. If the item is not found, insert it in the list.*

Items can be things such as numbers (student, account, employee, vehicle, and so on), names, words, or strings in general. For example, suppose we have a set of integers, not necessarily distinct, and we want to find out how many distinct integers there are.

We start with an empty list. For each integer, we look for it in the list. If it is not found, it is added to the list and counted. If it is found, there is nothing to do.

In solving this problem, a major design decision is how to search the list, which, in turn, will depend on how the list is stored and how a new integer is added. The following are some possibilities:

1. The list is stored in an array, and a new integer is placed in the next available position in the array. This implies that a sequential search must be used to look for an incoming integer. This method has the advantages of simplicity and easy addition, but searching takes longer as more numbers are put in the list.

2. The list is stored in an array, and a new integer is added in such a way that the list is always in order. This may entail moving numbers that have already been stored so that the new number may be slotted in the right place.

3. However, since the list is in order, a binary search can be used to search for an incoming integer. For this method, searching is faster, but insertion is slower than in the previous method. Since, in general, searching is done more frequently than inserting, this method might be preferable to the previous method.

4. Another advantage here is that, at the end, the integers will be in order, if this is important. If method 1 is used, the numbers will have to be sorted.

5. The list is stored as an unsorted linked list so must be searched sequentially. Since the entire list must be traversed if an incoming number is not present, the new number can be added at the head or tail; both are equally easy.

6. The list is stored as a sorted linked list. A new number must be inserted "in place" to maintain the order. Once the position is found, insertion is easy. The entire list does not have to be traversed if an incoming number is not present, but we are still restricted to a sequential search.

7. The list is stored in a binary search tree. Searching is reasonably fast provided the tree does not become too unbalanced. Adding a number is easy—it's only a matter of setting a couple links. An in-order traversal of the tree will give the numbers in sorted order, if this is required.

Yet another possibility is the method called *hashing*. As we will see, this has the advantages of extremely fast search times and easy insertion.

10.2 Solving the Search and Insert Problem by Hashing

We will illustrate how hashing works by solving the "search and insert" problem for a list of integers. The list will be stored in an array num[1] to num[n]. In our example, we will assume n is 12.

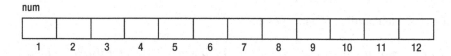

Initially, there are no numbers in the list. Suppose the first incoming number is 52. The idea behind hashing is to convert 52 (usually called the *key*) into a valid table location (k, say). Here, the valid table locations are 1 to 12.

If there is no number in num[k], then 52 is stored in that location. If num[k] is occupied by another key, we say a *collision* has occurred, and we must find another location in which to try to place 52. This is called *resolving the collision*.

The method used to convert a key to a table location is called the *hash function* (H, say). Any calculation that produces a valid table location (array subscript) can be used, but, as we shall see, some functions give better results than others.

For example, we could use H1(key) = key % 10 + 1. In other words, we add 1 to the last digit of the key. Thus, 52 would hash to 3. Note that H1 produces locations between 1 and 10 only. If the table had 100 locations, say, the function would be valid, but it may not be a good function to use.

Note also that H(key) = key % 10 would not be a proper hash function here since, for instance, 50 would hash to 0 and there is no table location 0. Of course, if locations started from subscript 0, then key % 10 would be valid, provided there were at least ten locations.

Another function is H2(key) = key % 12 + 1. The expression key % 12 produces a value between 0 and 11; adding 1 gives values between 1 and 12. In general, key % n + 1 produces values between 1 and n, inclusive. We will use this function in our example.

H2(52) = 52 % 12 + 1 = 5. We say, "52 hashes to location 5." Since num[5] is empty, we place 52 in num[5].

Suppose, later, we are searching for 52. We first apply the hash function, and we get 5. We compare num[5] with 52; they match, so we find 52 with just one comparison.

Now suppose the following keys come in the order given:

    52 33 84 43 16 59 31 23 61

- 52 is placed in num[5].

- 33 hashes to 10; num[10] is empty, so 33 is placed in num[10].

- 84 hashes to 1; num[1] is empty, so 84 is placed in num[1].

- 43 hashes to 8; num[8] is empty, so 43 is placed in num[8].

At this stage, num can be pictured like this:

num

84				52			43		33		
1	2	3	4	5	6	7	8	9	10	11	12

- 16 hashes to 5; num[5] is occupied and not by 16—we have a collision. To resolve the collision, we must find another location in which to put 16. One obvious choice is to try the very next location, 6; num[6] is empty, so 16 is placed in num[6].

- 59 hashes to 12; num[12] is empty, so 59 is placed in num[12].

- 31 hashes to 8; num[8] is occupied and not by 31—we have a collision. We try the next location, 9; num[9] is empty, so 31 is placed in num[9].

At this stage, num looks like this:

num

84				52	16		43	31	33		59
1	2	3	4	5	6	7	8	9	10	11	12

- 23 hashes to 12; num[12] is occupied and not by 23—we have a collision. We must try the next location, but what is the next location here? We pretend that the table is "circular" so that location 1 follows location 12. However, num[1] is occupied and not by 23. So, we try num[2]; num[2] is empty, so 23 is placed in num[2].

- Finally, 61 hashes to 2; num[2] is occupied and not by 61—we have a collision. We try the next location, 3; num[3] is empty, so 61 is placed in num[3].

The following shows the array after all the numbers have been inserted:

num

84	23	61		52	16		43	31	33		59
1	2	3	4	5	6	7	8	9	10	11	12

Note that if a number is already in the array, the method would find it. For example, suppose we are searching for 23.

- 23 hashes to 12.

- num[12] is occupied and not by 23.

- We try the next location, 1; num[1] is occupied and not by 23.

- We next try num[2]; num[2] is occupied by 23—we find it.

Suppose we are searching for 33; 33 hashes to 10, and num[10] contains 33—we find it immediately.

As an exercise, determine the state of num after the previous numbers have been added using the hash function H1(key) = key % 10 + 1.

We can summarize the process described with the following algorithm:

```
//find or insert 'key' in the hash table, num[1..n]
loc = H(key)
while (num[loc] is not empty && num[loc] != key) loc = loc % n + 1
if (num[loc] is empty) { //key is not in the table
   num[loc] = key
   add 1 to the count of distinct numbers
}
else print key, " found in location ", loc
```

Note the expression loc % n + 1 for going to the next location. If loc is less than n, loc % n is simply loc, and the expression is the same as loc + 1. If loc *is* n, loc % n is 0, and the expression evaluates to 1. In either case, loc takes on the value of the next location.

Alert readers will realize that we exit the while loop when either num[loc] is empty or it contains the key. What if neither happens so the while loop *never* exits? This situation will arise if the table is completely full (no empty locations) and does not contain the key we are searching for.

However, *in practice*, we never allow the hash table to become completely full. We always ensure that there are a few "extra" locations that are not filled by keys so that the while statement *will* exit at some point. In general, the hash technique works better when there are more free locations in the table.

How does the algorithm tell when a location is "empty"? We will need to initialize the array with some value that indicates "empty." For instance, if the keys are positive integers, we can use 0 or -1 as the empty value.

Let's write Program P10.1, which reads integers from a file, numbers.in, and uses a hash technique to determine the number of distinct integers in the file.

Program P10.1

```
import java.util.*;
import java.io.*;
public class DistinctNumbers {
   final static int MaxDistinctNumbers = 20;
   final static int N = 23;
   final static int Empty = 0;
```

```java
public static void main(String[] args) throws IOException {
    Scanner in = new Scanner(new FileReader("numbers.in"));
    int[] num = new int[N + 1];
    for (int j = 1; j <= N; j++) num[j] = Empty;
    int distinct = 0;
    while (in.hasNextInt()) {
        int key = in.nextInt();
        int loc = key % N + 1;
        while (num[loc] != Empty && num[loc] != key) loc = loc % N + 1;

        if (num[loc] == Empty) { //key is not in the table
            if (distinct == MaxDistinctNumbers) {
                System.out.printf("\nTable full: %d not added\n", key);
                System.exit(1);
            }
            num[loc] = key;
            distinct++;
        }
    } //end while
    System.out.printf("\nThere are %d distinct numbers\n", distinct);
    in.close();
} //end main

} //end class DistinctNumbers
```

Suppose numbers.in contains these numbers:

25 28 29 23 26 35 22 31 21 26 25 21 31 32 26 20 36 21 27 24 35 23 32 28 36

When run, Program P10.1 prints the following:

There are 14 distinct numbers

Here are some notes on Program P10.1:

- MaxDistinctNumbers (20) is the maximum amount of distinct numbers catered for.

- N (23) is the hash table size, a little bigger than MaxDistinctNumbers so that there is always at least three free locations in the table.

- The hash table occupies num[1] to num[N]. If you want, num[0] may be used; in this case, the hash function could simply be key % N.

- If key is not in the table (an empty location is encountered), we first check whether the number of entries has reached MaxDistinctNumbers. If it has, we declare the table full and do not add key. Otherwise, we put key in the table and count it.

- If key is found, we simply go on to read the next number.

10.2.1 The Hash Function

In the previous section, we saw how an integer key can be "hashed" to a table location. It turns out that the "remainder" operation (%) often gives good results for such keys. But what if the keys were non-numeric, for example, words or names?

The first task is to convert a non-numeric key to a number and then apply "remainder." Suppose the key is a word. Perhaps the simplest thing to do is add up the numeric value of each letter in the word. If the word is stored in a string variable, word, we can do this as follows:

```
int wordNum = 0;
for (int h = 0; h < word.length(); h++) wordNum += word.charAt(h);
loc = wordNum % n + 1; //loc is assigned a value from 1 to n
```

This method will work, but one objection is that words that contain the same letters would hash to the same location. For example, *mate*, *meat*, and *team* will all hash to the same location. In hashing, we must try to avoid deliberately hashing keys to the same location. One way around this is to assign a weight to each letter depending on its position in the word.

We can assign weights arbitrarily—the main goal is to avoid hashing keys with the same letters to the same location. For instance, we can assign 3 to the first position, 5 to the second position, 7 to the third position, and so on. The following shows how:

```
int wordNum = 0;
int w = 3;
for (int h = 0; h < word.length(); h++) {
    wordNum += word.charAt(h) * w;
    w = w + 2;
}
loc = wordNum % n + 1; //loc is assigned a value from 1 to n
```

The same technique will work if a key contains arbitrary characters.

In hashing, we want the keys to be scattered all over the table. If, for instance, keys are hashed to one area of the table, we can end up with an unnecessarily high number of collisions. To this end, we should try to use *all* of the key. For example, if the keys are alphabetic, it would be unwise to map all keys beginning with the same letter to the same location. Put another way, we should avoid systematically hitting the same location.

And since hashing is meant to be fast, the hash function should be relatively easy to calculate. The speed advantage will be diminished if we spend too much time computing the hash location.

10.2.2 Deleting an Item from a Hash Table

Consider, again, the array after all the sample numbers have been inserted:

num

84	23	61		52	16		43	31	33		59
1	2	3	4	5	6	7	8	9	10	11	12

Recall that 43 and 31 both hashed initially to location 8. Suppose we want to delete 43. The first thought might be to set its location to empty. Assume we did this (set num[8] to empty) and were now looking for 31. This will hash to 8; but since num[8] is empty, we will conclude, wrongly, that 31 is not in the table. So, we cannot delete an item simply by setting its location to empty since other items may become unreachable.

The easiest solution is to set its location to a *deleted* value—some value that cannot be confused with *empty* or a key. In this example, if the keys are positive integers, we can use 0 for Empty and -1 for Deleted.

Now, when searching, we still check for the key or an empty location; deleted locations are ignored. A common error is to stop the search at a deleted location; doing so would lead to incorrect conclusions.

If our search reveals that an incoming key is not in the table, the key can be inserted in an empty location or a deleted one, if one was encountered along the way. For example, suppose we had deleted 43 by setting num[8] to -1. If we now search for 55, we will check locations 8, 9, 10, and 11. Since num[11] is empty, we conclude that 55 is not in the table.

We can, if we want, set num[11] to 55. But we could write our algorithm to remember the deleted location at 8. If we do, we can then insert 55 in num[8]. This is better since we will find 55 faster than if it were in num[11]. We would also be making better use of our available locations by reducing the number of deleted locations.

What if there are several deleted locations along the way? It is best to use the first one encountered since this will reduce the search time for the key. With these ideas, we can rewrite our search/insert algorithm as follows:

```
//find or insert 'key' in the hash table, num[1..n]
loc = H(key)
deletedLoc = 0
while (num[loc] != Empty && num[loc] != key) {
    if (deletedLoc == 0 && num[loc] == Deleted) deletedLoc = loc
    loc = loc % n + 1
}

if (num[loc] == Empty) { //key not found
    if (deletedLoc != 0) loc = deletedLoc
    num[loc] = key
}
else print key, " found in location ", loc
```

Note that we still search until we find an empty location or the key. If we meet a deleted location and deletedLoc is 0, this means it's the first one. Of course, if we *never* meet a deleted location and the key is not in the table, it will be inserted in an empty location.

10.3 Resolving Collisions

In Program P10.1, we resolve a collision by looking at the next location in the table. This is, perhaps, the simplest way to resolve a collision. We say we resolve the collision using *linear probing*, and we will discuss this in more detail in the next section. After this, we will take a look at more sophisticated ways of resolving collisions. Among these are *quadratic probing*, *chaining*, and *double hashing*.

10.3.1 Linear Probing

Linear probing is characterized by the statement loc = loc + 1. Consider, again, the state of num after the nine numbers have been added:

num

84	23	61		52	16		43	31	33		59
1	2	3	4	5	6	7	8	9	10	11	12

As you can see, the chances of hashing a new key to an empty location decreases as the table fills up.

Suppose a key hashes to location 12. It will be placed in num[4] after trying locations 12, 1, 2, and 3. In fact, any new key that hashes to 12, 1, 2, 3, or 4 will end up in num[4]. When that happens, we will have a long, unbroken chain of keys from location 12 to location 6. Any new key hashing to this chain will end up in num[7], creating an even longer chain.

This phenomenon of *clustering* is one of the main drawbacks of linear probing. Long chains tend to get longer since the probability of hashing to a long chain is usually greater than that of hashing to a short chain. It is also easy for two short chains to be joined, creating a longer chain that, in turn, will tend to get longer. For example, any key that ends up in num[7] will create a long chain from locations 5 to 10.

We define two types of clustering.

- *Primary clustering* occurs when keys that hash to different locations trace the same sequence in looking for an empty location. Linear probing exhibits primary clustering since a key that hashes to 5, say, will trace 5, 6, 7, 8, 9, and so on, and a key that hashes to 6 will trace 6, 7, 8, 9, and so on.

- *Secondary clustering* occurs when keys that hash to the *same* location trace the same sequence in looking for an empty location. Linear probing exhibits secondary clustering since keys that hash to 5, say, will trace the same sequence 5, 6, 7, 8, 9, and so on.

Methods of resolving collisions that hope to improve on linear probing will target the elimination of primary and/or secondary clustering.

You may wonder if using loc = loc + k where k is a constant greater than 1 (for example, 3) will give any better results than loc = loc + 1. As it turns out, this will not alter the clustering phenomenon since groups of k-apart keys will still be formed.

In addition, it can even be worse than when k is 1 since it is possible that not all locations will be generated.

Suppose the table size is 12, k is 3, and a key hashes to 5. The sequence of locations traced will be 5, 8, 11, 2 (11 + 3 - 12), 5, and the sequence repeats itself. In other words, only relatively few locations will be probed in looking for an empty location. By comparison, when k is 1, all locations are generated.

However, this is not really a problem. If the table size is m and k is "relatively prime" to m (their only common factor is 1), then all locations are generated. Two numbers will be relatively prime if one is a prime and the other is not a multiple of it, such as 5 and 12. But being prime is not a necessary condition. The numbers 21 and 50 (neither of which is prime) are relatively prime since they have no common factors other than 1.

If k is 5 and m is 12, a key hashing to 5 will trace the sequence 5, 10, 3, 8, 1, 6, 11, 4, 9, 2, 7, 12—all locations are generated. A key hashing to any other location will also generate all locations.

In any case, being able to generate all locations is academic since if we had to trace many locations to find an empty one, the search would be too slow, and we would probably need to use another method.

Notwithstanding what we've just said, it turns out that loc = loc + k, where k *varies* with the key, gives us one of the best ways to implement hashing. We will see how in Section 10.3.4.

So, how fast is the linear method? We are interested in the average *search length*, that is, the number of locations that must be examined to find or insert a given key. In the previous example, the search length of 33 is 1, the search length of 61 is 2, and the search length of 23 is 3.

The search length is a function of the *load factor*, *f*, of the table, where

$$f = \frac{number\ of\ entries\ in\ table}{number\ of\ table\ locations} = \text{fraction of table filled}$$

For a successful search, the average number of comparisons is $\frac{1}{2}\left(1 + \frac{1}{1-f}\right)$, and for an unsuccessful search, the average number of comparisons is $\frac{1}{2}\left(1 + \frac{1}{(1-f)^2}\right)$. Note that the search length depends only on the fraction of the table filled, *not* on the table size.

Table 10-1 shows how the search length increases as the table fills up.

Table 10-1. *Search Length Increases as the Table Fills Up*

f	Successful Search Length	Unsuccessful Search Length
0.25	1.2	1.4
0.50	1.5	2.5
0.75	2.5	8.5
0.90	5.5	50.5

At 90 percent full, the average successful search length is a reasonable 5.5. However, it can take quite long (50.5 probes) to determine that a new key is not in the table. If linear probe is being used, it would be wise to ensure that the table does not become more than about 75 percent full. This way, we can guarantee good performance with a simple algorithm.

10.3.2 Quadratic Probing

In this method, suppose an incoming key collides with another at location loc; we go forward $ai + bi^2$ where a, b are constants and i takes on the value 1 for the first collision, 2 if the key collides again, 3 if it collides yet again, and so on. For example, if we let $a = 1$ and $b = 1$, we go forward $i + i^2$ from location loc. Suppose the initial hash location is 7 and there is a collision.

We calculate $i + i^2$ with $i = 1$; this gives 2, so we go forward by 2 and check location $7 + 2 = 9$.

If there is still a collision, we calculate $i + i^2$ with $i = 2$; this gives 6, so we go forward by 6 and check location $9 + 6 = 15$.

If there is still a collision, we calculate $i + i^2$ with $i = 3$; this gives 12, so we go forward by 12 and check location $15 + 12 = 27$.

And so on. Each time we get a collision, we increase i by 1 and recalculate how much we must go forward this time. We continue this way until we find the key or an empty location.

If, at any time, going forward takes us beyond the end of the table, we wrap around to the beginning. For example, if the table size is 25 and we go forward to location 27, we wrap to location $27 - 25$, that is, location 2.

For the next incoming key, if there is a collision at the initial hash location, we set i to 1 and continue as explained earlier. It is worth noting that, for each key, the sequence of "increments" will be 2, 6, 12, 20, 30.... We can, of course, get a different sequence by choosing different values for a and b.

We can summarize the process just described with the following algorithm:

```
//find or insert 'key' in the hash table, num[1..n]
loc = H(key)
i = 0
while (num[loc] != Empty && num[loc] != key) {
    i = i + 1
    loc = loc + a * i + b * i * i
    while (loc > n) loc = loc - n    //while instead of if; see note below
}
if (num[loc] == Empty) num[loc] = key
else print key, " found in location ", loc
```

■ **Note** We use while instead of if to perform the "wrap around" just in case the new location is more than twice the table size. For instance, suppose n is 25, the increment is 42, and we are going forward from location 20. This will take us to location 62. If we had used if, the "wrap around" location would be $62 - 25 = 37$, which is still outside the range of the table. With while, we will get the valid location $37 - 25 = 12$.

Could we have used loc % n instead of the while loop? In this example, we would get the correct location, but if the new location were a multiple of n, loc % n would give 0. This will be an invalid location if the table starts from 1.

With quadratic probing, keys that hash to different locations trace different sequences; hence, primary clustering is eliminated. However, keys that hash to the same location will trace the same sequence, so secondary clustering remains.

Here are some other points to note:

- If n is a power of 2, that is, $n = 2^m$ for some m, this method explores only a small fraction of the locations in the table and is, therefore, not very effective.

- If n is prime, the method can reach half the locations in the table; this is usually sufficient for most practical purposes.

10.3.3 Chaining

In this method, all items that hash to the same location are held on a linked list. One immediate advantage of this is that items that hash "near" to each other will not interfere with each other since they will not be vying for the same free space in the table, as happens with linear probing. One way to implement chaining is to let the hash table contain "top of list" pointers. For instance, if hash[1..n] is the hash table, then hash[k] will point to the linked list of all items that hash to location k. An item can be added to a linked list at the head, at the tail, or in a position such that the list is in order.

To illustrate the method, suppose the items are integers. Each linked list item will consist of an integer value and a pointer to the next item. We use the following class to create the nodes in the linked lists:

```
class Node {
    int num;
    Node next;

    public Node(int n) {
        num = n;
        next = null;
    }
} //end class Node
```

We can now define the array hash as follows:

```
Node[] hash = new Node[n+1]; //assume n has a value
```

We initialize it with this:

```
for (int h = 1; h <= n; h++) hash[h] = null;
```

Suppose an incoming key, inKey, hashes to location k. We must search the linked list pointed to by hash[k] for inKey. If it is not found, we must add it to the list. In our program, we will add it such that the list is in ascending order.

We write Program P10.2 to count the number of distinct integers in the input file numbers.in. The program uses *hashing with chaining*. At the end, we print the list of numbers that hash to each location.

Program P10.2

```java
import java.util.*;
import java.io.*;
public class HashChain {
   final static int N = 13;
   public static void main(String[] args) throws IOException {
      Scanner in = new Scanner(new FileReader("numbers.in"));

      Node[] hash = new Node[N+1];
      for (int h = 1; h <= N; h++) hash[h] = null;
      int distinct = 0;
      while (in.hasNextInt()) {
         int key = in.nextInt();
         if (!search(key, hash, N)) distinct++;
      }
      System.out.printf("\nThere are %d distinct numbers\n\n", distinct);
      for (int h = 1; h <= N; h++)
         if (hash[h] != null) {
            System.out.printf("hash[%d]:  ", h);
            printList(hash[h]);
         }
      in.close();
   } //end main

   public static boolean search(int inKey, Node[] hash, int n) {
   //return true if inKey is found; false, otherwise
   //insert a new key in its appropriate list so list is in order
      int k = inKey % n + 1;
      Node curr = hash[k];
      Node prev = null;

      while (curr != null && inKey > curr.num) {
         prev = curr;
         curr = curr.next;
      }
      if (curr != null && inKey == curr.num) return true; //found
      //not found; inKey is a new key; add it so list is in order
      Node np = new Node(inKey);
      np.next = curr;
      if (prev == null) hash[k] = np;
      else prev.next = np;
      return false;
   } //end search

   public static void printList(Node top) {
      while (top != null) {
         System.out.printf("%2d ", top.num);
         top = top.next;
      }
      System.out.printf("\n");
   } //end printList

} //end class HashChain
```

```
class Node {
    int num;
    Node next;

    public Node(int n) {
        num = n;
        next = null;
    }
} //end class Node
```

Suppose numbers.in contains the following numbers:

```
24 57 35 37 31 98 85 47 60 32 48 82 16 96 87 46 53 92 71 56
73 85 47 46 22 40 95 32 54 67 31 44 74 40 58 42 88 29 78 87
45 13 73 29 84 48 85 29 66 73 87 17 10 83 95 25 44 93 32 39
```

When run, Program P10.2 produces the following output:

```
There are 43 distinct numbers

hash[1]: 13 39 78
hash[2]: 40 53 66 92
hash[3]: 54 67 93
hash[4]: 16 29 42
hash[5]: 17 56 82 95
hash[6]: 31 44 57 83 96
hash[7]: 32 45 58 71 84
hash[8]: 46 85 98
hash[9]: 47 60 73
hash[10]: 22 35 48 74 87
hash[11]: 10 88
hash[12]: 24 37
hash[13]: 25
```

If m keys have been stored in the linked lists and there are n hash locations, the average length of a list is $\frac{m}{n}$, and since we must search the lists sequentially, the average successful search length is $\frac{m}{2n}$. The search length can be reduced by increasing the number of hash locations.

Another way to implement hashing with chaining is to use a single array and use array subscripts as links. We can use the following declarations:

```
class Node {
    int num;    //key
    int next;   //array subscript of the next item in the list
}

Node[] hash = new Node[MaxItems+1];
```

The first part of the table, hash[1..n], say, is designated as the hash table, and the remaining locations are used as an *overflow* table, as shown in Figure 10-1.

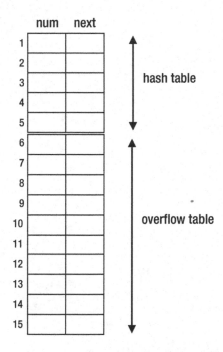

Figure 10-1. *Array implementation of chaining*

Here, hash[1..5] is the hash table, and hash[6..15] is the overflow table.
Suppose key hashes to location k in the hash table:

- If hash[k].num is empty (0, say), we set it to key and set hash[k].next to -1, say, to indicate a null pointer.

- If hash[k].num is not 0, we must search the list starting at k for key. If it is not found, we put it in the next free location (f, say) in the overflow table and link it to the list starting at hash[k]. One way to link it is as follows:

```
hash[f].next = hash[k].next;
hash[k].next = f;
```

- Another way to link the new key is to add it at the end of the list. If L is the location of the last node in the list, this could be done with the following:

```
hash[L].next = f;
hash[f].next = -1;    //this is now the last node
```

If we have to cater for deletions, we will have to decide what to do with deleted locations. One possibility is to keep a list of all available locations in the overflow table. When one is needed to store a key, it is retrieved from the list. When an item is deleted, its location is returned to the list.

Initially, we can link all the items in the overflow table as shown in Figure 10-2 and let the variable free point to the first item in the list; here, free = 6. Item 6 points to item 7, which points to item 8, and so on, with item 15 at the end of the list.

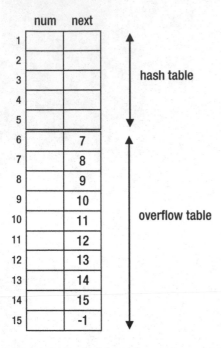

Figure 10-2. *Link items in overflow table to form "free list"*

Suppose 37 hashes to location 2. This is empty, so 37 is stored in hash[2].num. If another number (24, say) hashes to 2, it must be stored in the overflow table. First we must get a location from the "free list." This can be done with the following:

```
f = free;
free = hash[free].next;
return f;
```

Here, 6 is returned, and free is set to 7. The number 24 is stored in location 6, and hash[2].next is set to 6. At this stage, we have free = 7, with the tables having the values shown in Figure 10-3.

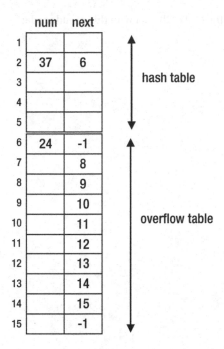

Figure 10-3. *After adding 24 to the overflow table*

Now, consider how an item may be deleted. There are two cases to consider:

- If the item to be deleted is in the hash table (at k, say), we can delete it with this:

```
if (hash[k].next == -1) set hash[k].num to Empty  //only item in the list
else { //copy an item from the overflow table to the hash table
  h = hash[k].next;
  hash[k] = hash[h];   //copy information at location h to location k
  return h to the free list   //see next
}
```

- We can return a location (h, say) to the free list with this:

```
hash[h].next = free;
free = h;
```

- If the item to be deleted is in the overflow table (at curr, say) and prev is the location of the item that points to the one to be deleted, we can delete it with this:

```
hash[prev].next = hash[curr].next;
return curr to the free list
```

Now consider how an incoming key might be processed. Suppose free is 9 and the number 52 hashes to location 2. We search the list starting at 2 for 52. It is not found, so 52 is stored in the next free location, 9. Location 6 contains the last item in the list, so hash[6].next is set to 9, and hash[9].next is set to -1.

In general, we can perform a search for key and, if not found, insert it at the end of the list with this pseudocode:

```
k = H(key)    //H is the hash function
if (hash[k].num == Empty) {
    hash[k].num = key
    hash[k].next = -1
}
else {
    curr = k
    prev = -1
    while (curr != -1 && hash[curr].num != key) {
        prev = curr
        curr = hash[curr].next
    }
    if (curr != -1) key is in the list at location curr
    else {  //key is not present
        hash[free].num = key    //assume free list is not empty
        hash[free].next = -1
        hash[prev].next = free
        free = hash[free].next
    } //end else
} //end else
```

10.3.4 Linear Probing with Double Hashing[1]

In Section 10.3.1, we saw that using loc = loc + k, where k is a constant greater than 1, does not give us a better performance than when k is 1. However, by letting k vary with the key, we can get excellent results since, unlike linear and quadratic probing, keys that hash to the same location will probe different sequences of locations in searching for an empty one.

The most natural way to let k vary with the key is to use a second hash function. The first hash function will generate the initial table location. If there is a collision, the second hash function will generate the increment, k. If the table locations run from 1 to n, we can use the following:

```
convert key to a numeric value, num (if it is not already numeric)
loc = num % n + 1       //this gives the initial hash location
k = num % (n - 2) + 1   //this gives the increment for this key
```

We mentioned before that it is wise to choose n (the table size) as a prime number. In this method, we get even better results if n-2 is also prime (in this case, n and n-2 are called *twin primes*, for example 103/101, 1021/1019).

Apart from the fact that k is not fixed, the method is the same as *linear probing*. We describe it in terms of two hash functions, H1 and H2. H1 produces the initial hash location, a value between 1 and n, inclusive. H2 produces the increment, a value between 1 and n - 1 that is relatively prime to n; this is desirable so that, if required, many locations will be probed. As discussed earlier, if n is prime, any value between 1 and n - 1 will be relatively prime to it. In the previous example, the second hash function produces a value between 1 and n-2. Here is the algorithm:

```
//find or insert 'key' using "linear probing with double hashing"
loc = H1(key)
k = H2(key)
```

---

[1]The technique is sometimes referred to as *open addressing with double hashing*.

```
while (hash[loc] != Empty && hash[loc] != key) {
    loc = loc + k
    if (loc > n) loc = loc - n
}
if (hash[loc] == Empty) hash[loc] = key
else print key, " found in location ", loc
```

As before, to ensure that the while loop exits at some point, we do not allow the table to become completely full. If we want to cater for MaxItems, say, we declare the table size to be bigger than MaxItems. In general, the more free locations in the table, the better the hash technique works.

However, with double hashing, we do not need as many free locations as with normal linear probe to guarantee good performance. This is because double hashing eliminates both primary and secondary clustering.

Primary clustering is eliminated since keys that hash to different locations will generate different sequences of locations. Secondary clustering is eliminated since different keys that hash to the same location will generate different sequences. This is since, in general, different keys will generate different increments (k, in the algorithm). It would be a rare coincidence indeed for two keys to be hashed to the same values by both H1 and H2.

In practice, the performance of any hashing application can be improved by keeping information on how often each key is accessed. If we have this information beforehand, we can simply load the hash table with the most popular items first and the least popular last. This will lower the average access time for all keys.

If we do not have this information beforehand, we can keep a counter with each key and increment it each time the key is accessed. After some predefined time (a month, say), we reload the table with the most popular items first and the least popular last. We then reset the counters and garner statistics for the next month. This way we can ensure that the application remains fine-tuned since different items may become popular in the next month.

10.4 Example: Word Frequency Count

Consider, once again, the problem of writing a program to do a frequency count of the words in a passage. Output consists of an alphabetical listing of the words with their frequencies. Now, we will store the words in a hash table using linear probing with double hashing.

Each element in the table consists of three fields—word, freq, and next. We will use the following class to create objects to be stored in the table:

```
class WordInfo {
    String word = "";
    int freq = 0;
    int next = -1;
} //end class WordInfo
```

We declare and initialize the table with this:

```
WordInfo[] wordTable = new WordInfo[N+1]; //N - table size
for (int h = 1; h <= N; h++) wordTable[h] = new WordInfo();
```

The table is searched for each incoming word. If the word is not found, it is added to the table, and its frequency count is set to 1. If the word is found, then its frequency count is incremented by 1.

In addition, when a word is added to the table, we set links such that we maintain a linked list of the words in alphabetical order. The variable first points to the first word in order. For example, suppose five words have been stored in the hash table. We link them, via next, as shown in Figure 10-4, with first = 6.

	word	freq	next
1	for	2	7
2			
3	the	4	-1
4	man	1	3
5			
6	boy	1	1
7	girl	2	4

Figure 10-4. *Words linked in alphabetical order (first = 6)*

Thus, the first word is boy, which points to for (1), which points to girl (7), which points to man (4), which points to the (3), which does not point to anything (-1). The words are linked in alphabetical order: boy for girl man the. Note that the linking works no matter where the hash algorithm places a word.

The hash algorithm first places the word. Then, regardless of where it is placed, that location is linked to maintain the words in order. For example, suppose the new word kid hashes to location 2. Then the link of kid will be set to 4 (to point to man), and the link of girl will be set to 2 (to point to kid).

We print the alphabetical listing by traversing the linked list. Program P10.3 shows all the details.

Program P10.3

```
import java.io.*;
import java.util.*;
public class WordFrequencyHash {
    static   Scanner in;
    static   PrintWriter out;
    final static int N = 13; //table size
    final static int MaxWords = 10;
    final static String Empty = "";

    public static void main(String[] args) throws IOException {
        in = new Scanner(new FileReader("wordFreq.in"));
        out = new PrintWriter(new FileWriter("wordFreq.out"));

        WordInfo[] wordTable = new WordInfo[N+1];
        for (int h = 1; h <= N; h++) wordTable[h] = new WordInfo();

        int first = -1; //points to first word in alphabetical order
        int numWords = 0;

        in.useDelimiter("[^a-zA-Z]+");
        while (in.hasNext()) {
            String word = in.next().toLowerCase();
            int loc = search(wordTable, word);
            if (loc > 0) wordTable[loc].freq++;
            else //this is a new word
```

```
            if (numWords < MaxWords) { //if table is not full
                first = addToTable(wordTable, word, -loc, first);
                ++numWords;
            }
            else out.printf("'%s' not added to table\n", word);
        }
        printResults(wordTable, first);
        in.close();
        out.close();
    } // end main

    public static int search(WordInfo[] table, String key) {
    //search for key in table; if found, return its location; if not,
    //return -loc if it must be inserted in location loc
        int wordNum = convertToNumber(key);
        int loc = wordNum % N + 1;
        int k = wordNum % (N - 2) + 1;

        while (!table[loc].word.equals(Empty) && !table[loc].word.equals(key)) {
            loc = loc + k;
            if (loc > N) loc = loc - N;
        }
        if (table[loc].word.equals(Empty)) return -loc;
        return loc;
    } // end search

    public static int convertToNumber(String key) {
        int wordNum = 0;
        int w = 3;
        for (int h = 0; h < key.length(); h++) {
            wordNum += key.charAt(h) * w;
            w = w + 2;
        }
        return wordNum;
    } //end convertToNumber

    public static int addToTable(WordInfo[] table, String key, int loc, int head) {
    //stores key in table[loc] and links it in alphabetical order
        table[loc].word = key;
        table[loc].freq = 1;
        int curr = head;
        int prev = -1;
        while (curr != -1 && key.compareTo(table[curr].word) > 0) {
            prev = curr;
            curr = table[curr].next;
        }
        table[loc].next = curr;
        if (prev == -1) return loc; //new first item
        table[prev].next = loc;
        return head; //first item did not change
    } //end addToTable
```

```
        public static void printResults(WordInfo[] table, int head) {
          out.printf("\nWords        Frequency\n\n");
          while (head != -1) {
              out.printf("%-15s %2d\n", table[head].word, table[head].freq);
              head = table[head].next;
          }
        } //end printResults

    } //end class WordFrequencyHash

    class WordInfo {
        String word = "";
        int freq = 0;
        int next = -1;
    } //end class WordInfo
```

Suppose wordFreq.in contains the following:

```
If you can trust yourself when all men doubt you;
If you can dream - and not make dreams your master;
```

Using a table size of 13 and MaxWords set to 10, when Program P10.3 was run, it produced the following output in the file wordFreq.out:

```
'and' not added to table
'not' not added to table
'make' not added to table
'dreams' not added to table
'your' not added to table
'master' not added to table


Words        Frequency

all              1
can              2
doubt            1
dream            1
if               2
men              1
trust            1
when             1
you              3
yourself         1
```

CHAPTER 10 ■ HASHING

EXERCISES 10

1. Integers are inserted into a hash table H[1..11] using the primary hash function
   h1(k) = 1 + k mod 11. Show the state of the array after inserting the keys 10, 22, 31, 4, 15,
   28, 17, 88, and 58 using (a) linear probing, (b) quadratic probing with probe function i + i2,
   and (c) double hashing with h2(k) = 1 + k mod 9.

2. Integers are inserted in an integer hash table list[1] to list[n] using linear probe with
   double hashing. Assume that the function h1 produces the initial hash location and the
   function h2 produces the increment. An available location has the value Empty, and a deleted
   location has the value Deleted.

   Write a function to search for a given value key. If found, the function returns the location
   containing key. If not found, the function inserts key in the *first* deleted location encountered
   (if any) in searching for key, or an Empty location, and returns the location in which key was
   inserted. You may assume that list contains room for a new integer.

3. In a hashing application, the key consists of a string of letters. Write a hash function that,
   given a key and an integer max, returns a hash location between 1 and max, inclusive. Your
   function must use *all* of the key and should not deliberately return the same value for keys
   consisting of the same letters.

4. A hash table of size n contains two fields—an integer data field and an integer link
   field—called *data* and *next*, say. The *next* field is used to link data items in the hash table in
   ascending order. A value of -1 indicates the end of the list. The variable top (initially set to -1)
   indicates the location of the smallest data item. Integers are inserted in the hash table using
   hash function h1 and linear probing. The data field of an available location has the value
   Empty, and no item is ever deleted from the table. Write programming code to search for
   a given value key. If found, do nothing. If not found, insert key in the table and *link it in its
   ordered position*. You may assume that the table contains room for a new integer.

5. In a certain application, keys that hash to the same location are held on a linked list. The
   hash table location contains a pointer to the first item on the list, and a new key is placed at
   the end of the list. Each item in the linked list consists of an integer key, an integer count,
   and a pointer to the next element in the list. Storage for a linked list item is allocated as
   needed. Assume that the hash table is of size *n* and the call H(key) returns a location from 1
   to *n*, inclusive.

   Write programming code to initialize the hash table.

   Write a function that, given the key nkey, searches for it if not found, adds nkey in its
   appropriate position, and sets count to 0. If found, add 1 to count; if count reaches 10, delete
   the node from its current position, place it at the head of its list, and set count to 0.

6. Write a program to read and store a thesaurus as follows:

   Data for the program consists of lines of input. Each line contains a (variable) number of
   distinct words, all of which are synonyms. You may assume that words consist of letters
   only and are separated by one or more blanks. Words may be spelled using any combination
   of uppercase and lowercase letters. All words are to be stored in a hash table using open

addressing with double hashing. A word can appear on more than one line, but each word must be inserted only once in the table. If a word appears on more than one line, then all words on those lines are synonyms. This part of the data is terminated by a line containing the word EndOfSynonyms.

The data structure must be organized such that, given any word, all synonyms for that word can be quickly found.

The next part of the data consists of several commands, one per line. A valid command is designated by P, A, D, or E.

P *word* prints, in alphabetical order, all synonyms of *word*.

A *word1 word2* adds *word1* to the list of synonyms for *word2*.

D *word* deletes *word* from the thesaurus.

E, on a line by itself, indicates the end of the data.

7. Write a program to compare quadratic probing, linear probing with double hashing, and chaining. Data consists of an English passage, and you are required to store all the distinct words in the hash tables. For each word and each method, record the number of probes required to insert the word in the hash table.

   Cater for 100 words. For quadratic probing and double hashing, use a table size of 103. For chaining, use two table sizes—23 and 53. For each of the four methods, use the same basic hash function.

   Print an alphabetical listing of the words and the number of probes for each of the four methods. Organize your output so that the performance of the methods can be easily compared.

Index

Get the eBook for only $10!

> Now you can take the weightless companion with you anywhere, anytime. Your purchase of this book entitles you to 3 electronic versions for only $10.

This Apress title will prove so indispensible that you'll want to carry it with you everywhere, which is why we are offering the eBook in 3 **formats** for only $10 if you have already purchased the print book.

Convenient and fully searchable, the PDF version enables you to easily find and copy code—or perform examples by quickly toggling between instructions and applications. The MOBI format is ideal for your Kindle, while the ePUB can be utilized on a variety of mobile devices.

Go to www.apress.com/promo/tendollars to purchase your companion eBook.